UNDERSTANDING THE MODERN PREDICAMENT

Dwight D. Murphey
Wichita State University

UNIVERSITY
PRESS OF
AMERICA

Library of Congress Catalog Card Number: **81-40345**

To all those good friends,
living, dead and yet unborn,
who share their radical solitudes
in art, reflection or literature
and who thereby become members
of that great fraternity which
conducts a dialogue over the ages

ACKNOWLEDGMENTS

The author wishes to express his appreciation for permission to reprint from the following material:

Permission for quotation from F. R. Cowell's The Revolutions of Ancient Rome (1963) has been granted by Thames & Hudson, Ltd.

Permission for quotation of specified experts from Moses Hadas' Humanism: The Greek Ideal and Its Survival has been granted by Harper & Row, Publishers, Inc. Volume Twenty-four of the World Perspectives Series, Planned and Edited by Ruth Nanda Anshen. Copyright © 1960 by Moses Hadas.

Permission for quotation from Bruno Snell's The Discovery of the Mind (1960) has been granted by the Harvard University Press. Reprinted by permission

Permission for quotation from Carl Roebuck's The World of Ancient Times (New York: Charles Scribner's Sons, 1966) has been granted by Charles Scribner's Sons. Copyright © 1966 by Charles Scribner's Sons; reprinted with permission of Charles Scribner's Sons.

Permission for quotation from T. G. Tucker's Life in Ancient Athens, The Social and Public Life of a Classical Athenian From Day to Day (1906) has been granted by The Macmillan Publishing Company, Inc.

Permission for quotation from George L. Mosse's The Crisis of German Ideology (1964) and Nazi Culture (1966) has been granted by George L. Mosse.

Permission for quotation from Henry May's The Discontent of the Intellectuals: A Problem of the Twenties (1963) has been granted by Henry F. May.

Permission for quotation from Jurgen Herbst's
The German Historical School in American Scholarship
has been granted by the Cornell University Press.
Copyright © 1965 by Cornell University. Used by
persmission of the publisher, Cornell University
Press.

Permission for quotation from Howard Becker's
German Youth: Bond or Free has been granted by
Routledge & Kegan Paul Ltd.

Permission for quotation from Werner Jaeger's
Paideia: The Ideals of Greek Culture has been
granted by the Oxford University Press.

Permission for quotation from M. Rostovtzeff's
A History of the Ancient World (1928) and The Social
and Economic History of the Hellenistic World (1941)
has been granted by the Oxford University Press.

Permission for quotation from Arturo Castiglioni's A History of Medicine, second edition, translated and edited by E. M. Krumbhaar, and from Eric
F. Goldman's Rendezvous With Destiny has been granted
by Random House, Inc., and Alfred A. Knopf, Inc.

Appreciation is also due to Mary MacBain of
Wichita, Kansas, for her invaluable work in preparation of the manuscript.

CONTENTS

PART I:

MAN'S IMMATURITY

1

THE PREDICAMENT

In my family we know my grandmother, Mrs.
Frank McDonough, Jr., by such various names as
Reata or "Shorty" or "Momo." The most recent
generation has even added another name--"Gigi,"
for "great-grandmother." She was ninety years old
last August 2, having been born an unbelievable
fourteen years before the beginning of this century. She was already twenty-eight when World
War I broke out in Europe.

In a reflective moment a year or so ago she
surprised me by saying that, if given the fanciful
option people sometimes talk about, she would not
choose to live her life over. "Once is enough,
thank you," she said, considering the wear and
tear that life, just in itself, entails.

That birthday was like many other happy days
going back beyond the reaches of my memory. She
was surrounded by a loving family. My grandfather
wasn't there, of course; he left us, survived powerfully by a gentle and manly presence which we
all feel even now, in 1964 after a life which was
itself long and worthwhile. For several years
after his death, Grandmother remained in the mountain home they had shared for so many years after
his retirement from the practice of law. Now on
her ninetieth birthday the frail vibrancy that
shone through her as she served everyone "Pepsi
floats" suggested the vitality which had been so
typical of her during her younger years.

It is probably not too presumptuous to say,
despite the negative she voiced on her speculated
option, that she has had an awfully good life.
It has not been touched, except briefly and not
too intimately, by war; and it has been free of
disease and of major tragedy. There has been a

steady flow of love and comfort and attainment.
She bore and raised four children; she took part
in innumerable community projects, helping others;
and for many years her work with pastels, doing
both landscapes and portraits, has been a source
of real satisfaction both to herself and to others.

My grandmother is worth keeping in mind as I
write about the "modern predicament." I will be
going into detail about the elaborately intertwin-
ed ingredients that make up modern society and
that determine our understanding of social reality.
In doing so, I will try to explain the divisions
and neuroses within modern civilization. But,
through it all, we will want to remember that this
complex and contradictory social structure has offered the setting for countless lives, such as
hers, which have been lived fully and well. Our
civilization is without a doubt the highest ever
attained by men, and nothing that I say by way of
trying to understand certain features of it should
detract from the reality of its achievements. And
"Shorty" has been one of those achievements.

The reader will not automatically know what I
mean when I refer to a "modern predicament." It
may be supposed that I mean all the disturbances
that have been so visible to everyone on a day-to-
day basis: two enormous world wars; assorted
other wars, some major in scope; a protracted Cold
War, which is not over despite our desire recently to bury it from sight; conflict of all types;
restless movements of social change. But I intend
the "modern predicament" to refer to all this and
much, much more. The disturbances are just the
outward, most visible signs. They reflect an inner
reality which is tremendously complicated, but
which is susceptible to being understood, at least
as to its long-term outlines.

It will be easiest to acquaint the reader
with this predicament by speaking specifically
about three aspects of it:

(1) In the first place, we need to think beyond the implicit notion about human life which we
so rightfully assume to be true in childhood and
of which we, in our continuing innocence, rarely
seem to be fully disabused. This is the notion
that there is a state of normalcy which represents
the well-meaning, conscientious, decent aspects of
human existence, and that everything that happens
to the contrary must be an exception, to be account-
ed for as an aberration. It is a sanguine notion
which is unhappily contradicted by an overwhelming
fund of human experience, which indicates instead
that human nature is seriously mixed.

I don't think we can really understand either
our own lives or modern civilization in adequate
perspective unless we appreciate that even in the
highest of times men are only partly "civilized."
I know that I can't supply a definition of what
full civilization and full maturity would entail,
but I do know that, whatever they are, men have
clearly not attained them, except in part.

In at least one of its dimensions, the reality
of modern life is defined by our origins and our
nature. This underscores the problematical fea-
tures--the "predicament"--of the contemporary
world. We must take into account the cosmic infancy of mandkind's peoples, institutions, ideas
and cultures. This is an infancy which colors all
contemporary life, just as it has all past life.
We have a rich heritage from the Greeks, the Romans and the Middle Ages, but even though this has
been immensely fertile and suggestive it has not
presented the modern world with a set of final solutions to the main human questions. It is a fact
of the utmost significance that we do not face
those questions bound together by paradigms from
the past.

Several years ago when I first read José Ortega y Gasset's The Revolt of the Masses, I was
struck by how closely his observations about contemporary man corresponded with my own experience.

He indicated that since the beginning of the nineteenth century Europe and America have been filled
to overflowing with ordinary men. The average man
has multiplied himself many times over, has become
far more affluent and assertive than ever before,
and has come to occupy all spaces, both physically
and socially. The effect has been to knock out
the old aristocracies. The modern "mass man" has
inherited an advanced civilization, but he neither
understands nor appreciates it. His psychology is
that of a shallow, rootless, self-satisfied "spoiled child," and this is a psychology which lends
itself to tantrum-like "direct action" techniques
which are fundamentally anticivilizational and are
conducive to totalitarianism.

I have seen a lot of this psychology in my
day-to-day contacts with other people, as well as
in the news-making events of our society. Accordingly, Ortega's analysis helps clarify the reality
in which we live. But I have nevertheless felt
that it would be a mistake to accept the analysis
given in The Revolt of the Masses by itself, without a still wider perspective. To take it at face
value might suggest that modern man has fallen and
has taken on a mediocrity which was absent before
the nineteenth century. But this would hardly tell
the story.

The explosion of the average man to a higher
level of life during the past two centuries simply
brings into view a shallowness which until then
had existed in the submerged corpus of mankind in
the form of thorough-going illiteracy, ignorance
and muteness. The earlier void had been veneered-
over by elites, but it is worthwhile to understand
that any such veneer was masking a bad situation.
Mankind was certainly problematical then; it was
problematical so long as it relied on veneers; and
the problematical nature of modern "mass man," far
from being anything new, is an extension of the
human condition as that condition came down to us
from the past.

6

None of this really contradicts Ortega. But
it supplements his insight in a way that is necessary if we are to understand exactly how profound
the problematical nature of modern man actually
is. If we see Ortega's mass man in the context
of the continuing infancy of the human race, we
can have no difficulty appreciating why it is that
mankind, even in so advanced a time as the twentieth century, is so self-lacerating.

(2) The second aspect of the predicament involves less of an overall perspective. It focuses
on certain specific ideas and movements which have
occurred during the modern period.

This aspect has to do with a social and intellectual fact which has been one of the salient
features of the modern age and which has served as
a catalytic agent of such power that all of our
ideas and institutions and movements have either
resulted from it or been altered by it. Its effects have been so far-reaching that I feel justified in saying (in anticipation of my third point)
that it has determined much of the underlying
ontology--i.e., the basic reality--of our civilization.

This fact has been the alienation of the
intellectual.

The intellectuals of the eighteenth and nineteenth centuries who supported aristocracy did not,
at least at that time, make their peace with the
incoming modern age and with the new "bourgeoisie"
of individualist, industrial society. They correctly saw such a society's incompatibility with the
values they cherished from the old order, with the
consequence that they excoriated the new order
before they gave it any real chance on its own.
This was continued without a break by the new intelligentsia of the Left, who in the middle of the
nineteenth century took up their stance outside
the predominant culture, denouncing it angrily and
formulating a variety of alternative models and

7

philosophies rationalizing change. Since that time,
this critique has been reiterated in tens of
thousands of volumes and films.

Several causes have combined to bring about
this alienation, but I ascribe it mainly to envy
and to the intellectuals' struggle for power and
status. The most important consequence of the
alienation has been the resulting alliance which
the modern intellectual subculture has struck with
the "have-nots" in society. This consequence has
been radically influential in determining the direction of the alienation itself. The main political and economic movements have sprung from this
alliance: Socialism and the Welfare State.

Such an alliance spawns its own worldview.
It is a worldview which sees millions of people as
entrapped and exploited by the stronger individuals
in a voluntaristic society. In its moral dimension,
its tone is to raise the needs of the have-not to
an ethical pinnacle and at the same time to deny
the work-oriented ethic of the middle class. The
State is seen as a liberating helpmate. Any sort
of relativism--and there have been many--is embraced, since relativism is the readiest intellectual
device by which to weaken a people's attachment to
existing values and social forms. And, too, the
worldview has its own special heroes and villains;
it interprets all men and events according to its
own lights. Enormities of the worst kind--such as
occurred under Stalin and Mao and are presently
occurring in Africa--can take place under its
blessing or its cloak of protective silence. At
the same time, other views, other forces, are
atrophied and turned aside by its overbearing
presence.

This is not to say that the alliance and its
corresponding worldview have won a total victory.
Despite their successes, they have had to race
alongside and to have their influence within the
whirling dervish of modern life--and that life has
its own mass, force and inertia. The result is

8

that although conservatives see the Left as having
changed the face of modern life, the Left itself
does not think of itself as having been particularly successful.

Because the alienation of the intellectual
and all that has flowed from it have been factors
of such potency, modern Western civilization must
be understood not as something solid, but as an
enormous system of antagonistic energies. It has
long been seriously divided, and this division has
spread to the remainder of the peoples of the
world through the influence of Western ideas.
There is no reason to suppose that a society founded upon such radically opposing energies has reached a final stasis. As much if not more so than
any other society, our civilization is transitory
and impermanent. It is a unique mixture, which in
all likelihood will not be repeated by any other
period of history.

(3) My third point about the predicament
focuses on the mental aspects of this division, in
the broadest meaning of "mental." The more I have
studied the intellectual history of the past two
hundred years, the more neo-Kantian I have become
in my view of the contemporary world (and indeed
of any society). By this I mean that social reality
is to a very large degree the product not of objective facts directly perceived, but of perceptions
and patterns of mental organization. This is true
in two ways: First, if we look at our own history
or at any process or problem within our society, we
understand it only through the large conceptual
framework that we bring to bear upon it. We do
not understand the reality directly; what we have
in our minds is a mediated reality. This mediation
involves an amount of selectivity and factual ar-
ranging that is far beyond what we usually acknowledge. There is a reality separate from ourselves,
which is the touchstone of what we are attempting
to understand, but the mediation itself makes up
a substantial portion of the reality as we finally
accept it. The second point I would make is that

9

a large part of the social reality we are trying
to fathom consists precisely of the mental states--
the perceptions, concepts and worldviews--of
millions of people. These mental states themselves
constitute a significant portion of the subject-
matter of human society. This means that the effect of the process of mediation is compounded.
There is first the aspect that our understanding
of reality is filtered, and then the aspect that
our understanding, as filtered, is a major datum
in our lives and in the lives of others.

Both of these aspects were well illustrated
by the Nazi phenomenon. The National Socialists
organized their perception of modern social reality
through concepts developed out of the earlier
German Romantic movement and German Volkish thought.
The reality they perceived and upon which they
acted was very different from reality as perceived
by others. From outside their system of belief,
we can see that their perceptions were a mixture
of a certain modicum of selected fact and a
generous portion of myth. If we apply the second
aspect to the National Socialists, we see that
their worldview became an extremely important datum influencing the structure of life both for
them and for others. The fact that they saw the
world as they did was itself a part of social
reality. It changed everything that touched their
society, creating the existential framework within which life went on. Indeed, for some twenty
million victims this was so potent a part of reality that it led to imprisonment and death.

The application of this second point to ourselves is obscured by the fact that we do not
readily see in our own context what is so evident
with regard to the Nazis. We know from a distance
that their worldview was in fact a motivating
force extraneous to reality which acted upon and
became a part of reality, changing events and the
whole makeup of the modern European experience.
What we don't realize, though, is that this is also true with regard to the ideas we ourselves

10

hold. It lies at the bottom of our natures to
assume those ideas to be true, to understand them
as an accurate reflection of reality rather than
as merely a mediation. But this is a mistake.
The existential frame of our own existence, both
on a day-to-day basis and as to the larger events
of our history, is largely formed out of our patterns of mental organization. And, whether we
like to acknowledge it or not, these patterns are
shot through with fictions. This is especially so
because of the presence of the ideologies which
have arisen out of the radical division within our
society. One cannot contemplate the vast ocean of
interrelated concepts, and their origin out of
tensions and tactical alliances, without becoming
impressed by the extent to which society strays
off into a miasma of figments. And this becomes
the social reality in which we live and with which
we must deal.

Thus the predicament of modern man goes profoundly to the depths of modern social reality and
to our understanding of it. It is a predicament
because the effect is only partly seviceable to
human values. Our society, like the neurotic individual, is able to get by and perhaps avoid being
institutionalized; but the neurosis, its origins
and consequences, define the life of the society
in terms which we can appropriately describe as a
"predicament."

* * * * * * * *

The reader will find it helpful to keep the
three aspects of the predicament in mind as he
follows the remainder of my writing:

Part I of the present volume has to do with
the immaturity of mankind and the absence of an
inherited consensus from the past.

Parts II and III pertain to the second aspect,

11

going into considerable detail about the alienation
of the intellectual and its causes and consequences.

My later writing, in which I review in detail
the worldviews of the different ideologies, should
be read and understood as an elaboration of my
third point. This enormous web of concepts and of
shadings defines our social reality existentially,
since we live according to our understanding.

2

MAN'S BASIC IMMATURITY

The gulf which separates the savage from the civilized man was illustrated with great force by the final scene of the motion picture <u>Mondo Cane</u>. Cargo planes were shown at an airfield in, I believe, New Guinea and were contrasted with some natives who looked through the fence with expressions of wonder and envy. The camera then shifted to the jungle where the natives had carved out a small airstrip and built a model cargo plane. Deep in the jungle, they worshipped the "God of the cargo plane."

The Cargo Cults are the fascinating subject of Peter Worsley's <u>The Trumpet Shall Sound</u>.[1] The cults came into existence independently at several places at the end of World War II, which gives us to believe that they were symptomatic of the basic mentality of Melanesian culture. According to Worsley they are "religious movements which have as their most characteristic feature the belief that spiritual agents will at some future date divert tremendous cargoes of the most sought-after manufactured wealth into the hands of the cult members." The cults were only partly the result of contact with the outside world; they reflected the spiritual and intellectual resources of the natives themselves. "When (the natives) visited Kainantu and saw the White man actually emerge from the Bird's belly, they believed them to be reincarnations of the spirits of the dead." The airplane had been personified into a bird.

The mentality of these primitive peoples is far removed from that of the engineers in Seattle or Wichita or San Diego who designed the cargo planes. If we consider these engineers, we see how far men have come across the gulf from their original primitivism.

Such an awareness of man's advance is a necessary counterweight to the main thrust of my observations, which will center on the continuing immaturity of humanity. We won't want to lose sight of the advances we have made while we review that immaturity.

Hardly a day passes, however, without fresh evidence of the residual immaturity of the human race even in Europe and America. Immaturity is so pervasive that it is one of the important facts about life. There is hardly an activity or a relationship that is not touched by it. We usually imagine that people are fundamentally sound and that each problem is explainable by a specific act of negligence or criminality, but this is hardly sufficient to account for the tone of life as we experience it. Something more must be said.

In everyday life the immaturity appears in countless petty ways. Few of them amount to anything in themselves, except for what they tell us about the people involved. The reader will notice that in giving the examples that follow, I am deliberately staying away from incidents reported in the newspaper, since the inherent selectivity of newspapers centers on the unusual. What I wish us to see is that the immaturity is a standard part of our lives. I am sure the reader can supply a great many similar examples from his own experience:

* A middle aged woman who lives down the block showed the immaturity when she threw a cup out of her car window in front of my house. No doubt the act itself was extremely minor. But its implications about her are extensive.

* Surely it was evident in the person who stole bulbs from our outdoor Christmas lights last Christmas.

* It was present in a man at a football game who occupied the wrong seat and then refused to move for me as the holder of the season ticket.

* I could see the immaturity in the father of
a teenage boy who had side-swiped my car when the
father felt no concern about the damage that had
been done.

* A student told me that while he was on his
motorcycle he had been hit by a car. The driver
stopped a block away, and then drove on.

* One night, sirens woke me and my wife. The
next morning we found that a man had been killed
driving the wrong way on the nearby interstate
highway, presumably while intoxicated.

* In the men's restroom near my office at the
University, cigarette butts are frequently ground
into the floor and a drain.

* We used to have neighbors who were from the
Phillipines. A strike occurred at the factory at
which the husband was employed. After a few days,
he and most of the other workers chose to return
to work. During the next two months his car wind-
shield was smashed out twice and his family-room
window once by someone acting in the early hours
of the morning.

* We bought a house and planted a lawn. A
month or so later a long strip of the lawn collaps-
ed three or four inches. It took six calls and
letters to the contractor to produce the explanation that the plumber had forgotten to tamp the
dirt after he had filled the ditch for the water
pipe. Almost all of the houses in the neighborhood
suffered the same unsightly problem. The concrete
driveway has since broken up completely where the
untamped ditch ran underneath it.

* In the Marine Corps the men in my platoon in
boot camp joined in a brawl outside the messhall
early one morning on the pretext that a member of
another platoon hadn't said "please" when he called for the butter to be passed.

15

* During my college teaching, the department chairman (since fired by the president of the University) declared a faculty slowdown, not allowing students to pre-register for a full load, because he thought classes were too large. Nine out of the eighteen faculty members in the department opposed the chairman's actions. They even met at one of their homes to discuss an opposing strategy. But when it came to a vote at the faculty meeting at which the chairman was present, eight of those nine voted to sustain the chairman.

* Quite a nice family my wife and I have known for several years have come to believe in demons, which they contend are real and which they go through long sessions "exorcising" from their bodies. A number of other friends profess a serious belief in astrology.

* The immaturity is evident in the cheating that goes on in a college classroom. It appears in the practice of law when at every turn there is pettiness, demagoguery, insensitivity to delay, inconvenience and cost, and when there is a profound lack of intellectual rigor on the part of both the bench and the bar. In academic life it is apparent in the childishness of many professors in their committee work and in the faculty senates, as well as in the pettiness of their departmental politics and in a mediocre level of commitment by many faculty members and students. On a broader level, the immaturity is obvious in the tone of politics in a democracy, not to mention in a society without a democracy. It shows itself daily in the catastrophes of the human race, such as have occurred in Ireland, in the bloodbath at the 1972 Olympics and in the many terroristic kidnappings, bombings and assassinations.

To the individual absorbed in his own life-span, civilization appears quite old. Six to ten thousand years seem a long time. But this perspective is deceptive; the six to ten thousand years of recorded history are placed in a more revealing

16

light if in our imaginations we jump ahead a hundred thousand or even a half a million years. An anthropologist looking back from such a vantage point will have a difficult time avoiding the thought that we are simply part of the bare beginnings of civilization. He will identify us with the beginning era. He may even adopt a classification which will say that we have not yet started on civilization, but only toward it. He will not be far amiss if he thinks of us as having been still groping toward a dim and distant light. No doubt such an anthropologist will give us due credit for our moon trips and organ transplants, and in fact for the entire gulf which separates us from the cargo cultists; but the converse is also true, that he will not fail to notice our totalitarianisms, wars, cultural vulgarity and general immaturity.

Those who have read Robert Ardrey's African Genesis will recall that he expressed a similar perspective. He asked his readers to imagine that they were standing on the beach west of Santa Barbara in California looking south across the 8000 miles of ocean extending to Antarctica. He observed that if every ten miles, which is the approximate distance to the horizon, were to represent a million years, the entire 8000 miles would represent only 800 million years--far less than the four or five billion years the earth has existed. On this time scale, the time of Christ would be only one hundred feet from the shore. The pyramids of Giza, Ardrey said, would be just one hundred and forty feet further. Five miles out into the ocean, even though only half the distance to the horizon, would measure back to the time of the African australopithecines.

It can be little wonder that man as a civilized creature is immature. Civilized man is the barest infant. It would be surprising if we were not to have gaping voids in our moral, intellectual and spiritual fabric. Because of this immaturity, mankind's condition is bound to be

17

mixed; it inevitably contains the contrasts of
creativity and destruction, nobility and servility,
grandeur and pettiness, clear-sighted vision and
muddled obscurantism. We are the child-man.

Of course, it would be a mistake to make too
much of this. We cannot deny the many excellent
things in life. I am painting a picture of residual cosmic immaturity, not complete barbarism.
Our friends who take astrology so seriously are
immature in their reversion to the mentality of
the cargo cultists, but they are fine, compassion-
ate, honest, hard-working people, far from a total
re-creation of pre-historic primitivism. But while
this is so, it is impossible to understand human
life without taking into account the continuing
child-like nature of men.

This immaturity is separate from the attributes of a given culture; it is not rooted in a
certain time or place. A cultural relativist may
argue that I am generalizing from characteristics
I see around me daily in a secular, hedonistic,
extroverted culture. But my reading of history
convinces me that immaturity has never been absent
among the human race. The eighteenth century was
not free of it. Nor was the sixteenth during the
Religious Wars. Nor Russia during the reign of
Ivan the Terrible, nor the ancient Romans, nor the
Greeks.

An author surprised the reading public in
Denver a few years ago by asserting that Colorado
is one of the desert states. This suggested a
wholly new perspective from that which Denverites
ordinarily have of their state. Going west from
Denver, there is a good deal of bare rock, particularly on the road to Central City, but what
stands out most are the lush alpine forests of
Loveland and Vail passes, the many streams and the
golden sunshine in the mountain air.

But if we approach Colorado from the other
direction, driving, say, from southern California

18

through Nevada and Utah and coming into Colorado from the west, the suggestion of continued desert takes on greater plausibility. The pine and aspen tend to grow only on the shaded north side of each mountain, where they can drink the water from slowly melting snow. The massive baldness of the desert mountains further west seems only superficially disturbed by these patches of forest. The craggy rocks take their place, too, as reminders of the preceding thousand miles.

Our perspective of civilization is similar to that of the Denverites; our eyes are not trained to see the continuation of past forms. We look back over the Renaissance, the Middle Ages and classical times and see the trees, the streams, the golden sunlight of civilized culture--and we count ourselves as part of an advanced civilization far removed from the Stone and Bronze Ages.

If we were able, though, to travel back in time and could live among the peoples of the past-- of a hundred thousand years ago, twenty five thousand years ago, ten thousand years ago; and then among the men of Phoenicia, Carthage and Rome--, we would be surprised by what we would see. Many of the outlines of earlier times would appear to continue unabated by the patchwork historic man has been able to put on them. It would seem that we have not completely revolutionized the human condition, but only irrigated, fertilized and pruned it. Much of the original human substratum would appear in the faces, the laughter, the neuroses, the strivings, the gaieties and tragedies, the hopes and fears and superstitions of men. From such a perspective we would wonder not so much about why mankind has turmoil, war, enslavement and oppression, as about how it has been able to achieve the many great things it has. It would be possible to appreciate that the events, both happy and tragic, of human life are rooted in the quality of the human material, and that this qualitative level is slower to change than are institutions, laws, ideologies and cultural forms.

19

Many thinkers have said what I am saying here.
My observation of the residual child-like nature
of mankind is by no means original.

Emerson expressed it in his essay "Politics"
when he said that "we think our civilization near
its meridian, but we are yet only at the cock-
crowing and the morning star. In our barbarous
society the influence of character is in its infancy."[2]

The seventeenth century French author LaBruyere wrote a single paragraph on the subject.
"If the world is only to last a hundred million
years," he said, "it is still in all its fresh-
ness, and has but just begun; we ourselves are so
near the first men and the patriarchs, that remote
ages will not fail to reckon us among them. But
if we may judge of what is to come by what is past,
what new things will spring up in the arts,
sciences, in nature, and, I venture to say, even
in history, which are as yet unknown to us!
What discoveries will be made! What various revolutions will happen in states and empires!
What ignorance must be ours, and how slight is an
experience of not above six or seven thousand
years."[3]

In The Betrayal of the Intellectuals, Julien
Benda said that "I cannot sufficiently admire
the rare mental value displayed by LaBruyere" in
the passage just quoted.[4]

A hundred years ago Sir Henry Maine saw the
continuity between the savage and the civilized
man. In a passage in Popular Government he said
that ". . . the differences which, after ages of
change, separate the civilized man from the savage
or barbarian, are not so great as the vulgar
opinion would have them. Man has changed much in
Western Europe, but it is singular how much of
the savage there still is in him, independently of
the identity of the physical constitution which
has always belonged to him . . . Like the savage,

20

he indulges in endless deliberation; like the
savage, he sets an extravagant value on rhetoric;
like the savage, he is a man of party, with a
newspaper for a totem, instead of a mark on his
forehead or arm; and, like a savage, he is apt to
make of his totem his God."[5]

Herbert Spencer believed man is changing his
"moral constitution," but that he has as yet only
partially lost his savage propensities: "It is
an indisputable fact that the moral constitution
which fitted men for his original predatory state,
differs from the one needed to fit him for this
social state to which multiplication of the race
has led. In a foregoing part of our inquiry it
was shown that adaptation is effecting a transition from the one constitution to the other. Living then, as we do, in the midst of this transition, we must expect to find traits of nature which
are explicable only on the hypothesis that humanity is at present partially adapted to both these
states, and not completely to either--has only in
a degree lost the dispositions needed for savage
life, and has but imperfectly acquired those needed for social life."[6]

At another point he wrote that ". . . the
lingering instincts of the savage are at this moment exhibited by about an equal percentage of all
classes."

John Ruskin exclaimed that "truly, it seems
to me, as I gather in my mind the evidences of
insane religion, degraded art, merciless war, sul-
len toil, detestable pleasure, and vain or vile
hope, in which the nations of the world have lived
since first they could bear record of themselves--
it seems to me, I say, as if the race itself were
still half-serpent, not extricated yet from its
clay."[7]

Countless other thinkers over thousands of
years have expressed disappointment at the qualitative level of men. The Roman historian Tacitus

21

commented on the "utter poverty of thought" around
him;[8] Johnathan Swift characterized men as barbarous Yahoos;[9] Shakespeare wrote of the human
condition as containing "the oppressor's wrong,
the proud man's contumely," all amounting to a
"weary life."[10] Edward Gibbon made a pessimistic
observation about human capability when he commented about education that "the power of instruction
is seldom of much efficacy, except in those happy
dispositions where it is most superfluous."[11] We
recall Schopenhauer's mournful lament about the
quality of human life.[12]

Mankind usually looks on these things with
dangerous simplicity. We are inclined to look for
scapegoats. We seek men with "black hats" and
compare them unfavorably with good men wearing
"white hats." This in turn feeds the fires of
human division and obscures an appreciation of
what is behind the dysfunctions in human life.

It would be more sophisticated to pull back
from mankind bitterly and say "a plague on both
your houses." If we cast a negative vote, we
must condemn virtually all of mankind for sharing
the qualities which produce so much horror. It
is not simply the active participant in horror who
is responsible; those are responsible also who do
not do all they can to elevate themselves and to
provide in a principled way in advance to mitigate
the horrors of mankind.

But without giving up our capacity for righteous anger, there is another more beneficial attitude to adopt. This is the attitude stated so
profoundly by Christ on the cross: "Father, forgive them; for they know not what they do."

What better summarizes the human condition?
What more compassionately points to the child-like
nature of mankind? We may detest the malignancy
of men and may strive all our lives to overcome it
and work diligently to be decent ourselves, but
over and above all the "sound and the fury" we are

22

well advised to accept with ultimate serenity the tragic, the mundane and the joyful; they are all part of life as we know it.

In "Fiddler on the Roof" the playwright showed the simultaneous vulnerability, lovableness and limitation of ordinary people. We cannot ignore the follies and vices of mankind--do not wish to ignore them--and would be forfeiting our responsibility were we to do so, but it leads to greater mercy and reconciliation if we permit ourselves to view humanity compassionately.

NOTES

1. The quotations here from Worsley are from Peter Worsley, The Trumpet Shall Sound (London: MacGibbon & Kee, 1957), pp. 44 and 201. See also the Encyclopedia Brittanica, 1966, entry on "Cargo Cults."

2. Ralph Waldo Emerson, The Portable Emerson (Viking Press, 1946), p. 201.

3. LaBruyere, Characters, trans. Henry Van Laun (London: Oxford University Press, 1963), pp. 238-9.

4. Julien Benda, The Betrayal of the Intellectuals (Boston: The Beacon Press, 1930), p. 158.

5. Sir Henry Sumner Maine, Popular Government (New York: Henry Holt & Co., 1886), pp. 143-4.

6. Herbert Spencer, Social Statics and Man Versus the State (New York: D. Appleton and Company, 1897), pp. 88, 102.

7. Peter Quennell, Selected Writings of John Ruskin (London: Falcon Press, 1952), p. 88.

8. Tacitus, The Complete Works of Tacitus (New

23

York: Modern Library, 1942), p. 761.

9. Jonathan Swift, <u>Gulliver's Travels</u> (New York:
Modern Library, 1931), pp. 251-337.

10. Hamlet's "To be or not to be" soliloquy in
William Shakespeare's <u>Hamlet</u>.

11. Edward Gibbon, <u>The Decline and Fall of the
Roman Empire</u> (1776), Vol. I, chapter 4, para. 3.

12. Arthur Schopenhauer, <u>The Philosophy of
Schopenhauer</u> (New York: Modern Library, 1928),
p. 376.

3

THE MISSING PARADIGM: GREECE

Despite the profound contributions the ancient Greeks made to Western civilization, they did not provide later humanity with final solutions to the main human questions.

We are not armed in the modern period with a ready-made paradigm--i.e., model--provided by the Greeks (just as we are not from the Romans and the Middle Ages, although that will be the subject of the ensuing two chapters). None was paradigmatic--and this has the important consequence that in the modern age we face the perennial problems of mankind anew. This leaves us free to be existentially at odds with ourselves.

The history of the ancient Greeks tells of a continuing struggle with the basic problems of life. More effervescently perhaps than others, they shared the cosmic immaturity of the human race. The many-sided, diverse nature of their experience affords an excellent example of the "shaking out process" through which mankind has been passing.

Every aspect of Greek life contained diversity, change and conflict. This was true as to each separate feature--its philosophy, its culture, its drama, its economics and politics. There was diversity from city-to-city and even within a given city from period to period. To suggest a homogeneous Greek thrust is to simplify away the differences among them.

In this chapter I will want to look at their achievements and their limitations, to show in greater detail just why it is that their heritage to us is one of richness, but not of solution.

25

Some Greek Achievements

Man the Measure. Protagoras' comment that
"man is the measure of all things" is the classic
expression of humanism. The Greek experience
was anthropocentric, although this was by no
means unmixed. There was a decided turn away from
the irrational, demonic world -- and here the gulf
opened between the reality-oriented modern mind
and the primitivism of the Cargo Cults. Once
this step was taken, a vast number of others became possible.

Bruno Snell has written that "the heroes of
the Iliad . . . no longer feel that they are the
playthings of irrational forces" and that "they
acknowledge their Olympian gods who constitute
a well-ordered and meaningful world."[1] He admits
that "they continued throughout to preserve a belief in magic," but magic was not a controlling
theme: "All those who helped to advance the new
era had as little regard for it as Homer."
Thucydides indicated his own separation from the
irrational when he said that "for those who put
their faith in oracles, here is one solitary
instance of their having been proved accurate."[2]

Man was elevated rather than debased. Snell
points to an "immense difference" between Greek
and Oriental religion, observing that "throughout
his poems Homer has his gods appear in such a
manner that they do not force man down into the
dust; on the contrary, when a god associates with
a man, he elevates him, and makes him free, strong,
courageous, certain of himself." Werner Jaeger
confirms this when he writes that "the homeric
epics contain the germ of all Greek philosophy.
In them we can clearly see the anthropocentric
tendency of Greek thought, that tendency which
constrasts so strongly with the theomorphic philosophy of the Oriental who sees God as the sole
actor and man as merely the instrument or object
of that divine authority. Homer," he says,

26

"definitely places man and his fate in the fore-
ground."[3] Still further, T.G. Tucker has noted
that "there never were minds more free from the
anguish of moral yearnings, or ideals of self-
mortification, than those of classical Athens."[4]

Again, this was not unmixed. There was much
to contradict it, although at least during the pre-
Christian era these contradictions did not reverse
the emphasis. Herodotus repeatedly stated a
doctrine which, if it had not been balanced by
other factors, could have inhibited the creativity
of ancient man: "God is envious of human prosperity . . . what a chancy thing life is . . .
Great wealth can make a man no happier than moderate means, unless he has the luck to continue
in prosperity to the end . . . until he is dead,
keep the word 'happy' in reserve."[5] He was quoting Solon, but elsewhere he stated on his own behalf that "in this world nobody remains prosperous
for long."

Snell reports that vestiges of the original
belief in "the uncanny and the spooky, the belief
in ghosts and magic" remained in Homer. A belief
in fate was a major theme: "In Homer," Snell says,
"the outstanding feats of man are said to spring,
not from his individual character or from his
special gifts, but from the divine force which
flows through him." This was not without its impact on the individual: "There are personal fates,
but no personal achievements . . . Helplessness is
a fundamental motif in the early Greek personal
lyric."

Accordingly, Moses Hadas has quoted E. R.
Dodds that "the Greeks were as continuously and
deeply concerned with the supernatural as any
people in history."[6] Although Hadas points out
that "uncompromising intellectuality does in fact
characterize much of the best Greek work," he sets
off against this an observation that "we must be
aware that rationalism was never the sole nor even
the dominant outlook in Greece itself, and that

27

later ages which insisted that it was were only
seeking buttresses for their own outlook."

Just the same, Hadas' overriding message in
The Greek Ideal and Its Survival is that the Greeks
did make "man the measure." He emphasizes that
despite important opposing elements the Greek religious view was such that men still felt it not
only possible to live energetic lives on this
earth, but were impelled to do so. "What we have,
in effect, is a world of gods and men in which
each party attends to its own business and according to its own standards. That is why, though the
gods of the (Homeric) epic are potent, the poem is
still anthropocentric." The gods became mere data:
"Because the Greeks set about doing with all their
might what their hands found to do, accepting
divine intervention as an ineluctable hazard, not
as a law and promise, they were able to achieve
the things they did achieve."

Hadas notes two features which were picked up
by Machiavelli and Spinoza and which influenced
Renaissance thinking. First, the separation between the sphere of men and the sphere of the gods
lent itself naturally to a separation of church
and state. "The first step in making man rather
than external authority the measure of all things
is to separate government from religion, and this
was done, most explicitly and thoroughly, by
Machiavelli." Second, the Greeks had not developed
an organized priestly class. "The second step is
to separate religion from an organized authority
based on a specific revelation, and this was done,
most explicitly and thoroughly, by Spinoza."

Because of Christianity, for many centuries
the main Greek influence on later Western civilization was not anthropomorphic, but Platonic. But
Hadas makes the surprising point that Plato and
even Aristotle were the exceptions and not the
rule in Greek life. "Plato is in fact a deviation.
Unquestioning submission to a spiritual authority
and aspiration toward an undefined goal is not
what sets the Greeks apart from other men . . .
In Greece itself, apparently, Plato's influence

28

was limited. His Academy was, as we shall see, exclusive and to a degree esoteric. Virtually all of the literary figures of the next generation were alumni not of the Academy but of the school of Isocrates." He reports that "Aristotle himself is virtually unheard of in the Hellenistic age and was revived only in the Roman period. The most widespread philosophic tendencies of the Hellenistic age were the Stoic and the Epicuriean."

Through Plato, the Greeks contributed much to Christianity; but through what was otherwise an anthropocentric view they contributed to the secular foundations of the modern age.

Intellectual Variety. The Greeks did not present later man with an intellectual consensus; what they did do was to foretell later ideas: there was little that they did not explore first. According to Hadas "the major genres and subject matter of literature, as of philosophy and plastic art, have been laid down by the Greeks."

We can get some idea of the extent to which modern thinking was foretold by taking a single area such as political philosophy; one who is absorbed in the discussions of the modern era can only be surprised to learn how much of that discussion was taken up in Greek thought.

It was not new when nineteenth century socialists such as Marx launched attacks on monogamous marriage and discussed in detail the idea of collectivizing child-rearing. Two thousand years ago Aristophanes' comedy Ecclesiazusae presented precisely such a scheme.[7] A character in the comedy fervently endorses a radically egalitarian system of sex-on-demand and a community of parentage. More profoundly, this idea comes from Plato. When the modern anarchist John Henry Mackay advocates such a plan, he has substantial precursors in Greek thought.

Collectivist thought in general has important

29

roots in several aspects of Greek life and thought:
in the communal, barracks life of the Spartan as
established by Lycurgus; in the writing of Xeno-
phon praising the Spartan state; in the Republic
of Plato, which reflects Plato's admiration for
the Spartan system; in Plutarch's later writing
painting the Spartan constitution as ideal. And
although the Athenian example was very different
from the Spartan and was characterized in Pericles'
time by personal freedom and the Rule of Law,
there was even there an ideal of devotion to the
community which carries over in modern socialist
writing and particularly in democratic socialism.

The nineteenth century classical liberal
Frederic Bastiat ascribed much of the collectivist
thought of the seventeenth and eighteenth centuries to the study of ancient civilization, including the Greeks. "Antiquity presents everywhere--
in Egypt, Persia, Greece, Rome--the spectacle of
a few men molding mankind according to their whims,
thanks to the prestige of force and of fraud,"
Bastiat wrote.8 Modern man did not look back upon
them and learn exclusively liberating notions.

But monarchical thought, partially distinguishable from these collectivist ideas, also received support from the Greeks. Rostovtzeff
relates that "Greek philosophy in early Hellenistic
times added . . . the theory that kingship was
the best form of government and that kings were
identical with the State and, as it were, an incarnation of it. Various schools . . . vied with
each other in finding arguments to prove that
monarchy, from the philosophical standpoint, was
the best possible form of government."9

Set off against socialism and monarchism,
however, were significant contributions to later
classical liberal ideals. F.A. Hayek looked upon
Athenian ideals as an historical source for what
he takes to be the central idea behind classical
liberal thought--the concept of Isonomia, later
known as the Rule of Law.

It was the achievement of the Greeks that
they became in their diversity the fount, not
certainly of a consensus, but of the contending
branches of political thought. The multi-tracked
intellectuality was present in the other major
areas of thought, as well.

Intellectual Method. The Greeks did not
"solve" the major questions of intellectual method
--but they did go far into rational method to open
up avenues which are pertinent today.

Snell says of Hecataeus, for example, that
"it remains his particular achievement that he
placed knowledge, as it was understood by him, in
a position whence it could be advanced and
augmented. Like Xenophanes, only more concretely
he holds that knowledge consists of the data
gained from inquiry and search." Snell tells us
that "this enthusiasm for knowledge lives on in
Herodotus. For him experience forms the one and
only basis of knowledge. He distinguishes between
what he has seen himself, what he has heard from
eye-witnesses, and what he has learned merely as
rumor."

At the same time, Snell acknowledges that
this was just a beginning, that real empirical
science did not develop in ancient Greece. Again
we see the contradictions in the Greek experience
when Snell attributes this lack of empirical
science "in no small measure" to Parmenides, "who
cast aside human knowledge, i.e., sense experience,
and sought a direct access to divine knowledge."

Empirical science as we know it may not have
been rising, but strides were nevertheless made in
the applications of reason. Euclid developed a
logical system of plane geometry, arithmetic and
stereometry; Archimedes formulated his principles
of differential calculus; and Apollonius established his theory of conic sections. In drama and
history, Abbott writes, "the achievements of the
age of Pericles have never been surpassed,"[10]

31

though consistently with the diversity of movement
this praise is leavened by a later observation of
Abbott's that Greek youth learned from the sophists
"to question everything, bringing the deepest
feelings of man to the touchstone of a formal and
ill-developed logic."

Although the sophists deserve and have
received considerable criticism, Werner Jaeger
credits sophistic culture with having made "one of
the greatest discoveries which the mind of man has
ever made: it was not until it explored these
three of its activities (grammar, rhetoric and
dialectic) that the mind apprehended the hidden
law of its own structure."

Foretelling the moderns, specialization was
the hallmark of much Greek thought. Hadas remarks
of Plato that "specialization was a cardinal
principle in his social thinking." He adds that
"in respect to educational theory Aristotle went
beyond Plato in specialization."

Snell stresses the gradual formulation of a
language fitted to logical thought. He traces
the movement from purely proper nouns, which denote
a single object, to concrete nouns, which denote
classes of objects . . . and then to abstract
nouns through the use of mythical names and the
figurative use of concrete nouns . . . and still
further the development of connecting parts of
speech. He refers to a "strange threefold development": "At first the logical element is merely
understood from the context; as a second step, certain words which had at first had a different
function came to represent the latent logic; and
finally this logic, now overtly expressed, becomes
an object of reflexion." We see how subtle and
yet pivotal the contributions may be that a culture such as that of Greece has made to Western
civilization.

Heroic Emulation. The Greek contributions
were by no means entirely cerebral. The other

dimensions of life were equally creative.

Competitiveness for honor was a major factor
in Greek creativity. It is amusing to read of the
horror expressed, according to Herodotus, by a
certain Tritantaechmes: "Good heavens, Mardonius,
what kind of men are these that you have brought
us to fight against--men who compete with one
another for no material reward, but only for honor!"
Heroic emulation was given a high place in Pericles'
funeral oration: "What made (Athens) great was
men with a spirit of adventure, men who knew their
duty, men who were ashamed to fall below a certain
standard . . . Famous men have the whole earth as
their memorial . . . their memory abides and grows.
It is for you to try to be like them."

"The Homeric ideal is summarized in a single
line," Hadas says, "--'to strive always for excellence and to surpass all others.'" He adds that
the "most striking feature of the Homeric ethos
is the enormous importance attached to individual
prowess, individual pride, individual reputation."
Snell tells us that "since the days of Jacob
Burckhardt the competitive character of the great
Greek achievements has rightly been stressed . . .
From his earliest boyhood the young nobleman is
urged to think of his glory and honor; he must
look out for his good name." Jaeger adds that the
hero was considered the highest type of humanity.

Although I have no theory to explain the ultimate origins of Greek creativity, this heroic
competition was clearly a major spur to it. The
competitiveness in athletics and military action
is, of course, legendary, and Tucker speaks of
this competition as a cause also of the greatness
of Greek sculpture. "Nothing could foster great
sculpture," he says, "better than this--first, a
deliberate aim at the representation of ideal humanity; second, a constant stimulus of rivalry
on all sides towards its perfect attainment."
Jaeger refers to the competitiveness as a key to
Greek drama and poetry.

Artistic Flowering. This rivalry for honor
took place within a leisured life which was made
possible by the economic base founded on slavery
and by a high level of state aid. These brought
a new splendor to cultural pursuits during the Age
of Pericles. Abbott relates that "by direct or
indirect means Pericles made the state the pay-
master of a vast number of citizens, and the state
was practically himself . . . At the same time the
public festivals of the city were enlarged and
adorned with new splendor." Under Pericles'
patronage, Pheidias the sculptor and Ictinus the
architect worked to produce "the unrivalled triumph of architectural skill," the Acropolis, in
honor of Athena. This flowering was a quick one;
Abbott remarks that "this magnificence was not the
result of centuries of toil; it was the work of
fifty years. In 479 B. C. Athens was a heap of
blackened ruins; in 429 B. C. all the great works
of the Periclean age had been accomplished except
the Erectheum. Athens indeed became a vast workshop." But this development was typical; the
encouragement of the arts was common among the
Greek tyrannies.

This spendor was entirely public. It wasn't
shared by private life. Tucker says there was
"no magnificence of streets or private houses,"
and speaks of the "insigificance of the private
dwellings."

The beauty of Greek sculpture and architecture
lay in its idealization and simplicity. Tucker
comments that "throughout all the truly classical
period you will find nothing embodied by Athenian
artists in stone or in metal which does not carry
with it some feeling of majesty and dignity, heroism or other loftiness, or else stir the mind to
keen pleasure in the contemplation of physical and
mental perfection." Seeking to explain this,
Tucker reflects that "their choice of these higher
and healthier themes was intuitive or inbred, the
spontaneous outcome of a judgment sane and true;"
it was almost certainly related to the humanistic

idealism of Greek religion and to the heroic conception held of man.

Balance and Harmony. Broad conceptions of balance, harmony, beauty and justice entered into the Greek mentality. Snell reports that behind the world of the gods the Greeks perceived "an even more universal plan which controlled the life of man and gave it meaning." He goes so far as to assign this perception a place of central importance in the development of Western civilization when he says that "our European culture may well be said to rest on the discovery of the Greeks that this plan takes different manifestations: to the intellect it appears in the shape of law, to the senses it is beauty, to the active spirit it is justice. The persuasion that truth, beauty and justice exist in the world, even though their appearance is largely hidden, is our ever-present heirloom from the Greeks."

Werner Jaeger has similarly written about the role played by Greek harmony: "The subsequent influence of the conception of harmony on all aspects of Greek life was immeasurably great. It affected not only sculpture and architecture, but poetry and rhetoric, religion, and morality; all Greece came to realize that whatever a man made or did was governed by a severe rule, which like the rule of justice could not be transgressed with impunity--the rule of fitness or propriety."

Economics and Technology. Characteristic Greek energy extended also into economics. Herodotus spoke with pride of the Samians as being "responsible for three of the greatest building and engineering feats in the Greek world: the first is a tunnel nearly a mile long, eight feet wide and eight feet high, driven clean through the base of a hill nine hundred feet in height. The whole length of it carries a second cutting thirty feet deep and three broad, along which water from an abundant source is led through pipes into the town . . . Secondly, there is the artificial harbor

35

enclosed by a breakwater . . . and, last, the
island has the biggest of all known Greek temples."

Although he notes that during the Hellenistic
period there was a slow economic erosion caused
by a number of factors, Rostovtzeff describes a
high level of attainment: "Greece, in spite of
her poor natural resources, had developed these
remarkably by the long and steady efforts of her
people. There is not the slightest doubt that
even in the third century Greece was one of the
best cultivated countries in the world. Her
vineyards and olive-groves, her fruit-gardens and
kitchen gardens were famous. The standard of her
agriculture and the quality of her pasturage were
very high. Thousands of men turned to account the
wealth of the sea: there was abundance of fish,
salt, sponges, and shell-fish for dyeing, and their
exploitation was well organized. Mines and quar-
ries were worked as long as there were minerals
. . . Greek artisans were still the most efficient
and the most artistic. Trade relations were firmly established between the various parts of the
Greek world." Poland, Reisinger and Wagner relate
that "the third century became the age of inven-
tions and discoveries and the flourishing period
of the sciences."[11]

Transmission of Culture. The Greeks were the
great cultural source. According to Jaeger, they
became during the Hellenistic period "the teachers
of all succeeding nations. Greece," he adds,
"is the school of the western world." The conquests of Alexander the Great in the East were
followed by deep cultural influence, so that, as
Reisinger and Wagner have observed, "henceforth
the Greek language and civilization formed the
bond of union which embraced the kingdoms of his
successors." Still later the Romans appropriated
and continued to spread Greek culture.

Greek culture came to transcend a given city
or nation. Hadas writes that "what enabled the
Greek ideal to survive was its detachment from

36

national sovereignty and its transformation into
something like a religious cult," and he notes that
"what was transmitted, naturally, was neither of
the classical Greeks' strains separately--Chthonic
or Olympian, mystic or rational, Platonic or
Isocratean--but an amalgam compounded of the two
along with new ingredients contributed by the
subjects of the cultural empire."

Isonomia. F. A. Hayek has presented the dual
concepts of personal liberty and "Isonomia" as of
primary importance in the struggle within Western
civilization for individual liberty. In The
Constitution of Liberty he contests the common
assertion that the ancients did not enjoy individual liberty; "This is true of many places and
periods even in ancient Greece, but certainly not
of Athens at the time of its greatness . . . surely
not of those Athenians to whom Pericles said that
"the freedom which we enjoy in our government
extends also to our ordinary life . . . 'and whose
soldiers, at the moment of supreme danger during
the Sicilian expedition, were reminded by their
general that, above all, they were fighting for a
country in which they had "unfettered discretion to
live as they pleased.'"[12]

Herodotus reports a debate among advocates of
democracy, oligarchy and monarchy. The advocate
of democracy asked his listeners to "contrast with
(monarchy) the rule of the people: first, it has
the finest of all names to describe it--isonomy,
or equality before the law; and, secondly, the
people in power do none of the things that monarchs
do." He added that "I have no wish to rule--or to
be ruled either."

Pericles' funeral oration emphasized this:
"Our constitution is called a democracy because
power is in the hands not of a minority but of the
whole people. When it is a question of settling
private disputes, everyone is equal before the
law." He added that "in public affairs we keep to
the law. This is because it commands our deep

37

respect." Abbott tells us that the Greek attitude
was that "bad or good, the law must be strictly
obeyed. If it worked ill it might be corrected,
but obeyed it must be."

The courts were a primary institution. The
body of jurors was known as the Heliaea. Abbott
comments with regard to Pericles and the Heliaea
that "above all, he established the majesty of
law, and claimed for it the support of the whole
nation. Every Athenian had now a direct reason for
knowing what the law was, and for helping to maintain it. The reign of the Heliaea was the reign
of law."

Even this had its imperfections, sometimes
severe, according to present standards. The law
was said to be equal, but the jurymen had discretion in practice about how to interpret it.
Abbott takes some of the gloss off when he tells us
of the type of things to which a "legal realist"
would point today: "The rich offered the most
tempting victims to courts largely composed of the
very poor. The establishment of such courts was
a step onwards in the development of class-hatred,
ranging the rich and poor on opposite sides; for
though the law was the same for all, the administration of it was now as entirely in the hands of
the poor, as it had once been in the hands of the
rich. And along with this inequality went the
degradation of moral sentiment, which could not
fail to arise in men who were engaged from morning
to night not only in listening to legal quibbles,
or falsehoods, but in deciding for hire on the
lives and properties of others without the least
responsibility or control." In such a situation
demagoguery would run high.

Nevertheless, equality before the law has been
one of the central concepts in Western law and in
the history of liberty, as Hayek has emphasized.
The Greek application of it was not perfect, but
the Athenian concept was important to later generations; it has been a leading principle within

classical liberalism and was important in medieval
thinking. It is a major Constitutional principle
in American jurisprudence.

The connection between the Rule of Law and
the liberty of the individual in the sense of the
lack of arbitrary restraint is apparent. Snell
argues that there is no incongruity between the
Athenian's personal absorption into the community
and this personal liberty; the Rule of Law was the
key. "It should not surprise us that the cogni-
zance of individuality and the communal establishment of the polis are contemporary events; for to
be a citizen is not the same as belonging to a
mass of retainers. The law is the new link which
binds men together.

And Yet, the Child Man

These and still other achievements have come
down to us. Their value cannot be diminished and
ought not to be debunked. And yet, each has rarely involved a clear, unmixed blessing; even in the
areas of greatest achievement, there have been
human blemishes, combined with much complexity and
contradictory tendencies. The Greeks themselves
were child-men. They did not resolve the problematic nature of life for us.

No Social, Economic Paradigm. In the social
and economic areas they adopted make-shift solutions which we would be unwilling to accept as a
paradigm in modern Western civilization. Hadas
makes the point that "we are stirred by the democratic ideals of Athens as set forth in Pericles'
Funeral Oration, but we are aware that the entire
system rested upon the institution of slavery, that
citizenship was rigidly exclusive, and that women
were relegated to an inferior legal and social
status." Abbott distinguishes between the Greeks'
solution and our own aspirations with the observation that "the most obvious point of difference in

39

Greek civilization, when we compare it with out own, is the existence of slavery. There were slaves everywhere; in every workshop and every household; on the farms and in the mines; the police were slaves, the clerks in public offices were slaves."

It may have been true, as Rostovtzeff states, that "the free play of economic forces . . . with which the State very seldom interfered" was "the essence of the Greek economic system," and that this was akin to laissez-faire capitalism--and further that this economic freedom was the key to the progress the Greeks made in the economic area--, but a "capitalism" involving slave labor would not have pleased Adam Smith, Richard Cobden or the other modern proponents of capitalism. Nor would such advocates of free-trade have been happy with the protectionist economic policies adopted by the various cities; Rostovtzeff says that "none of the Greek cities abolished its restrictive measures against its neighbors or its oppressive customs-duties." Still further, modern business enterprise would not welcome the condition Rostovtzeff tells us about when he says that "organized bands of pirates had their own well-protected harbours (not only in Crete) and were welcomed in all commercial ports when they appeared laden with their booty."

The Greeks during the Age of Pericles were able at least temporarily to put together a com-bination of factors which helped them overcome some of the major questions which have plagued Western civilization. They had personal absorption into the state, and yet liberty; democracy, but not egalitarian levelling; a leisured, aristocratic life, but a pluralism of types within the leisured group; the free play of economic forces, but still a lifestyle which was not typically bourgeois.

Abbott ascribes this mainly to slavery, though other factors must be taken into account, since obviously slavery existed elsewhere without producing the same combination of cultural factors. Abbott asks "what was the effect of slavery on the

Athenian democracy?" and he answers "as a first and obvious effect it allowed the citizen an amount of leisure which without it would have been impossible. While the slave was at work, the master was in the Ecclesia, or in the law-courts, or in the market-place, or in one of the numerous portocoes." Slavery and the state payment for certain services rendered to the citizen permitted leisure even to the poor citizen. This in turn, according to Abbott, blunted any tendency Athenian democracy may have had to turn toward socialism.

This slave-based leisure negated the predomi-nance of a commercial lifestyle, so there was no fifth century Sinclair Lewis to pen his dissatis-faction with an Athenian Babbitt. The "capitalism" of Athens produced a culture which was more in keeping with the ideal which intellectuals have sought than has been the busy, work-ethic type of capitalism known to modern times. Instead of pre-paring a student for business, Athenian schools centered on "self-culture and worthy citizenship." "The daily life of the Greek, especially the Athe-nian, was often spent in busily doing nothing."

Perhaps in the leisure produced by modern technology we will be able to find a cultural form akin to this, unless our own spiritual imperfec-tions cause us to degrade our leisure into less-than-noble uses; but in the absence of such a plateau for leisure it is difficult to emulate the Greeks. We would hardly wish to adopt the slavery which permitted such a life.

No Solution to Class Antagonism. There was a certain stability in Periclean Athens in the ab-sence of a thrust toward socialism, but a centuries-long perspective of Greek experience makes it clear that the Greeks found no solution to the antagonism between the haves and the have nots. There is a reminder of the nicknames given the groups within the French Revolution in Abbott's description of the men of the Plain, the Shore and the Mountain, as taken from Plutarch: "the men of the Plain

were chiefly . . . rich landholders of a strict
conservative type, who wished to retain unimpaired
all their ancient rights and privileges. The men
of the Mountain were the poor goatherds . . .
They were the radical party . . . whose only hope
of improving their condition lay in breaking the
power of their opponents, and removing the
barriers of birth and privilege."

Jaeger tells of class conflicts in the seventh
century B.C. and he traces them through the sixth
century, in which the landowning nobility was displaced by men of commercial wealth. The fifth
century continued the social upheaval. And Rostovtzeff says that in the third century "class war was
rife and the sharp social contrast between rich
and poor led to acute conflicts in many cities."
Though I cannot agree with Marx that this conflict
overshadows all else in history, class warfare was
typical of the Greeks, as contemporaneously it was
of the Romans. The ancients bequeathed no panacea
here.

The Changing Concept of Areté. Throughout
Greek history, emphasis was placed on virtue, excellence, a sense of the noble -- areté. This
concept went hand in hand with heroic emulation.

No one view of the ideal man comes down from
this Greek conception. Over the centuries, the
Greeks themselves changed their view of it. In
the Iliad of Homer, it was totally in line with the
early aristocratic level of Pindar. But Hesoid
introduced the areté of working class virtue, the
excellence of "righteousness and work." In praise
of Sparta, Tyrtaeus exalted the heroic patriot,
and made the state the measure. "Whatever helps
the state is good, whatever injures it is bad,"
was Tyrtaeus' view according to Jaeger. Solon
recognized a pluralism of virtues, allowing for
various goals. A primary tendency as time passed
was to shift from the ideal of physical excellence
to moral and intellectual excellence. The Odyssey
exalts both warlike valour and intellectual merit;

42

Xenophanes recommended "his 'wisdom' as more profitable to the State" than "wrestling and boxing and running," thereby rejecting Pindar. In the time of Socrates the identification of the individual and the state tended to break up, according to Jaeger, with individual virtues becoming important. Intellectualizing the matter, Plato ascribed all separate virtues to a single one -- knowledge.

The upshot is that the existential problem is not solved for us by a consensus arrived at by Greek culture. The argument over values and life-styles which goes on in modern thought was typical also of the Greeks.

Paideia. Werner Jaeger's monumental two-volume Paideia: The Ideals of Greek Culture tells of a similar evolution in the Greek concept of Paideia. For centuries, Homer was the paramount educational instrument; the purpose of education was not to learn a craft or profession, but to receive from the past the heritage reflecting Greek values, although Jaeger says that the deliberate formation of character in keeping with a cultural ideal began as late as Pericles. When at that time introspective intellect was turned on Greek society, the Sophists caused the Greeks to become conscious of their own culture. The concept of paideia became enlarged in meaning; it came to include not just education, but the totality of culture, including "all the artistic forms and the intellectual and aesthetic achievements of their race." In Socrates it took still another twist: it came to refer to the inner life of a man, as though it were a personal possession which could be protected against the outside world. This was a spiritualization of paideia.

No Final Religious Paradigm. If there is anything paradigmatic in Greek religion, it is its openness -- its lack of a paradigm --, although the portion of it assignable to Plato contradicts even this. The predominant Greek tendency was not

43

to insist on a single religious form or to seek to convert others to a "true" view; "dispersed as they were over various lands, they worshipped their god in many shapes and under many names."

Tucker speaks of the many "inconsistent and even incompatible elements" in Greek religion, and ascribes this to the Greeks' origins. "We have already observed that the classical Greek was the outcome of a blending of northern invaders, akin to the Teutons and Celts, with earlier denizens of the country, who were of a quite alien Mediterranean stock. Greek religion was equally the outcome of a blending of the two." One of these original sources had had a religion based on "the powers of nature and their personification" and the other had been based instead on "a worship of ancestors and their ghosts."

The upshot was polytheism and a certain ambiguity even about the gods that were believed in. Hadas reflects that "even on the question of position, there is ambiguity; sometimes Zeus is sovereign, bound by no will but his own, and sometimes he is subordinate to Fate and only the executive arm for the decrees of Fate."

As with other facets of Greek society, there was no final formulation; Greek religion changed with time. The totemic aspects had dropped out prior to Homer; with Homer the gods were thought close enough to man to encourage a "robust confidence in man's own godlikeness"; this was shaken in the fifth and sixth centuries when moral qualities were ascribed to the gods, raising them high above the human level and giving man himself less confidence; however, with the advent of tragedy man was put on his own, "no longer protected by the gods' heavenly radiance," and began to make his own decisions. There came an age of scepticism in which the Sophists "abolished all ties of religion and custom by branding them mere conventions." Euripidean intellectualism criticized "not only the gods, but the whole mythology," according to Jaeger.

44

"There is no greater proof of the fact that his generation questioned everything and believed nothing, than the disintegration of all life and tradition into discussion and philosophizing."

Then came the rise of Platonism and its opposite, the Epicurean view. These were followed by the Stoics. During the Hellenistic Age which followed, the Stoic and Epicurean philosophies predominated. Stoicism constituted, according to Hadas, a fusion of the Platonic with the non-Platonic. It was Epicureanism, Hadas says, which truly represented the Greek tradition; but the Platonic view related most to the Christianity which later swept the Roman world.

In religion as in other things the Greeks left us not a "solution," but a variety of rich sources.

The Exuberant Child-Man. There are a number of other ways in which Greek culture left open questions -- as in their failure to settle upon a final political model, their continuous harsh warfare, the nonparadigmatic implications of their small size and scale; this discussion has been by no means complete. My overall impression, particularly as I have read the histories written by their own historians, has been that the Greeks were childlike. I was about to write "delightfully, interestingly, exuberantly childlike." but such a judgment can only be made at a distance. Had we lived among them, we might have found many aspects neither delightful nor interesting in a favorable sense. Those annihilated in the sacking of a city or who survived to be pressed into slavery had occasion, in fact to rue the exuberance.

But from a distance they were indeed delightful and exuberant and deeply interesting. Their accomplishments were great, but they were people, subject to the ordinary foibles. We smile when we read of the phallic processions and the statues of Hermes with an erect penis. We smile again

45

when we read Herodotus' believing account of the comparative casualties supposedly suffered by the Greeks and the Persians at Platae: "... of the 300,000 men (of the Persians), not 3,000 survived. The Spartan losses in the battle amounted to 91 killed; the Tegeans lost 16, the Athenians 52." Humanity at large is reflected in Thucydides' accounts of the fickleness of Athenian character, as when he reports a letter from Nicias observing that "I know the Athenian character from experience: you like to be told pleasant news, but if things do not turn out in the way you have been led to expect, then you blame your informants afterwards." He tells of the voters at Athens who will permit their judgments to be swayed "by any clever speech designed to create prejudice," and of Nicias' choice "to meet his own death himself at the hands of the enemy" rather than to "be put to death on a disgraceful charge and by an unjust verdict of the Athenians."

There was indeed Olympian elevation, but Euripides saw fit instruments for his realism in "lying, treachery, malice, uncleanness, jealousy, rage, vengeance, envy." The public taste in 5th century Athens was reflected in Aristophanes' comedies which were "distinguished by three characteristics: the direct attacks on public characters; the extravagant forms assumed by the choruses; and the nakedness of their indecency."

Jaeger writes of the human weakness which accompanied the nobility and energy of the late 5th century; even among so fine a flowering he finds "something inexpressibly sad about the hypocrisy which was the necessary price for all that brilliance, and the moral rootlessness of a world which would give anything and do anything for outward success."

Sadness, however, does not best summarize the Greeks; at least, not a sadness differing from the sadness inherent in any review of humanity's immaturity. From our distance they are immensely

entertaining and enjoyable. They involved all
that goes into a good play. Most assuredly they
hold the mirror up to ourselves.

NOTES

1. So that I can avoid the pedantry of including
hundreds of footnotes, I will be footnoting to a
given source only once in each chapter. The single
footnote will cite all the pages to which I would
otherwise refer by specific footnotes. The references to Snell, for example, are as follows:
Bruno Snell, The Discovery of the Mind (New York:
Harper & Row, 1960), pp. 22, 32, 61, 35, 100, 143,
147, 144, 236, 159-160, 258, 69, 174, 177, 24, 201,
179, 108, 180. The pages are referred to in the
order in which I have cited material from Snell in
the chapter.

2. Thucydides, History of the Peloponnesian War,
trans. Rex Warner (Baltimore: Penguin Books,
1954), pp. 324, 121, 117, 440, 462.

3. Werner Jaeger, Paideia: The Ideals of Greek
Culture, (New York: Oxford University Press, 1939),
Vol. I, pp. 51, 311, 90, 265, 229, 163, 134, 224,
171, 69, 89, 272, 300, 348, 331; Volume II: pp. 5,
157, 160, 70.

4. T. G. Tucker, Life in Ancient Athens, The
Social and Public Life of a Classical Athenian
From Day to Day (New York: The Macmillan Company,
1906), pp. 210, 298, 47, 282, 183, 204-205, 209.

5. Herodotus, The Histories, trans. Aubrey de
Selincourt (Baltimore: Penguin Books, 1954), pp.
25, 15, 507, 199-200, 210, 212, 122, 123, 579.

6. Moses Hadas, The Greek Ideal and Its Survival
(New York: Harper Colophon Books, 1960), p. 10,
referring to E. R. Dodds' The Greeks and the Irrational; pp. 8, 50, 104-105, 126-127, 82, 1, 86, 87,

18, 21, 98, 93-94, 11, 77, 89, 36, 97, 98.

7. Aristophanes' comedy is set out in Joseph B. Gittler, _Social Thought Among the Early Greeks_ (Athens, Georgia: University of Georgia Press, 1941), pp. 150-157. It is a delightful spoof on socialist thought. The theme of the socialist model argued by one of the characters is illustrated by the following passages:

> "Praxagora: First, I'll provide that the silver, and land, and whatever beside each man shall possess, shall be common and free, one fund for the public, then out of it we will feed and maintain you, like housekeepers true, dispensing, and sparing, and caring for you . . . No girl will of course be permitted to mate except in accord with the rules of the State. By the side of her lover, so handsome and tall, will be stationed the squat, the ungainly and small."

8. Frederic Bastiat, _The Law_, trans. Dean Russell (Irvington-on-Hudson: Foundation for Economic Education, 1950), p. 50.

9. M. Rostovtzeff, _The Social and Economic History of the Hellenistic World_ (London: Oxford University Press, 1941), pp. 268, 210, 212, 273, 185, 196, 209.

10. Evelyn Abbott, _Pericles and the Golden Age of Athens_ (New York: G. P. Putnam's Sons, 1891), pp. 308, 325, 135-136, 304, 150, 262, 264-265, 342, 343, 344, 9, 320, 328.

11. F. Poland, E. Reisinger and R. Wagner, _The Culture of Ancient Greece and Rome_ (Boston: Little, Brown and Company, 1926), pp. 122, 68, 240.

12. F. A. Hayek, _The Constitution of Liberty_ (Chicago: University of Chicago Press, 1960), pp. 164-166.

4

THE MISSING PARADIGM: ROME

The point I am making in these chapters is
preliminary to my discussion of modern society.
It is that modern civilization began not on a
firm foundation, but on the basis of a still-im-
mature humanity and without definitive models from
the past. The non-paradigmatic nature of all
previous societies suggests that history has consisted of a series of make-shifts.

A society which endured, as Rome did, for a
thousand years in the West and considerably longer
in the East may seem to contradict the "make-shift"
theory. And yet, Roman history is the story of
an entire series of make-shifts. During those
thousand years Rome never became settled upon a
satisfactory foundation. There was at all times
a void underneath the surface.

Gibbon didn't begin his study of the decline
of Rome until the age of Augustus, and although
he saw the working of certain "slow and secret
poisons" even during the early Empire, he didn't
consider the decline itself to have occurred until
after the reign of Marcus Aurelius. In a similar
vein, Carl Roebuck concludes that "the earliest
signs of weakness seem to have appeared at the
time when the Empire was outwardly very strong
and stable, in the second century after Christ."[1]

I would say, though, that it is difficult
really to understand the decline without tracing
the weakness back through almost the entirety of
Roman history. José Ortega y Gasset's perceptive
eye went more to the heart of the matter when he
saw the "desperation of ancient man" as having
begun in the first century B.C.[2] This desperation
was the result of earlier weaknesses, which can
be traced back through the Gracchi and beyond. I

49

believe that those who would understand Rome's
fall almost seven centuries later must start in the
second century B.C., just as Americans must begin
with the generation of Emerson and Thoreau if they
are to understand the civil dissension in later
twentieth century America.

The Early Period

The scepticism of some modern scholars has
cast doubt on the exact year in which the Romans
threw off their kings and established the Republic.
The date traditionally assigned has been 509 B.C.,
but the event may have occurred somewhat later.
In either case, almost a thousand years elapsed
from the beginning of the Republic to the time when
the last Roman emperor in the West was deposed by
the barbarian Odacer in 476 A.D.

The Republic's beginning centuries were con-
sumed by the "Struggle of the Orders," through
which the Plebeians gradually gained political
equality with the Patricians. During those centuries Roman society moved toward equality and
away from its original aristocratic complexion.

The Punic Wars severely tested the Republic.
The first were continued for twenty-three agonizing
years, the second for seventeen. Hannibal ravaged
Italy for several years before he was finally de-
feated by Scipio at Zama in 202. The Third Punic
War involved still another four years of war, and
resulted in the destruction of Carthage in 146 B.C.
There were also wars with the Samnites before those
with Carthage, and later there were wars with
Macedonia.

These military struggles had significant internal effects. The powers of government were
brought into the hands of the Senate as a body
offering experience and continuity. The upshot
was that the earlier democratic gains were undone;

50

the old dichotomy of Patrician versus Plebeian no
longer existed, but there was a new Senatorial
aristocracy, the Nobiles, which consisted of the
magistrates and their descendants.

A Cohesive Society: the MOS MAIORUM

As a small city-state under the pressures of
constant war, the Romans became tightly knit.
Mommsen's comment that "life in the case of the
Roman was spent under conditions of austere restraint, and, the nobler he was, the less he was
a free man," indicates that the community was
proud and austere.[3] Mommsen goes on to say that
"all-powerful custom restricted (the Roman of this
period) to a narrow range of thought and action;
and to have led a serious and strict or, to use
the characteristic Latin expressions, a sad and
severe life, was his glory." There was a "collective sense of dignity in the noble families of
Rome" which "swelled into that mighty civic pride,
the like of which the earth has never seen again."
And there was a strong veneration of family and
ancestors.

It was from this that the conception of the
mos maiorum arose; the mos maiorum--or "the tradition of our ancestors"--was an image of close cultural unity by which the Romans perceived their
society. This unity contained several elements.

To Polybius, "a scrupulous fear of the gods
is the very thing which keeps the Roman commonwealth together." He remarked that the religious
devotion was carried to "an extraordinary height
. . . both in private and public business," although he expressed his belief that religion was
used by the nobility to control the remainder of
the people.[4] Roebuck says "the highest Roman virtue was pietas, the proper observance of obligations to the gods, to the state and to the family,
and the most important quality of Roman character
was gravitas, a serious dignified attitude to life."

R. E. Smith confirms that Rome "was essentially a religious society."[5]

The upper class in particular had a close family life which Roebuck says was "characterized by strong patriarchal authority." Smith informs us that the virtue of disciplina, which stressed the duty to obey those in authority, was fundamental; and he points out that their histories often told stories that reinforced this commitment. In particular, the army rested on complete obedience. Severe punishments were meted out to those who did not obey. The individual was in various ways absorbed into a cohesive society. There was a collective ideal, with the individual finding meaning primarily through membership in and subordination to the society as a whole. Smith underscores the importance of the family when he says that the city's greatness had stemmed very much from the "sacredness of family life."

Behavior was closely controlled. "The Romans thought that no marriage, or rearing of children, nay or feast or drinking-bout, ought to be permitted according to everyone's appetite or fancy, without being examined and inquired into," according to Plutarch. He says the Romans were of the opinion "that a man's character was much sooner perceived in things of this sort than in what is done publicly and in open day." The result was that "they chose, therefore, two persons, one out of the patricians, the other out of the commons, who were to watch, correct, and punish, if anyone ran too much into voluptuousness, or transgressed the usual manner of life of his country; and these they called Censors."[6]

The Rome of the mos maiorum amounted to what we would today call a "closed society." This is well illustrated by Smith when he tells us that there were men who considered themselves guardians of Rome as a tightly-knit society and who imposed a strict censorship to bar any outside influences that might break up the hegemony of Roman society.

52

These men especially wished not to allow in any foreign thinking or manners that would prove inconsistent with Rome's. They certainly did not want extensive Greek influence.

Expression of all types was strictly controlled (although this wasn't totally accomplished). According to Smith, the control of literature was easy, since this depended on wealthy patrons and the nobles were the educated and leisured class: "Those who might have been antagonistic did not have the opportunity to express themselves." Plautus found it prudent to circumvent the restraints by making Greece rather than Rome the locale for the plots of his plays; and Naevius was imprisoned and then banished because he didn't toe the mark.

The purpose of the control was not malevolent, since a serious ideal lay behind it. A spirit of duty, of noblesse, pervaded Roman life. The restraints followed naturally in a community in which the ideal was, Smith says, "to be the leading man in the State in war and peace, to hold the highest office and the most important military command, to acquire wealth honorably and to have children to carry on the family."

Panaetius gave the mos maiorum at least some theoretical basis, but for the most part the Romans were practical, not contemplative. Panaetius was the exception when "he took the Roman ethos and the aristocratic ideal and gave them a philosophic basis; Stoicism and the ideal became fused in his interpretation."

Rome was governed almost exclusively by the nobiles. It is apparent from the statistics cited by Smith that a novus homo -- a "new man" -- was rare. During the century that ended when Tiberius Gracchus was tribune, 159 of the consulships were held by members of 26 families. Ninety-nine were held by members of just ten families. Only four new men became consuls during the fifty-four years

53

between 200 and 146 B. C.; and each of these attained that office only with the help of the noble
families. Polybius was something of an ancient
Montesquieu when he wrote about a "mixed constitution" involving a check and balance among monarchy,
aristocracy and democracy; but in fact Rome was
overwhelmingly aristocratic.

The economy was based on the small family
farm. Rostovtzeff says "the citizen farmer lived
on his land and tilled it with the help of his
family, or perhaps with a few slaves who formed
part of the family from the economic point of view."

All of these ingredients together show the
nature of the Republic's concordia during the
Punic Wars and for a few years thereafter. But
what are we to think of the soundness of such a
social order?

The mos maiorum was a tight little island of
social mores and thought. Because it depended upon
insulation, it was foredoomed to eventual dissipa-
tion; it couldn't last and history shows that it
didn't last. Such a closed society could not be
sustained once the unique conditions upon which it
was based had shifted. Eventually a flood of alien
ideas and influences poured in upon it from the
rest of the world. Such a society would only be
an anachronism under changed conditions, but it
could hardly last even as an anachronism, since its
unique characteristics could not be sustained in
an open setting. In the section which follows I
will trace its disintegration under those outside
forces.

The mos maiorum was, from the point of view
of virtually all later Romans, the best time in
Roman history. It is also a time in which Roman
society contained all of the elements Burkean conservatism would desire for a society: social
hierarchy, tradition, a strong religious center,
private property, community, control over will and

appetite, and an integrative-type state. There is, therefore, considerable significance in my conclusion that it was little more than an impermanent make-shift founded on uniquely insulated conditions. Such a conclusion is not only at odds with Burkean conservatism but leaves Roman civilization existentially naked. It means that even the best part of the Roman experience was non-paradigmatic. The Roman concordia was valuable for its own purposes, but those purposes were transient.

Disintegration of the MOS MAIORUM

The historian Polybius, although a Greek, lived in Rome during the second century B.C. He made two contradictory predictions: he estimated that the "mixed constitution" which he praised would keep licentiousness in check, but he is better remembered for his other and more prophetic prediction foretelling the dissolution of the mos maiorum: "The future of the Roman polity . . . is quite clear, in my opinion . . . When a commonwealth, after warding off many great dangers, has arrived at a high pitch of prosperity and undisputed power, it is evident that, by the lengthened continuance of great wealth within it, the manner of life of its citizens will become more extravagant; and that the rivalry for office, and in other spheres of activity, will become fiercer than it ought to be. And as this state of things goes on more and more, the desire of office and the shame of losing reputation, as well as the ostentation and extravagance of living, will prove the beginning of a deterioration. And of this change the people will be credited with being the authors, when they become convinced that they are being cheated by some from avarice, and are puffed up with flattery by others from love of office. For when that comes about, in their passionate resentment and acting under the dictates of anger, they will refuse to obey any longer, or to be content with having equal powers with their leaders, but will demand to have all or far the greatest them-

55

selves. And when that comes to pass the constitution will receive a new name, which sounds better than any other in the world, liberty or democracy; but, in fact, it will become the worst of all governments, mob-rule."

After the Punic Wars the changes which would shatter the mos maiorum did occur. With the pressure of war removed, the need for senatorial continuity was less urgent and the demand for military virtue declined. It became possible to relax again. The cauldron of war was no longer mixing the brew of pietas and gravitas.

Where economic causation is involved, there is a temptation to assign the effects exclusively to it. Such a single-minded explanation is a mistake in the Roman context as elsewhere, but this does not mean that the economic factors were not of major importance. They helped shatter the underpinnings of the old order.

Rome now had extensive overseas provinces which provided a continuous flow of indemnity, slaves and booty. Cowell says "a new economy based upon money, foreign booty, cheap imports and skillful slaves were all signs that the Romans were embarking upon a new and feverish pursuit of wealth and luxury."[7] Heitland places considerable emphasis on the economic and social impact of the provinces when he says that "in promoting the private self-seeking and public impotence that foiled all efforts for reform, the provincial system played a great part, and it was through the influence of the Provinces that the Roman Republic came to a violent and unlamented end."[8] Roebuck adds that "too many governors saw only an opportunity for their own aggrandisement and made very considerable personal gain."

Slaves poured in from the provinces, altering the economic base. An "agricultural revolution" occurred as large slave plantations, the latifundia, replaced the family farm. "This agricultural

56

revolution helped to create an idle mob in Rome
with serious political and military effects for
the state." Roebuck explains that "because the
plentiful supply of slave labor drove free men
from the large farms and public works projects,
Romans and Italians of the lower class consequently faced unemployment in both the country and the
city." Nor was it just the small farmers and the
laborers on the large estates who migrated to the
city to form the new proletariat; the slaves themselves were often freed and became part of the
same urban element. Smith gives a good description: "The growth of latifundia . . ., the absen-
tee landlord running his farm with slave labor,
the conscription of the yeoman class for war service,
were all combining to create social distress, and
to take away from a large number of people their
means of livelihood. The persons thus dispossess-
ed came to Rome, where they contrived to eke out a
livelihood as hired laborers in public works and
as clientes of the nobles."

The estates became larger as, according to
Heitland, "there was in this period a marked
tendency to give up tillage for grazing." As
to the manual trades, he says that just as "slavery
was driving out free labor in the country . . .
the same was taking place in the manual trades,
though we hear less of it." He adds that "old
prejudices against bodily labor other than agriculture helped to give our handicrafts to the
slave-artisan."

The result was that "if we try to discover
what were the occupations of ordinary Roman citizens in this period, we come upon three lines of
life, (a) soldiering with an eye to profit,
(b) finance, including a certain amount of commerce,
(c) acquiescent pauperism." In the next century
the Marian army reforms made soldiering for profit
a seriously disruptive force. It remained so for
six centuries, creating and destroying demagogues
and later setting up and pulling down emperors.
The "acquiescent pauperism" grew to massive

proportions; by the time of Augustus there were 200,000 people supported by subsidized grain. The growth of so large a dependent proletariat was certainly incompatible with the mos maiorum. Heitland points out that with "the mere dependence of the poor as poor upon the rich as rich, the quest for corporal sustenance rather than social protection, was already beginning." Political opportunism took full advantage of "cheap grain," as we see during the first century B.C. in the conduct of Rullus and Clodius.

Nor was cheap corn the only manipulative instrument. The appeal to the proletarians included lavish free entertainment and "above all," Dickinson says, "outright bribery."9 The corrupting influences which the mos maiorum had sought to suppress were intensified. "Human blood was first shed for sport in the Roman forum in 490 (264 B.C.)," Mommsen says. Such "amusements" began as funeral games, and as they became more vulgar they were opposed by the nobles. In 268 B.C. the "government carried a decree of the people prohibiting the bringing over of wild beasts to Rome, and strictly insisted that no gladiators should appear at the public festivals," but Mommsen says this wasn't enforced. Heitland describes the entertainments as "demoralizing" and cites the indecencies of the actresses (slaves under orders) at the ludi Florales." The gladiatorial fights in which slaves killed each other were for a long time an "irregular private affair," but they eventually became public spectacles. When they later became a political instrument, "the people of Rome were cultivated by new techniques of mass bribery and propaganda."

A commercial middle class developed during the Punic Wars. Smith says that instead of being a positive force they had little sense of "Community"; they "took no part in Rome's government, and were untouched . . . by moral scruples." The aristocracy voiced a theme which has been important throughout Western civilization: it "despised"

58

commerce and remained a landed nobility.

"As government contractors, as financiers, and as business men plying their business in many parts of the world, (the Equites) became a rich and influential class." At first their political thinking and alignment "was unformed," but Gaius Gracchus sought their support and later they became a major power behind Julius Caesar. As "a party of material interest without past traditions of ancestral virtue," they weren't fitted to sustain the tightly knit mos maiorum.

The aristocracy itself was slowly transformed by a number of forces which at the same time affected the entire society. Its austere virtues were slowly dissolved. By the time Cicero and Cato the Younger attempted to rally those loyal to the Republic almost a century later, the Senate was just a shadow of what it had been. This weakness was not entirely due to the civil wars or even to the competition for demagogic glory which predominated during the first century B.C., although these were important factors. Although Smith criticizes Sallust for assigning to the nobles of 112 B.C. the same debasement they embodied in 60 B.C., it is evident that the decay began before the Gracchi.

Hellenization was an influence which was general but which had its main effect on the nobility. As Rome lost its preoccupation with purely Italian affairs and became a world power, its educated leisure class came in touch with the intellectual ferment which had so long existed in Greece. "Among the upper classes," Roebuck tells us, "a steady change in education and manners set in." Cato the Elder had been right in thinking that Greek influence would help shatter the mos maiorum; he had tried to block the influx of Greek ideas. To prevent such an influx "they exercised a vigilant censorship, aimed to exclude anything that might destroy the harmony of Roman society." Prompted by Cato, a party of Reform

59

arose which sought unsuccessfully to erect barriers
to shelter the distinctive Roman culture. In 186
B.C. the Senate suppressed the worship of Dionysus,
which was conducted through secret societies with
an orgiastic ritual. The worship of Bacchus, also
characterized by secret rites and nightly orgies,
flourished mainly in the Greek district, and it
too was suppressed. A few years later in 157 B.C.
the Senate suspended the construction of a permanent theater, since according to Mommsen "the
Roman drama was, at this epoch when men were
wavering between the old austerity and the new
corruption, the academy at once of Hellenism and
of vice." Rome didn't have its first permanent
theater until a century later. In 161 B.C. the
Senate banished rhetoricians and philosophers.
Seven years later three Greek philosophers --
Carneades a sceptic, Diogenes a stoic, and Crito-
laus a peripatetic -- visited Rome as ambassadors
of Athens, but were "hustled untimely out of Rome,"
according to Smith, "their business having been
rushed through the Senate at Cato's instigation."

    These measures were an effort - ultimately
futile - to preserve the mos maiorum. To keep
this effort in perspective, it is worth noting
Mommsen's view that, though culturally conservative,
the Catonian party was not unnecessarily bigoted:
"Cato was by no means chargeable with an opposition
to culture and to Hellenism in general. On the
contrary it is the highest merit of the national
party, that they comprehended very clearly the
necessity of creating a Latin literature and of
bringing the stimulating influences of Hellenism
to bear on it; only their intention was, that
Latin literature should not be a mere copy taken
from the Greek . . ."

    The influx of Greek culture was manifested
best in the education of Publius Cornelius Scipio,
known as Scipio the Younger, who was one of the
soundest men of the second century. Roebuck says
of him that "Scipio was representative of a new
type of young Roman just emerging in this period,

well educated along Greek lines and with a broader, more international outlook than the farmer-senators, men of Fabius' type, who constituted a majority of the Senate."

The overall effect, though, was socially unsettling; Hellenization introduced, through rationalism, a relativism and an individualism which were inconsistent with the old concord and austerity. Mommsen tells us that "the tragic drama of this period and its principal representative Ennius displayed . . . an anti-national and consciously propagandistic aim." He goes on to say that "this Attico-Roman comedy, with its prostitution of body and soul usurping the name of love -- equally immoral in shamelessness and in sentimentality -- with its offensive and unnatural generosity, with its uniform glorification of a life of debauchery, with its mixture of rustic coarseness and foreign refinement, was one continuous lesson of Romano-Hellenic demoralization, and was felt as such."

The corruption is evident in this passage from Mommsen. The following statements by Smith show the rationalistic questioning and the advent of individualism (neither of them necessarily bad, but both inconsistent with the cultural insularity of the mos maiorum): "The nobles began to seek in reason a foundation for their social customs and beliefs, and the individual began to assume a position of greater importance." He says that Lucilius was "the first instance of an individual writer" who recounted "his own views and experiences," and says that "his appearance at this time has a certain symbolic quality, for the Gracchi, like himself, were in their individualism the product of their age; but he was in sympathy with, they in revolt against, their society.

The rapid increase in sensuality was another general influence. The "glorification of a life of debauchery" was thoroughly at odds with the Roman virtues of pietas, gravitas and disciplina.

Paterculus states that "when their dread of Carthage was at an end, and their rival in empire was removed, the nation, deserting the cause of virtue, went over, not gradually, but with precipitation, to that of vice; the old rules of conduct were renounced, and new introduced; and the people turned themselves from activity to slumber, from arms to pleasure, from business to idleness."[10] Polybius also spoke of "the general deterioration of morals," and related that "some had wasted their energies on favorite youths; others on mistresses; and a great many on banquets enlivened with poetry and wine, and all the extravagant expenditure which they entailed." He added that "to such monstrous lengths had this debauchery gone among young men, that many of them had given a talent for a young favorite."

Plutarch wrote in the same vein later when he said that "he was very rare who would cultivate the old habits of bodily labor, or prefer a light supper, and a breakfast which never saw the fire, or be in love with poor clothes and a homely lodging, or could set his ambition rather on doing without luxuries than on possessing them. For now the state, unable to keep its purity by reason of its greatness, . . . was fain to admit . . . new examples of living. With reason, therefore, everybody admired Cato, when they saw others . . . grow effeminate by pleasure."

A number of scandals occurred during the ten years between 179 and 169 B.C., particularly in the conduct of officials overseas; and two years previously, in 181, a law had been enacted to limit the size of private parties. "It is said," Heitland tells us, citing Macrobius, "that gluttony grew fast, with disastrous effect on the morals of young men, and that the example of their betters led to an epidemic of drunkenness among the common people." Mommsen elaborates this point when he says that "hitherto the Romans had perhaps drunk pretty deeply at supper, but drinking-banquets in the strict sense were unknown; now formal revels

62

came into vogue, on which occasions the wine was little or not at all diluted and was drunk out of large cups . . . In consequence of this debauchery dice-playing, which had doubtless long been in use among the Romans, reached such proportions that it was necessary for legislation to interfere." In 173 two men were expelled "for preaching Pleasure as the rule and guide of life."

Slavery played a role in this evaporation of the moral values of the mos maiorum. Heitland reports that "from gratifying the wishes of their owners it was an easy step to create in them new desires and then provide the satisfaction . . . The Roman once roused was apt to take his pleasure with a riotous appetite, to which his slaves ministered with the mature vitiosity of the East. But in no respect were the oriental slaves more mischievous than in their treatment of the young. It was their immediate interest to curry favor with the rising generation, and their means of doing so was a course of indulgence and secret connivances, demoralizing from the first, and becoming worse as the children grew up."

The moral decline was most immediately harmful in its effect on the nobility. Mommsen comments that "the government of the aristocracy was in full train to destroy its own work." He says that "there was a profound meaning in the question of Cato, 'What was to become of Rome, when she should no longer have any state to fear?'"

The point was reached at which there existed "a degenerate oligarchy and a democracy still undeveloped but already cankered in the bud." According to Heitland the moral collapse made reforms useless, since "there was no point at which to make the beginning of a fruitful crusade." He observes that "it was a moral force that was the mainspring of the whole machine, and it was precisely this moral force that was now failing fast." Once this was true, it would do no permanent good to elect the best men, to punish the worst abuses,

to enforce honesty by law. Once the positive was
gone, a void remained.

The same trends were present in the decline of
the family. Mommsen relates that "the ties of
family life became relaxed with fearful rapidity.
The evil of grisettes and boy-favorites spread
like a pestilence." Much later Augustus sought to
reestablish sexual mores which would strengthen
family ties, but during the period we are discussing "the loose relations between the sexes among
the higher classes of society was one of the most
obvious consequences of the disintegration." Women
had earlier been confined tightly within the patriarchal, family, but there was now a movement
toward their emancipation. Mommsen comments on it,
but Heitland provides the following description.
"The Roman ladies of the period had . . . fallen
away from the solid moral type of earlier days . . .
Their extravagance and love of display were becoming a marked feature of the age. In the scandal
of the Bacchanalian orgies women of position had
played a leading part, and it was believed that in
that affair vice had been followed by crime:
those whose secrecy was doubted had been silenced
by poison."

The mos maiorum's religious base eroded at
the same time. Mommsen says that "towards the
end of this epoch, complaints were loudly made
that the lore of the augurs was neglected, and,
that, to use the language of Cato, a number of
ancient auguries and auspices were falling into
oblivion through the indolence of the college."
He adds that "the Hellenistic irreligious spirit
found free course," and observes that the government began to use religion as a manipulative device, treating "the national religion in accor-
dance with the view of Polybius as a superstition
useful for imposing on the public at large." The
growing Hellenism introduced scepticism: "The
first great blow to the current theology was dealt
by Ennius, who lived into the middle of this
period. He translated into Latin the work of

64

Euhemerus, and drove home the sceptical attack by applications in his own works."

Another factor was that the Roman constitution was clearly insufficient for the broadened circumstances which now existed. Rome had grown beyond a city-state, but retained its earlier governmental mechanism. This was unsuited for governing all of Italy, much less a major portion of the Mediterranean world. Citizens were required to come to Rome to vote. Heitland concludes that "the constitution was no longer sufficient for the needs of the time," although he sees that there was no chance for successful reform, since the human material needed for that purpose was no longer present: "It had come to this, that no privilege could be successfully assailed or defended without resorting sooner or later to the use of the sword. And military revolution meant monarchy."

The power of the Senate was founded entirely on consent and had no further legal basis. In 287 B.C. the Hortensian Law had "recognized the plebiscites of the Tribal Assembly as valid and binding on the whole state, without senatorial ratification." Necessity had set aside this democratic standard during the Punic Wars and placed power in the Senate, but after the wars the Senate lacked constitutional justification for exclusive power. The day was approaching when senatorial hegemony could not be maintained. Senatorial control was in difficulty the moment it was seriously challenged.

There was an incubation first of anarchy and then of despotism as the replacements for the mos maiorum. The tendencies I have traced were only the beginning: the ensuing ninety years of civil disorder magnified each of them until finally there could be no social order without the cements of military dictatorship.

65

The Beginning of Political Disorder: The Gracchi

Tiberius Gracchus was elected tribune in 133 B.C. Most historians describe the personal characteristics of the Gracchi brothers favorably. Rostovtzeff refers to Tiberius as "highly educated, absolutely honest, and remarkably able." Mommsen says that Gaius "was very different from his brother, who was about nine years older. Like the latter, he had no relish for vulgar pleasures and vulgar pursuits; he was a man of thorough culture and a brave soldier; . . . But in talent, in character, and above all in passion he was decidedly superior to Tiberius." Plutarch said about both that "the greatest detractors and their worst enemies could not but allow that they had a genius to virtue beyond all other Romans, which was improved also by a generous education." Although the moral and social disintegration provided the setting for the civil disorder which began with the Gracchi, the Gracchi brothers themselves did not embody the profligacy.

Although he was a member of the Senate, Tiberius' purpose in becoming a tribune was to bypass the Senate. He proposed to reassert the old Licinian-Sextian law which had limited the amount of public domain anyone could occupy to five hundred acres. When another tribune vetoed the bill, Tiberius unconstitutionally obtained a vote removing him from office. The Senate refused to finance the administration of the land statute and Tiberius was threatened with impeachment as soon as he left office. Tiberius accordingly announced his candidacy for reelection, even though the reelection of the tribune would be unconstitutional. During the ensuing campaign he and three hundred of his supporters were killed and their bodies were thrown in the Tiber. Dickinson says that this enormity "was the first act of political violence, the first instance of resort to extralegal force, in the course of nearly four centuries of the history of the republic." But Scipio, who was probably the greatest Roman of his day, commented favorably by repeating a line from Homer: "Even so perish all who do the same."

Just the same, Tiberius had left his mark. The land reform was continued by a senatorial "middle party" headed by Scipio himself. But it satisfied neither the reform nor the opposition factions; significantly, Scipio was assassinated by a member of the Gracchan party and the efforts of the "middle party" were cut short.

The reform party lacked leaders and remained quiet for nine years after Tiberius' death, but in 123 B.C. his brother Gaius Gracchus was elected tribune. His mother foresaw "the country's ruin" and urged him to hold back, but he came forward with a program which Mommsen had described as "nothing else than an entirely new constitution." It included (a) a provision permitting the re-election of tribunes, (b) distribution of cheap corn in Rome, (c) changes in the order of voting in the <u>comitia</u> <u>centuriata</u>, (d) a proposal to establish colonies in Italy and overseas, (e) modifications in army recruitment, (g) a measure for the diminution or remission of debt, (h) the establishment of a "middle man" system for the collection of taxes in the provinces, (i) a public works program that included extensive road projects, and (j) a transfer of the functions of the jurymen from the nobility to the equestrian order. The program was based on an assumption of tribunician democracy, and therefore repudiated the central role of the Senate.

Mommsen observes, however, that democracy was not viable in the Rome of that time and that what Gaius actually sought was an absolute monarchy "in the form of a magistracy continued for life by regular reelection and rendered absolute by an unconditional control over the formally sovereign comitia, an unlimited tribuneship of the people for life." Interestingly, Mommsen approves such a move, saying that it was precisely a monarchy that was needed; but he criticizes Gaius for his tech-

67

niques, which continued to stimulate the incipient class warfare. For my part, I wonder how Gaius could otherwise have created a monarchy. To do so without a class war would have required senatorial support. Monarchy eventually came into being, but not because everyone agreed to it amicably; it followed ninety years of conflict which exhausted the Roman people and gave military predominance to one man.

Gaius soon found that the demagogic bidding for public favor is a game many can play. Cowell reports that the Senate promptly "persuaded another tribune, Livius Drusus, to overbid Gaius." Plutarch comments that Drusus set about "playing the demagogue in opposition to (Gaius) and offering favors contrary to all good policy." We are told that "when Gaius required those getting land allotments to pay the State a rent, Drusus proposed that there should be no rent. When Gaius proposed two colonies Drusus suggested twelve."

Gaius was reelected in 122 B.C. but was defeated for the next year. Not surprisingly, he began to keep a bodyguard with him. This alarmed the Senate into empowering the Consuls to "take all necessary measures for the safety of the State." One of the Consuls then killed Gaius and, incredibly, three thousand of his supporters -- another in an accumulating string of outrages which were creating embittered division within Roman society. Gaius' body was also thrown into the Tiber.

An evaluation of the Gracchi's careers must contain many elements. The most important is to realize that the catastrophe which began at this time arose only superficially from their efforts. We recall Tolstoy's later observation that great men merely ride a wave and have no more influence on the direction of events than would a bubble moving with the wave.[11] The Gracchi were creatures of their time. Given the conditions which had come into existence, it is probable that if the

Gracchi had not done what they did, the same role
would have been played by someone else. Scipio's
"middle party" was the most constructive alternative, but Scipio's assassination tells a great
deal about the viability of anything really constructive. During the period of affluence which
preceded the Gracchi the Romans had developed the
"child-man" psychology which Ortega had described
with reference to twentieth century Europeans.[12]
They felt expanded desires with an urgent need for
immediate satisfaction, but without real appreciation for the roots of their society or the
principles necessary to social order. The "direct
action" techniques reflected the psychology of
the typical man of the day. A hundred years
later the state became the most powerful "direct
action" tool, absorbing life into itself, as
Ortega has said, as an anti-vital influence.

Smith says that "the Gracchi by the means
they adopted in pursuit of their needs precipitated a spiritual crisis in Rome which was the first
cause of all that followed. The crisis was
largely spiritual, but we may doubt whether the
Gracchi created it, except superficially. They
reflected it and acted on the basis of it. Once
the consensus of the mos maiorum had disintegrated,
things could not be put back in their old form.
It was a unique growth which men could not arti-
ficially recreate.

Gaius and Drusus learned from each other
that demagogic techniques feed on each other.
Most leaders of the first century B.C. turned to
demagoguery, although men such as Cicero and Cato
the Younger were exceptions. This demagoguery had
begun with the Gracchi. Roebuck shows how the
older brother had set the pace: "A current of
doctrinaire humanitarianism and political theory
became increasingly apparent in (Tiberius')
speeches and conduct. Tiberius' appeal to the
urban poor in Rome was an embittered call to class
strife. 'The savage beasts in Italy (Tiberius
said) have their particular dens . . . but the men

69

who bear arms, and expose their lives for the safety of their country, enjoy in the meantime nothing
more in it but the air and the light; and having
no homes or settlements of their own, are con-
strained to wander from place to place with their
wives and children . . . They were styled the
masters of the world but in the meantime had not
one foot of ground which they could call their own.'"

Gaius adopted the same inflammatory manner,
perfecting it to indicate his rejection of the
Senate. Plutarch reports that "while he was arguing for the ratification of this law, his behavior
was observed to show in many respects unusual
earnestness, and whereas other popular leaders had
always hitherto, when speaking, turned their faces
toward the senate house, and the place called the
comitium, he, on the contrary, was the first man
that in his harangue to the people turned himself
the other way, towards them, and continued after
that time to do so. An insignificant movement and
change of posture, yet it marked no small revolution in state affairs, the conversion, in a manner,
of the whole government from an aristocracy to a
democracy, his action intimating that public
speakers should address themselves to the people,
not the senate."

Ninety Years of Civil War

Constant agitation, conspiracy, proscription,
murder and demagoguery continued until in 31 B.C.
Octavius gained sole power by defeating Antony and
Cleopatra at Actium. As a first step in reviewing
this extended period of civil disorder, it is to
be noted that Marius, the Consul elected in 108
B.C., radically altered the nature of the Army.
"The people assumed the right to assign important
military commands to particular individuals by
direct popular vote," Dickinson informs us. At the
same time, the army was professionalized. The
army would thereafter serve its generals, who would
simultaneously be popular demagogues. The army

70

played an increasingly important role in internal politics. Under the Empire it was often the army itself, or the Praetorian guards, that named the emperor.

For our purposes, it is sufficient just to review the highlights of the disorder of the first century B.C.:

With their armies behind them, Marius and Sulla fought for personal supremacy. Each proscribed many of his opponents. Saterninus, a tribune, and Glaucia, a praetor, were murdered. Drusus was assassinated. Sulla sought as dictator to reestablish the constitution, but after his retirement the accumulated bitterness proved irrepressible. Pompey and Caesar rose as competing leaders. The Catilinian conspiracy failed; Cataline himself died in battle. The First Triumvirate was formed by Caesar, Pompey and Crassus. Cicero was exiled. Crassus was killed at Carrhae. Caesar was assassinated. The Second Triumvirate consisting of Octavius, Antony and Lepidus defeated Brutus and Cassius at Philippi. Octavius, renamed Augustus, established his Principate after Antony and Cleopatra were defeated and committed suicide at Actium.

It is clear (except perhaps to the Nietzschean glorifiers of violence from whom we hear so much in nineteenth century thought) that the first century B.C. didn't offer a paradigm for later civilization to follow.

Military Reconstruction: The Age of Augustus

The Punic Wars had pressed Rome into the tightly knit mos maiorum, but the slaughter of the first century had no similar effect; the degeneration continued to grow, increased by the brutality of civil war and the effects of continued demagoguery. When the disorder ended, the Roman who

71

emerged was far removed from the austere virtue and noble dedication of the old Roman. If we believe a solid base was reestablished, we are misled by the Republican forms assumed by the Augustan military hegemony. The Augustan Age gave respite from disorder and provided world-wide Pax Romana, but the moral fabric was characterized by sycophancy and debasement.

Historians give varied interpretations to the Augustan period. To Smith, Rome "awoke to the fulfillment of her destiny after the nightmare of the first century B.C." Rome as now a "world power" and enjoyed a "cosmopolitan philosophy and sense of moral responsibility which came eventually after a century of bloodshed." In his opinion "the Augustan Age was true to Rome," and he speaks of "the faith and confidence in Rome" which summed up the spirit of the age. He believes that "the Age of Augustus gave back to men the opportunity -- for the wish had long been there -- to live once again in conformity with their former moral code, to take up again the ideas and ideals of their happier past and give them life and purpose in an even greater future."

Cowell, on the other hand, interprets the times differently, although he acknowledges that there was "a sudden bound forward" after order was reestablished. He observes that "what was essentially a military tyranny was veiled by the use of old Republican forms and labels" and asserts that historians who take a totally favorable view are forgetting the nature of absolutism.

A few senators showed some spirit, Cowell says, shouting that "senators ought to be free to talk about the Republic," but they were a minority. He shows Augustus to have been a hypocrite: "A close examination of the reality behind this stock recital of his virtues, soon reveals elements of exaggeration and falsity in so synthetic a beatitude, for it is not difficult to paint another picture compounded out of the man's

72

cruelty, vindictiveness and hollowness, his hypocritical attempts to enforce high standards of
conduct, in sexual relations for example, to which
he was not himself willing to conform, and worst
of all, of having set the Romans on the fatal path
of no return that was to lead them through military
dictatorship into the foulest form of arbitrary
monarchical absolutism." Though the Senate was
strengthened, it was "mere stage property." Most
senators were habitually subservient.

In my opinion, Cowell has the better of the
argument. We can test the Augustan Age by its
fruits; we know what followed in the reigns of
Tiberius, Gaius, Claudius and Nero. If the Augustan Age had been followed by a viable Roman
community, we could conclude that such strength
had its origins under Augustus. Instead, Rome
receded into debauchery and a downhill slide which
culminated in the Dark Ages. There were many
symptoms of a void: 200,000 people lived off
the corn dole and Rostovtzeff reports that the
proletariat was "kept in good humour by giving
them . . . a constant supply of amusements and
occasional doles of money;"[13] amazingly, a law
was thought necessary to require that each Roman
raise a family, since the birth rate was precipi-
tously declining in the upper classes; and
reference to the growing "despair of ancient man"
is reflected in Rostovtzeff's statement that "the
mental attitude of the directing classes had
undergone a complete change: men ceased to take
an interest in the state and public affairs . . .
The idea of civic freedom had become, in the
minds of most men, inseparable from the anarchy
and confusion which were still so fresh in the
memory of the generation contemporary with Augustus . . . A dark shade of pessimism covers all the
thought and literary production of this period."

Ferguson speaks of "the Golden Age of Latin
literature" which "reached its full development
in the tranquillity of the Augustan Age;"[14] this
was the period of Virgil, Horace, Ovid and Livy.

73

Rostovtzeff reports "a vastly increased activity
in all departments of economic and intellectual
life." But Cowell again places the time in perspective, observing that "it is true that the Augustan Age boasts the imperishable glory of Virgil,
Livy, Horace and adornments such as Ovid, Tibullus
and Propertius. But Virgil and Horace were
middle-aged at the Battle of Actium and Livy was
then already 28 years old. They, like all the
greatest figures in Roman literature, were Italians
not Romans, and they were products of the dying
Republic rather than of the rising Empire."
Tacitus said that after these literary giants "a
hush has come upon eloquence as indeed it has on
the world at large."[15] The period from the death
of Augustus to the death of Marcus Aurelius is no
longer known as the Golden Age, but as a "Silver
Age." Ferguson describes the decline, saying
that "compared with the creative vigor of the
Golden Age, the literature of this period seems
thin and self-conscious, artificial and pedantic."
Tacitus lived in the late first century and early
second century A.D. and was the last great author.
He was deeply alienated from the milieu in which
he lived.

Smith points to at least one demographic
basis for regeneration during the Augustan period.
Augustus had founded the new Roman state not on
Rome alone, but on the whole of Italy, thus
broadening the base. Accordingly, "the Augustan
revolution represented the conquest by the politically unrepresented Italians over the selfish
political power-holders of Rome . . . The spiritual
and moral reformation at which Augustus aimed represented the attempt by the countryside and towns
to conquer Rome in that province too." A broadened "positive" came in to forestall the void at the
center.

74

Power and Decadence: The First Two Centuries

This "positive" was not sufficient to place
Rome on a permanently satisfactory foundation.
The history after Augustus is tragic, even though
the drowning civilization enjoyed a respite during
the reigns of the "five good emperors" in the
second century, a respite which caused Gibbon to
date the decline from the death of Marcus Aurelius
in 180 A.D. After Augustus, Nero and Caligula
rather than Marcus Aurelius were most representative of the remaining centuries of the Empire.

The recitals of Tacitus, who is called "somewhat jaundiced" by Ferguson but who is praised
by Rostovtzeff, are worth noting; Tacitus writes
of the "profligacy of women" and tells of a law
requiring that no noble woman "should get money
by prostitution." He says the emperor Tiberius
"feared freedom while he hated sycophancy" and
rendered speech "restricted and perilous." So
servile were the senators that Tiberius "as often
as he left the Senate-House used to exclaim in
Greek, 'How ready these men are to be slaves.'"
The "dishonesty of contractors and the negligence
of officials" caused roads to become impassable.
Although the first years of Tiberius' reign had
been mild, he became a "cruel tyrant" in reaction
to the intrigues of the praetorian cohorts. Tacitus states as fact the surmise that Tiberius' son
Drusus was poisoned by Sejanus, the prefect of
the praetorian guard. Summarizing, Tacitus groans
under the subject matter: "I have to present in
succession the merciless biddings of a tyrant, in-
cessant prosecutions, faithless friendships, the
ruin of innocence . . . I am everywhere confronted
by a wearisome monotony in my subject matter."
For page after page he tells of accusations, executions and suicides, and relates that the emperor
Claudius' own "taster" poisoned him, that Nero
visited brothels disguised as a slave and staged
orgiastic spectacles, at one time openly consummat-
ing marriage with a man. To be sure, Tacitus does
refer to the reigns of Nerva and Trajan as "times

75

when we may think what we please and express what
we think," but he also complains of the emptiness
of prevailing conversation, saying that his contemporaries could think only of actors and gladiators. He speaks of the "utter poverty of thought."

    I doubt if it is fair to put Tacitus down
as "jaundiced"; his alienation reacted against the
"insanities" of his age. He was one of the few
vital men of his time. Roebuck gives too easy
an explanation when he attributes the virtually
universal alienation of intellectuals from the
society of the Empire to the pro-Republican biases
of their wealthy patrons. Such an explanation
fails to appreciate that sensitive men could feel
a sincere antipathy to the prevailing conditions.

    It is not just Tacitus' temperament that
created the voids of the first two centuries. Numerous barbarisms appeared: that it was the praetorian guard which installed Claudius as emperor,
that Nero committed suicide, that Seneca was executed, that superstition ran rampant in the
lower classes, that Caligula was mentally deranged.
Although Gibbon also speaks of the strong features,
he recognizes the void. The void continued long-
existing weaknesses, but to Gibbon it was just
beginning: "This long peace, and the uniform
government of the Romans, introduced a slow and
secret poison into the vitals of the empire. The
minds of men were gradually reduced to the same
level, the fire of genius was extinguished, and
even the military spirit evaporated."[16] He continues to say that "the decline of genius was
soon followed by the corruption of taste" and that
the "diminutive stature of mankind . . . was daily
sinking below the old standard, and the Roman
world was indeed peopled by a race of pigmies."
Even though the Age of the Antonines enjoyed good
rulers, a shadow presaged the future: "The fatal
moment was perhaps approaching, when some licen-
tious youth, or some jealous tyrant, would abuse,
to the destruction, that absolute power which they
had exerted for the benefit of their people."

76

This occurred, in fact, when Marcus Aurelius selected his son Commodus as the next emperor.

Ortega acknowledges that even "in the times
of the Antonines the State overbears society with
its anti-vital supremacy. Society begins to be
enslaved, to be unable to live except in the
service of the State." Rostovtzeff tells that
under the earlier Julian and Claudian dynasties
the paranoia of the emperors more than once
caused the massacre of the leading members of the
nobility. "Thus one by one the noblest families
vanished from the scene forever." Families re-
placing these died out after two or three generations, since the upper classes were unwilling to
have children. At the same time, the proletariat
continued to grow. From all of this the result
was, according to Rostovtzeff, that "a stagnation
is perceptible throughout the empire, a paralysis
even of the desire for gain."

During these first two centuries a slow
economic decline began. By the fourth century,
through the combined effects of technological
regression, military disaster, plagues and the
growth of large estates, the open cities had
shrunk to small, walled towns. The urban society
gave way to a vast rural community, setting the
stage for medieval life. "In spite of the increase
of arable area," Rostovtzeff says, there was in
the first two centuries "no improvement, but
rather a falling off, in agricultural skill."
He tells that "in mining and metallurgy the
Romans did not improve upon the methods of the
Hellenistic Age, but even lost ground." In manu-
factures of all types "the quality grows inferior:
there is less both of mechanical skill and beauty."
Earlier discoveries fell into disuse. While
Rostovtzeff assigns this economic decline to a
diffusion of industry arising out of increased
local self-sufficiency, it is still another manifestation of an even more pervasive loss of
vitality. Other authors sometimes attribute the
decline to pestilence and war. Certainly these

77

were important contributing factors, but it is
a mistake to make them the primary explanations,
since Rostovtzeff's observation is to be remembered that "even before the time of war and pestilence in the reign of Marcus Aurelius, we mark in
the whole of intellectual life not merely a
pause but even a backward movement." In this case
the sickness of the mind cannot be explained by
the sickness of the body.

Even the political system rested on a void.
There could be no assurance that the succession
of good emperors in the second century would continue. The string was ended when Marcus Aurelius
named his son successor. Roebuck says that
"Commodus' reign is usually regarded as the turn-
ing point." There was no orderly system for
transferring power after his death. Gibbon writes
of forty years of tyranny after Aurelius. There
was a thirteen year respite under Severus Alexander, but this was followed by fifty years of
anarchy during which there were more than fifty
rivals and twenty-seven recognized emperors, most
of whom died violently.

Gibbon describes Commodus' way of life: "He
valued nothing in sovereign power except the un-
bounded license of indulging his sensual appetites.
His hours were spent in a seraglio of three
hundred beautiful women and as many boys, of every
rank and every province; and, wherever the arts
of seduction proved ineffectual, the brutal lover
had resource to violence. The ancient historians
have expatiated on these abandoned scenes of
prostitution, which scorned every restraint of
nature or modesty; but it would not be easy to
translate their too faithful descriptions into the
decency of modern language."

The Approach of the Dark Ages

In the third century, according to Rostovtzeff, "the last signs of civil freedom disappeared. The state was governed by a bureaucratic swarm of imperial officials who had graduated in the school of the army; and they included secret police who took a leading part in terrorizing the subjects." The army was the power behind the throne -- and it consisted of the most uncivilized elements. "Emperors sought to buy the favor of the troops by lavish bribes which ruined the treasury and doomed their successors who might be murdered if they lacked the means of overbidding the men they succeeded," Cowell reports. "The Roman armies were largely comprised of the dregs of the people and of barbarians." At one time many worthwhile persons had been induced to join the army to gain Roman citizenship, but when Caracalla extended universal citizenship this inducement disappeared. Army recruitment was thereafter "from among the more violent and uncivilized groups of the population or outside the Empire altogether," according to Roebuck. One emperor pragmatically spelled out the realities to his sons when he counselled them to "be of one mind: enrich the soldiers: trouble about nothing else." As both a consequence and a further cause of these developments, "the officers, the last representatives of a higher culture, disappeared from the army." The effect was that a significant social movement was taking place: the "state, relying upon the army or, in other words, upon the lower classes, defeated the upper classes and left them humiliated and beggared." To Rostovtzeff this was "a fatal blow to the aristocratic and urban civilization of the ancient world."

Under these circumstances it is hardly surprising that the old Principate, which had retained the forms of a Republican constitution, even though hypocritically, was replaced by an unabashedly oriental-style absolutism. "The reign of the Syrian relatives of Severus began one of the

saddest chapters in the history of the empire,"
Rostovtzeff says. "Elagabal, or Heliogabalus, as
the Romans called him, was a religious fanatic who
introduced into Rome the manners and customs of
his Syrian theocracy." Eventually the point was
reached at which "all who were admitted to the
sacred presence had even to fall on their faces
and kiss the hem of the royal raiment." This was
the practice under Diocletian. "He wore a special
costume for state occasions," Roebuck says about
him, "a jeweled diadem and dress of purple with
threads of gold." Cowell indicates some of the
chants the Senate had to sing to the emperor in
the fifth century:

"Augustuses of Augustuses,
    the greatest of Augustuses."

        repeated eight times

"God gave you to us! God gave you for us!"

    repeated twenty-seven times

"Our hope is in You, You are our salvation!"

    repeated twenty-six times

    There was some spiritual reawakening near the
end of the third century because of a final willingness to defend the empire from the barbaric invaders, but the basic trend continued afterwards,
aided by untold disasters in the form of famine,
disease and invasion. Gibbon wisely ascribes the
famine, though, to the "rapine and oppression,
which extirpated the produce of the present and the
hope of future harvests." The pestilence, in
turn, followed the famine.

    The Roman state had been keeping the barbarian
invaders out for hundreds of years. There had
been an invasion of Gauls in 400 B.C. and in 111
B.C. "Numerous Celtic and Germanic peoples had
crossed the Rhine River." But where Rome had pre-

viously been able to withstand them, it now could not. The sack of Rome by Alaric in 410 A.D. was due more to Roman decay than to external causes.

The Middle Ages approached. Because vast areas were deserted, the emperor Constantine issued laws in the fourth century "binding the agricultural worker, and his children after him, to the land he worked." The same happened with the artisan. Laws were issued "forcing the merchant or artisan to continue in his occupation." The result was that "the workers in each trade formed an hereditary caste." Learning and the arts continued their decline. The despair became so overpowering that men lost faith in reason, with the result that anti-rationalism and superstition became rampant. Ortega observes that "from a certain height and a certain distance the Cynic agitators and the Christian converts could be mistaken one for the other." With the predominant philosophies counselling withdrawal, it became a time similar in a sense to that described futuristically in Ayn Rand's Atlas Shrugged. "To withdraw from public life to a serene unruffled seclusion, avoiding excess in order to escape the pain when balance was established, was the life to which (Epicureanism) exhorted men to aspire," Smith tells us. Roebuck says that "men tended to reject the rationality of Greco-Roman civilization and moved into a world dominated by superstition and religion." Rostovtzeff repeats this when he says that "the best men . . . came to distrust reason; their ideals were trampled under foot; and they either sank into the slough of a coarse materialism or sought salvation in mystical religions."

So we come to the end of six centuries of make-shift. The mos maiorum had not possessed permanency, and nothing which succeeded it had established a truly viable system. What is amazing is that with such a void at its center Rome was able to survive as long as it did. We do not ordinarily think of Rome as having fallen in the

81

West until the last emperor was replaced by Odacer as the first barbarian King of Italy in 476 A.D. In the East we consider Justinian in the sixth century the last emperor, giving way then to the Byzantine Empire. But all such classifications are arbitrary. These classifications are based primarily on continued territorial sovereignty. Were criteria used which would take into account the quality of life and of culture, we would wish to draw the line a good deal earlier.

It remains true that Rome required a long time to die. Rostovtzeff explains best the dynamic of its continuation and death when he writes that "the state, supporting itself upon the relics of past greatness, went on existing just so long as its culture and organization were superior to those of its enemies; when that superiority disappeared, new masters took control of what had become a bloodless and effete organism. Any creative power that remained turned away from this world and its demands and studied how to know God to be united with Him."

NOTES

1. Carl Roebuck, The World of Ancient Times (New York: Charles Scribner's Sons, 1966), pp. 725, 436, 556, 485, 489, 488, 495, 504, 497, 467, 446, 507-8, 589, 695, 664, 682, 665, 683, 697, 449, 515, 666. A plague continued for fifteen years during the reign of Marcus Aurelius, and Roebuck, p. 664, reports an estimate of a million killed. Later the Empire was hit by earthquakes and by still another plague, so that Roebuck says, at p. 682, that "in the 270's, the population had been reduced by a third."

2. José Ortega y Gasset, Man and Crisis (New York: W.W. Norton & Co., Inc., 1962), pp. 129, 133.

3.   Theodore Mommsen, <u>The History of Rome</u> (New York: Charles Scribner's Sons, 1895), Vol. III, pp. 104, 126, 162-3, 204-5, 173, 163, 123, 298, 121, 112, 342, 324, 337-8, 343, 344, 357, 358, 360.   At p. 324, Mommsen speaks of Tiberius Gracchus' reelection as a tribune as an "unconstitutional prolongation."

4.   Polybius, <u>The Histories of Polybius</u>, trans. Evelyn S. Shuckburgh (London: Macmillan and Company, 1889), Vol. I, pp. 506-7, 466-8, 474, 506; Vol. II, p. 454.   The incorrect prediction I have referred to in the text appears in Vol. I at p. 747:   "Nay, even when these external alarms are past, and the people are enjoying their good fortune and the fruits of their victories, and, as usually happens, growing corrupted by flattery and idleness, show a tendency to violence and arrogance,--it is in these circumstances, more than ever, that the constitution is seen to possess within itself the power of correcting abuses.   For when any one of the three classes becomes puffed up, and manifests an inclination to be contentious and unduly encroaching, the mutual interdependency of all the three, and the possibility of the pretensions of any one being checked and thwarted by the others, must plainly check this tendency: and so the proper equilibrium is maintained by the impulsiveness of the one part being checked by its fear of the other . . ."

5.   R.E. Smith, <u>The Failure cf the Roman Republic</u> (Cambridge University Press, 1955), pp. 9, 24, 13, 126, 19, 25, 11, 25, 6, 61, 65, 8, 95-6, 19, 23, 13, 14, 126, 7, 5, 76, 152, 162, 163, 143, 137.

6.   Plutarch, <u>The Lives of the Noble Grecians and Romans</u> (New York: Modern Library), pp. 422, 414, 1019, 1007.

7.   F.R. Cowell, <u>The Revolutions of Ancient Rome</u> (New York: Frederick A. Praeger, 1963), pp. 20, 84, 99, 103-4, 171, 176, 182, 196, 193, 208.   As to the date upon which the Republic was established,

Cowell speaks at p. 20 of "510-509 B.C. or considerably later as some scholars now maintain . . ."

8. W.E. Heitland, The Roman Republic (Cambridge
University Press, 1923), Vol. II, pp. 220, 236,
240, 241, 243, 253, 222, 230, 233, 211, 224, 228,
224, 254.

9. John Dickinson, Death of a Republic (New York:
Macmillan Company, 1963), pp. 22, 18, 20.

10. John Selby Watson, trans., Sallust, Florus
and Velleius Paterculus (London: Henry G. Bohn),
pp. 444, 8.

11. In War and Peace, Tostoy departed from his
novel several times to discuss his fatalistic
philosophy of history. It isn't to be inferred
from my comment in the text that I fully endorse
Tolstoy's view, since I am by no means a fatalist;
and yet Tolstoy's perception has some portion of
the truth in it. It emphasizes the underlying
corpus of mankind, which we certainly know today
to be very relevant, and directs our attention to
the massive changes that can take place within the
broad spectrum of life itself. Such a view is
closely related to the classical liberal "vitalist
perspective," which sees mankind as containing
a great deal more than can easily be grasped by,
say, a socialist planner.

12. José Ortega y Gasset, The Revolt of the Masses
(New York: W. W. Norton and Company, Inc. 1957);
see particularly his description of modern man
as a "spoiled child" on p. 98; other references
are to p. 121.

13. M. Rostovtzeff, A History of the Ancient World
(Oxford at the Clarendon Press, 1928), Vol. II,
pp. 97, 193, 290, 107, 193, 183, 198, 224, 213,
216, 293, 294, 296, 297, 299, 301, 241, 318, 306,
315, 366, 307, 323, 310, 362, 366.

14. Wallace K. Ferguson and Geoffrey Brunn, A
Survey of European Civilization (Boston: Houghton
Mifflin Company, 3d ed., 1962), pp. 73-4, 75-6, 82.

15. Tacitus, The Complete Works of Tacitus, trans.
A. J. Church and W. J. Brodribb (New York: Modern
Library, 1942), pp. 99, 100, 137, 119, 144, 147,
148, 163, 283, 298, 376, 420, 758, 761.

16. Edward Gibbon, The History of the Decline and
Fall of the Roman Empire (London: Methuen & Co.,
4th ed., 1906), Vol. I, pp. 58, 78, 152, 92, 281.

5

THE MISSING PARADIGM: THE MIDDLE AGES

From the preceding two chapters, we have seen
that the role of human immaturity has been essential to understanding both the Greek and the Roman
experiences. In the present chapter we will see
that the same is true with regard to the Middle
Ages; it was a period in which "what was missing"
was every bit as important as the factors which
were actually present. The Burkean conservative
believes the medieval model to contain a paradigm
which satisfies permanent truths about the human
condition, but I find this far from acceptable.

It may seem that a relatively pessimistic
view of the Middle Ages, mitigated only slightly
by a recognition that certain advances were made
during the period, is easy to justify. But this
is no longer the case. Since the early nineteenth
century historians have become more appreciative
of the Middle Ages. This greater appreciation,
which contrasts so sharply with the view held by
the humanistic historians of the fifteenth and
subsequent centuries, has often bordered on apolo-
getics. The result is that I am flying in the
face of the modern tendency when I point to the
void which underlay the Middle Ages.

Opposing Views of the Middle Ages

Some important progress was in fact made during the Middle Ages. To the extent the Renaissance
historians failed to emphasize this progress they
overstated the "darkness" of the period. Such an
overstatement is to have been expected; with
society once again on the move with the exhilarat-
ing sense of freedom which came from an expansion
of mental effort and the rediscovery of ancient
learning, the tendency, understandably, was to

overreact.

Yet, it is hard to read the recent literature about the Middle Ages without feeling that there has been an overreaction in the opposite direction. The effort is to put the best possible face on the period. Its worst features are passed over or explained away. We still have not arrived at a good historical understanding. As to this favorably oriented distortion, there is the testimony of Karl Morrison that "medievalists have laboriously tallied references to Cicero and Virgil, reconstructing curricula of instruction, and registered any outbursts of what Highet calls the 'sense of beauty,' seeking to establish as fact that the humane spirit, the knowledge and admiration of the classics, and the secularism of the Renaissance were present in the early Middle Ages."[1]

The following apologia is found, for example, in Loren MacKinney's The Medieval World published in 1938: "The Italian humanists of the fifteenth and sixteenth centuries, misunderstanding the period from the decline of the Roman Empire in the West to their own time, assumed that those centuries constituted an interlude of cultural darkness and barbarism. The humanists gave to this period the name 'Middle Ages,' and to the term 'medieval,' the sense of a long dark period of barbarism and ignorance in sharp contrast to the highly developed civilization of the ancient world and of their own 'modern' age . . . In recent years, however, the entire medieval period has been viewed as an age of active reconstruction."[2]

The view that the period was one of "active reconstruction" is a possible interpretation. But MacKinney often stretches his analysis out of shape to justify it. He reports that "throughout (the tenth) century, historical literature flourished." He gives as supporting evidence the fact that monasteries kept yearbooks "in which local events were briefly recorded." He says these yearbooks were "the seeds from which real histories grew."

We feel some letdown, then, when he informs us that "often the record for an entire year fills less than half a page of modern print." This does not justify a conclusion that historical literature flourished, even though he has shown that historical records had not entirely died out. The critics writing in the fifteenth century seem to have been closer to a correct inference from the facts.

MacKinney's emphasis is again apparent when he pleads that "the truth is that, at its worst, the tenth century was by no means a total loss to civilization." Surely it is possible to admit this much and still rank the tenth century very poorly in comparison with either the ancient or the modern world.

Many recent historians have taken the position that "each age must be judged by its own standards." This reflects at least in part an historicist philosophical position. This perspective is evident in Morrison's statement that "if the early Middle Ages seem dark, or a period of 'gloomy and almost static barbarism' to students of classical learning, it is because they are applying to that age goals and standards which the age itself did not acknowledge or strive after."

But such a reflection is only half true. Its validity depends upon the historian's purpose. There may be times we will accept the value-system of an epoch itself, but if we seek to evaluate matters of life and death, health and disease, knowledge and ignorance, anarchy and order, what we seek is an evaluation according to our own values and understanding. A relativistic perspective will not be the appropriate method. When "judged by his own standards," even the life of a slave or of the worst barbarian may be perfectly acceptable. Such relativism is particularly out of place in an analysis of the "voids" underlying a period of history, since it would deprive us of the standards we seek to apply.

According to the editors of Lord Acton's
essays on the history of freedom, his reaction to
modern historiography was similar to my own.
They report that "the second tendency against
which Acton's moral sense revolted, had arisen
out of the laudable determination of historians to
be sympathetic towards men of distant ages and of
alien modes of thought. With the romantic movement the early nineteenth century placed a check
upon the habit of despising medieval ideals, which
had been increasing from the days of the Rennais-
sance and had culminated in Voltaire. Instead
of this, there arose a sentiment of admiration for
the past, while the general growth of historical
methods of thinking supplied a sense of the rela-
tivity of moral principles . . . It became almost
a trick of style to talk of judging men by the
standard of their day and to allege the spirit of
the age in excuse for the Albigensian Crusade
or the burning of Hus. Acton felt that this was
to destroy the very bases of moral judgment and
to open the way to a boundless scepticism."3

The apologetic treatment of the Middle Ages
has been the result of a combination of factors.
These have included the Romantic reaction to humanism in the early nineteenth century, the tendency of historians of a scientific frame of mind
to view men of other ages from a clinical perspective, the relativisitic outlook of Historicism,
and the more or less natural bias of men specializ-
ing in the medieval period.

Another major contributing factor has been
the tendency of socialist authors to identify with
the Middle Ages. Two main reasons have existed
for this tendency: First, the socialist intellectual has found that medieval thought and values
had much in common with his own doctrine and at-
tachments. Second, because of their tactical
position vis a vis capitalism, socialist authors
have found it necessary to portray the Industrial
Revolution in the blackest terms. For this purpose it has been necessary to rehabilitate the

Middle Ages so that the factory system will seem a deterioration or at least not an improvement.

The writings of R. H. Tawney give a good example of this socialist perspective. In The Acquisitive Society he urged the organization of society on the basis of "functions" (a "socially useful service") rather than on "acquisitive rights." In Religion and the Rise of Capitalism he reviewed feudalism and found much to his liking, although he did call it "exploitive" and would not have carried it bodily into the present. He admired the Middle Ages for its "functional view of class organization, and the doctrine of economic ethics."[4] He went so far as to say that "the last of the Schoolmen was Karl Marx,"--although we could add R. H. Tawney. He told that during the Middle Ages "society was interpreted, in short, not as the expression of economic self-interest, but as held together by a system of mutual, though varying, obligations. Social well-being exists, it was thought, in so far as each class performs its functions and enjoys the rights apportioned thereto." He said "there is no place in medieval theory for economic activity which is not related to a moral end." In the medieval view "the ideal -- if only man's nature could rise to it -- is communism." With regard to technical economic doctrine he particularly liked the medieval "teaching with regard to the just price and the prohibition of usury." He summed up his position with an analogy to socialist thought, saying that "the medieval insistence that riches exist for man, not man for riches, (and) the argument of the Socialist who urges that production should be organized for service, not for profit, are but different attempts to emphasize the instrumental character of economic activities by reference to an ideal which is held to express the true nature of man."

91

An Epistemological Void

Those who seek to rehabilitate history's
verdict about the Middle Ages are not without some
supporting evidence. There were areas of progress;
everything wasn't bleak. Over a long period a
"revolution" in agricultural methods prepared
the way for the Industrial Revolution. Although
Forbes and Dijksterhuis have spoken of "a deplor-
able lack of written evidence on the arts and
crafts of the Middle Ages," a major development
took place in "the introduction of prime movers
to take the place of muscle energy in moving
machinery and tools."[5] There were less than a
hundred watermills in Great Britain in the tenth
century; the Domesday Book a century later shows
5624. In addition to the watermill, the windmill
came into extensive use. The horse began to take
the place of the ox; horseshoes were in general
use by the tenth century. The modern horse harness, "which eventually added much to the prosperity of northern agriculture," was developed under
Charlemagne.[6] The eleventh century produced the
whipple-tree, which was "essential to the full
development of horse traction" and thereby improved
land transportation. "By the fourteenth century a
new carvel-built type of ship became common;
gradually driving the older types from the seas.
However, apart from the stern-rudder, the introduction of the floating magnetic compass was perhaps the most momentous invention to promote sail-
ing the ocean. It was known in the twelfth century, but came into general use about one century
later." Pottery containers were replaced by tuns
and wooden barrels. Cheese and butter came into
use, particularly among the rich. Metallurgy was
improved in the eleventh and twelfth centuries by
mechanizing various operations through the use of
water power, including the introduction of water-
moved bellows for the smelting furnaces. Even as
early as the seventh century dikes were used in
the Low Countries to keep out the sea.

Any view which fails to consider these advanc-

92

es is to that extent deficient, but a recital of
such achievements can only be part of the picture.

Ludwig von Mises observed that one of the
characteristics of life based on capitalism and
technology is that the amenities of life are enjoyed not just by the wealthy, but by the average
citizen.[7] Forbes' and Dijksterhuis' History of
Science and Technology illustrates the extent to
which this did not occur during the Middle Ages:
"Hardly any progress," they indicate, "was made
in improving the amenities of life during the
Middle Ages. The only light sources were still
the torch, the candle, and the oil lamp. Good
beeswax and tallow candles were now available, but
they were mainly used in churches and the houses
of the rich; the poor used oil lamps or went to
bed early. Neither did the latter profit from the
invention of spectacles around 1290, because for a
long time they remained too expensive except for
the very few." They continue, saying "the open
firearms of the hearth was still the only means
of heating the house . . . Neither were there any
great changes in food. Butter took the place of
oil, beef fat, or lard. In general bread, vege-
tables, and fish formed the mainstay of the medieval diet, meat appearing irregularly on the table
even of the rich."

Knowledge and technique is not always gained
or even retained; it can be lost. The early
thirteenth century surgeon Gilbert discovered a
method for the repair of severed intestines which
was lost and not rediscovered until centuries later
when John B. Murphy popularized his "Murphy's
Button" as the technique for end-to-end anastomosis.
A medical historian points out that this "does
suggest that many great discoveries have in fact
been born, lived, died, and been forgotten by all
the world, as Gilbert's alder button was forgotten."[8] Much of the Middle Ages is noted for its
loss of knowledge.

The most significant criticism of the medieval

period lies in its having encouraged habits of thought which repealed the epistemological basis for civilization, and further in its having actively obstructed the redevelopment of a sound epistemology. Dampier went to the heart of the matter with an expressive metaphor when he said that "the scattered seedlings of science had to grow in a vast and confused jungle which was always threatening to choke them, and not in the open healthy prairie of ignorance which seems to be envisaged by some historians of science."[9]

History records an inexhaustible chain of fascinating and yet morbid examples of the suppression of creative thought. The tone was set by Tertullian's earlier "I believe, because it is impossible."[10] Men of the most constructive bent were often hounded, tortured or killed.

In the seventeenth century the Inquisition condemned Galileo's theory that the earth revolved around the sun.[11] In 1616 he was forced to assert that his theory was false and to promise not to republish it. G. F. Young tells that "Galileo was therefore in 1633 charged with having gone back on his promise of 1616, and summoned to appear before the Inquisition in Rome, to answer for his writings which, in maintaining the fixed position of the sun and the movement of the earth round it, propounded a doctrine which was declared by the Pope to be in flat contradiction to the Bible."[12] Young says that "at Rome Galileo, now seventy years old and broken in health, was threatened with torture by the Inquisition; his theories were formally condemned, he was made to recant on his knees his so-called errors, and especially to declare his doctrine as to the movement of the earth false, and was kept a prisoner."

Twelve centuries earlier, Arabian science had benefited from the Greek, Roman and Egyptian medical classics which Bishop Nestor of Constantinople had taken with him when he fled to Syria after being excommunicated by the Church of Rome.

94

We are told, too, that "anything savouring of Atomism inevitably aroused suspicion in the Middle Ages because it always suggested Epicureanism and thus heresy." William of Conches ran into opposition on this account in the twelfth century for his Philosophica mundi, which contained "corpuscular considerations."

In the sixth century, Boethius was executed for treason by Theodoric; in prison he had written The Consolation of Philosophy. Three centuries later the monk Gottschalk was tortured and sentenced to life imprisonment in a monastery for arguing that "if one followed Augustine's theology to its logical conclusion, men were predestined to hell as well as to heaven." A century later "a grammarian of Ravenna was actually burned as a heretic, for accepting the classical poems as articles of religious faith and for claiming that Virgil, Horace, and Juvenal had appeared to him in a vision and promised him a part in their Paradise." In the sixteenth century Michael Servetus described the circulation of the blood through the lungs in a book which included his thoughts on theology. He was burned at the stake by Calvin. The verdict of the court declared that "we condemn thee, Michael Servetus, to be bound and to be led to the place of Shampell, there to be fastened to a stake and burned alive, together with thy heretical book, as well written by hand as printed, even until they be reduced to ashes, and thus wilt thou finish thy days to furnish an example to others who might wish to commit the like."

The Greek physician Galen wrote more than 500 medical treatises in the second century A.D. As the Middle Ages set in his work became revered, with the effect that it became impossible to question him. Galen became the established authority. His anatomy was followed for almost fourteen centuries, until finally in the sixteenth century Andreas Vesalius secretly dissected human bodies in graveyards and at places of execution. A medical historian notes with appropriate emphasis the

95

startling discovery Vesalius made: "Then Vesalius made a major discovery. He obtained the skeleton of a monkey and found that it conformed to Galen's anatomical ideas about humans. Now he understood! Galen's anatomy had been based on the dissection of lower animals! He had not really observed cadavers! No wonder he was full of errors -- and how criminal it had been to canonize those errors so solemnly!"[13]

But this remarkable discovery -- that the anatomy so slavishly followed for almost fourteen centuries was based on monkeys instead of men -- was not appreciated. In 1543 Vesalius published his De Humani Fabrica, but "from then on," we are told, "his life was a downhill slide." An old teacher attacked him, the medical profession opposed him. He burned the manuscript of a new book and withdrew, becoming a drifter. Later "the Inquisition closed in on him, it is said, and he was saved by the Emperor, on condition that he journey to the Holy Land in atonement for his 'crime.'"

The fact that during the reign of Henry VIII in England a law was enacted entitled "An Act for Abolishing Diversity of Opinion" tells us something about the mentality of the period.

A plague swept across Europe just before the middle of the fourteenth century. Florence is said to have suffered one hundred thousand dead and Paris and Avignon each had more than fifty thousand deaths. At Oxford the student population was reduced from thirty thousand to six thousand.[14]

Castiglioni reports in his History of Medicine that "various theories were proposed as to the cause of this terrific scourge. Among the most prominent was that it was owing to the conjunction of Saturn, Jupiter, and Mars on the 24th of March 1345." He says that "another natural reaction was the belief that the scourge was due to the poisoning of wells, especially by the lepers and the Jews."

96

There is a fascinating incident about this plague in Atkinson's Magic, Myth and Medicine. The story of the Jewish physician Balavignus is surely one of the more tragic in history. "Following the sanitary laws as set down in Leviticus, Balavignus had all refuse burned. Naturally the rats left the ghettos and gravitated to gentile quarters in search of food. The Jews consequently suffered less from the disease than did their Christian neighbors, the mortality in the ghettos being five per cent of what it was among the Christians." The result was that "this was so noticeable that Jews at once fell under suspicion. It was observed that they covered their wells and took away their buckets. This led to the belief that they were not only escaping the plague themselves but were in a conspiracy to destroy the Christians by the disease. One day it was said that someone had seen a Jew deposit a bag containing poison in a well. This report so infuriated the people that a general massacre of the Jews was begun. Hecker tells us: 'In this terrible year an unbridled spirit of fanaticism and thirst for blood caused the death of nearly all the Jewish population in Strassburg . . . At Eslengen the whole Jewish community in despair burned themselves in the synagogue."

Balavignus himself was tortured, forced to confess and then burned at the stake. "Soon in the smoking embers lay the mortal remains of this great man who, had his advice been heeded, would have proved to be one of the world's greatest benefactors."

This wasn't the only time militant ignorance prevented the use of sanitation to stop the plague. Balavignus' lesson was suppressed and three centuries later it was still being suppressed. The following passage about the plague of 1629 appears in Young's account of the Medici: "The pestilence raged for thirteen dismal months, during which time in and around the city twelve thousand people died. Ferdinand established a Board of Health, and this

97

body issued many wise regulations, while they also forced the inmates of the immense number of monasteries and convents with which the city was crowded both to obey sanitary rules, and also to bear their share in receiving and helping those who were convalescent. But Ferdinand's sound sanitary regulations were denounced by the priests as impious; the Pope demanded that the Board of Health should be censured, and required that a severe penance should be exacted from its members."

Aristotle's writings exercised a dominant influence in Scholastic thought (so much so that it became a serious obstacle to further inquiry, as any philosophy would when applied by an authoritarian mentality). But even his works had at first been condemned. Although the University of Paris adopted his writings in 1225, this was only after a Provincial Council in Paris had condemned them in 1209.

It was also in the thirteenth century that Roger Bacon, who understood so well the role of experimentation in science, analyzed the causes of man's intellectual failure to be "Undue Regard to Authority, Habit, Prejudice, and False Conceit of Knowledge." At first, Bacon received the protection of Pope Clement IV, but after Clement's death he was imprisoned for fifteen years by Pope Nicholas IV.

Although much of the persecution of thoughtful men came from the Church as a dominant institution, the persecution was by no means limited to the Counter-Reformation, when the Church was under stress. My examples have covered the entire medieval period. During the Roman Empire, Christianity was first tolerated, then persecuted, then actively supported by the Emperors. For its own sake, when it gained ascendancy, Christianity was not a tolerant religion. Thorndike says that "finally, with Constantine, Christianity triumphed; and soon began in its turn to persecute all pagans and heretics."[15]

Considerable dispute existed over matters of doctrine within the early Church, particularly about the Trinity and the divinity of Christ. The Council of Nicaea was convened by the Emperor Constantine in the fourth century and "anathematized" the Arians who did not believe in the Trinity. "Thus, early in Christian history conservatism triumphed," MacKinney says, "and branded as heretical all who believed in unitarianism or denied the absolute divinity of Christ." The state combined with the Church to persecute heretical groups, which included the Donatists, Circumcellions, Montanists, Priscillians, Manicheans, Novations, Meletians, Nestorians, Monophysites and Pelgians. We are reminded of Gibbon's remark that "the appellation of heretic has always been applied to the less numerous party."

It has not always been the Church that has persecuted intellect. We have seen the role the Roman state played in combination with the early Church. We vividly recall the treatment Socrates received at the hands of Athenian democracy. Cicero quite literally lost his head in later Republican Rome. And the modern age is not without its Billy Mitchells and Boris Pasternaks.

It was Calvin, a Protestant, who burned Servetus. Even empiricists have not been immune to brutality, as we see in the case of the Emperor Frederick II in the thirteenth century. "He is accused," we discover from Taton, "of having performed such inhuman experiments as placing a prisoner in a closed barrel in order to see whether his soul departed when he died, of raising children in absolute silence to find out what language they would speak spontaneously, or again of disembowelling two men to discover the respective effects of sleep and movement on their alimentary canal."[16] Frederick's language experiment with the children is a repetition of one made, according to Herodotus, by Psammetichus of Egypt.[17] The problem of intolerance, brutality, lack of empathy for others is so deeply rooted in human nature that it cannot

99

be ascribed to any one institution or doctrine.
It reflects immaturity -- a civilizational void.
In the Middle Ages this void gaped particularly
wide.

Nor do we need to look only at persecutions.
The point is also illustrated by a number of
instances in which ideas became stagnant under
authoritarian acceptance. A grammar written by a
fourth century teacher in Rome, Donatus, was used
for twelve centuries. Priscian's fifth century
grammar was used throughout the Middle Ages. We
have already seen how Galen's anatomy was accepted
without question for almost fourteen centuries.
Ptolemy dominated astronomy until the sixteenth
century, while medieval astronomers occupied
themselves primarily by calculating tables.[18]

Medicine was thoroughly dogmatic. Castiglioni
tells us that "the Church solemnly affirmed the
principle that the canonical writings should be
regarded as a supreme indisputable authority, not
only in matters of faith but also in science.
Medicine oriented itself rapidly in this direction.
The first Christian physicians . . . preached the
all importance of faith and recognized the complete
authority of the Nazarene, whose gospel is addressed to suffering humanity awaiting salvation."

Later, the medical knowledge of the school at
Solerno was put into the form of a poem, the
famous Flos medicinae or Regimen sanitatis Saler-
nitanum. This was memorized by thousands of doc-
tors "for whom each of these verses had the
quality of Holy Writ." Although the poem itself
contained "useful, simple and true maxims," the
authoritarian nature of its acceptance makes it
easy to understand why medieval medicine remained
in a barbaric state for so long.

This barbarism is illustrated by Taton when he
tells us that "the Leech Book of Bald is a good
example of this mixture of ancient, Christian, and
popular beliefs. Its cure for snake-bite, for

100

instance, was a snake soaked in holy water." Castiglioni reports that in the early Middle Ages "there was formed a Christian religious medicine in which prayer, the imposition of hands, unction with holy oil, were regarded as the most important remedies, those to which the faithful should have exclusive or almost exclusive recourse in seeking divine aid for the cure of bodily ills." Many saints were thought to have healing powers and it was long thought that the kings of England and France could cure scrofula by a touch of the hand. Atkinson relates that "the Anglo-Saxon believed that disease was either the result of an elf shot or of demons, or was due to the destruction of the body by worms; these worms are pictured in their manuscripts as monstrous creatures and they, as well as the demons and elf shots, were to be dealt with by charms or by the administration to the patient of nauseating and repulsive remedies which were meant to disgust the elfish enemies and thus drive them away."

In the late Middle Ages, Scholasticism was elevated to an unchallengeable position. Edwin Hoyt shows that it consisted of Aristotelianism planted in a sterile soil. He says that "at its highest point Scholasticism was founded on the philosophy of Aristotle. But what an arid ground that philosophy came out upon when it was deposited in Europe."[19] He says "the Scholastics . . . began to hold that there was no greater knowledge than Aristotle's." According to Taton "the Aristotelian dialectic came to be considered tantamount to science and reason." Castiglioni adds that "here science became progressively crystallized in the rigid forms of scholasticism; neither clinical observation nor attempts at experimental investigation could have the sightest effect on this solid edifice."

The Collapse of Ancient Man

This review of both the persecution of some

ideas and the authoritarian acceptance of others
has shown the extent to which the medieval period
abused the epistemological preconditions of
civilization. The causes for this mental reversal
went deep and point to the existence of a broad
void at the end of the ancient era. Christianity
was a symptom, not itself the underlying cause, of
this void.

The insights of José Ortega y Gasset are
helpful. In Man and Crisis he interprets the
crisis. The "system of convictions" which held
men together shattered and men came to hold only
"negative convictions." Having lost their bearings, they despaired of themselves, so that "the
problematical thing was the very self of the subject himself."[20] To Ortega, "this is the state of
mind which led men to the Christian solution."
He makes an analogy between the Christian converts
and the Cynic agitators.

Men fled from the world. With regard to the
Christian converts, Ortega tells us that "in the
radicalism of their speeches they all agree.
They preach against the wealth of the rich, the
pride of the powerful; they are against learned
men, against the established culture, against com-
plications of every type. In their minds, he is
most right and of most value who knows nothing,
who has nothing -- the simple man, the poor man,
the humble man, the churchless." The result was
"to turn all values inside out. If wealth does not
give happiness, poverty will; if learning does not
solve everything, then true wisdom will lie in
ignorance." Christianity was itself born out of
the desperation of ancient man which according
to Ortega began in the first century B.C. and grew
during the Empire. There are later analogies in
history in the nihilism of the nineteenth century
Russian intelligentsia and of the German Youth
Movement before World War I and of the New Left in
American and Europe in the late 1960's.

In this escapist atmosphere, supernaturalism

had strong appeal as a radical solution. When all else proved false, concern for the "other world" and a denial of this one seemed a desirable refuge. Man returned to his more primordial beginnings; there was a regression to the mental processes of the cargo cultists.

It is something of a mistake, though, to say that the men of the fourth and fifth centuries had "returned" to supernaturalism. A truer perception would be that much of mankind has never been fully away from it. We need merely to read Plutarch's references to divine omens to know that this is so. Even at its most advanced, ancient civilization (as indeed our civilization today) was mixed. It retained a strong underlay of residual barbarism. When he turned extravagantly to supernaturalism, the despairing man of ancient times merely grabbed hold of something which was already familiar to him and used it to negate the civilizational elements which no longer commanded his confidence.

Christian tradition understandably takes the most favorable possible view of this development. In its view Christianity was a positive force bringing renewal to man. If this were correct, a great positive stepped in at the end of Roman civilization to take the place of the decay and desperation.

Facts and logic, though, require a very different interpretation of Christianity. It would be a momentous contradiction that the finest development in man can have come from the most debased human materials. Simple cause-and-effect suggests that Augustinian Christianity was of the same quality as the men who formulated it (though this could not be conclusive against it, since as an argument the observation would be ad hominem). An honest appraisal cannot be flattering: Augustinian Christianity was a form of reemergent barbarism.

MacKinney says "there are many curious tales

103

which illustrate the ardent Christian asceticism
of this period. One pious hermit was said to have
gone without bread for eighty years; another revel-
ed in such filth that he was covered with vermin;
another, in order to escape all worldly influences,
resolved never to look at his own body, and refused even to take off his clothes. All of the
holiest of the hermits resorted to drastic physical tortures in order to fight off the temptations
of the Devil . . . By standing in ice cold water,
rolling in thorns, or lashing themselves with
whips, the true soldiers of Christ were usually
able to defeat the wiles of the Evil One."

Is it possible that such men were the carriers
of a higher culture? Were they the precursors of
advanced civilization? To say so is to argue a
paradox and to make cultural pathology a paradigm.

St. Simeon Stylites "was reputed to have lived
for years on the top of a sixty-foot pillar." It
can be argued that as an extremist he was not
representative of early Christianity, and it is
true that the behavior of the hermits and the
stylites went beyond that of many others. But we
know also that St. Augustine held predominant influence for eight centuries, and that his Confessions suggest an extremism akin to that of the
hermits and the stylites; he was their intellectual mentor, if not an imitator of their behavior.
"The friendship of this world is fornication
against Thee," he was able to say.[21]   He "despised earthly happiness;" "deliver me out of the
bonds of desire, wherewith I was bound most
straitly to carnal concupiscence, and out of the
drudgery of worldly things." "Not even the infant
whose life is but a day upon the earth" is free of
sin; men in general are wicked; the life of this
world is marred by "the muddy concupiscence of the
flesh."

Augustine labelled empirical curiosity about
the world "the lust of the eyes," arguing that
"the soul hath . . . a certain vain and curious

desire, veiled under the title of knowledge and learning . . . of making experiments through the flesh. The seat whereof being in the appetite of knowledge, and sight being the sense chiefly used for attaining knowledge, it is in Divine language called The lust of the eyes . . . (T)he general experience of the senses, as was said, is called The lust of the eyes . . . Hence men go to search out the hidden powers of nature (which is besides our end), which to know profits not, and wherein men desire nothing but to know . . . (T)he theatres do not carry me away, nor care I to know the courses of the stars."

This involves, of course, a matter of values. The Augustinian view is defensible if we care to do nothing practical about disease, filth and suffering, and if we wish to know nothing about "the courses of the stars," the roundness of the earth, the chemical composition of helium. But if we see the humanistic value of low infant mortality, of a man sleeping peacefully under anesthetic during an amputation, of the ability to walk on the moon, of clean clothes and a washed body, then we must wonder whether Augustinianism was not in fact the voice of the internal barbarism which both contributed to and emerged from the collapse of Roman civilization.

We analyze these things dispassionately. To obtain their true meaning in terms of values, however, it is necessary to permit ourselves a more subjective perspective. If we do this, it becomes apparent that if we had lived during those times and had been at all sensitive, it would have seemed that we lived not in a civilized community, but in something more closely resembling an ant-heap. All that our contemporaries would have viewed as sanity we would have perceived as terribly distorted. Surely it would have been appropriate for Balavignus, Servetus, Vesalius, Galileo and Roger Bacon, as they sat in prison or went to the stake, to have cried "This is insane!" There is irony in the fact that hundreds of thousands of people died

105

of the plague without any knowledge that it was
their own primitivism that was the real sine qua
non of their deaths. Most died thoroughly committed to the "insanity" -- the condition of epistemological pathology -- which they insisted was normal
and right.

Such reflections shouldn't make us smug. We
are not divorced from the infancy of mankind.
Although the Middle Ages were the most pronounced
manifestation of humanity's barbaric residuals, it
is impossible to come to grips with human life
even today without appreciating them.

NOTES

1. Karl F. Morrison, "The Church, Reform, and
Renaissance in the Early Middle Ages," Life and
Thought in the Early Middle Ages, Robert Hoyt (ed.)
Minneapolis: University of Minnesota Press, 1967),
pp. 144, 158.

2. Loren Carey MacKinney, The Medieval World
(New York: Rinehart & Company, Inc., 1938), pp.
3, 291, 298, 262, 293-4, 282, 66-69, 53, 94, 95.

3. John Dalberg-Acton, The History of Freedom and
Other Essays (Freeport: Books for Libraries
Press, Inc., 1967), Introduction by John Neville
Figgis and Reginald Vere Laurence, pp. xx, xxi.

4. R. H. Tawney, Religion and the Rise of Capitalism (New York; Mentor Books, 1960), pp. 27, 39,
29, 35, 39, 233.

5. R. J. Forbes and E. J. Dijksterhuis, A History
of Science and Technology (Baltimore: Penguin
Books, 1963), pp. 129, 130, 132, 136, 134, 139,
141, 142-3, 109, 148.

6. Lynn White, Jr., "The Life of the Silent
Majority," Life and Thought in the Early Middle

<u>Ages,</u> Robert Hoyt (ed.) (Minneapolis: University
of Minnesota Press, 1967), pp. 93, 96.

7.   Ludwig von Mises, <u>The</u> <u>Anti-Capitalist</u> <u>Mentality</u>
(Princeton: D. Van Nostrand Company, Inc., 1956),
pp. 79-80.

8.   D. T. Atkinson, <u>Magic</u>, <u>Myth</u> <u>and</u> <u>Medicine</u>
(Greenwich: Premier <u>Books</u>, 1956), pp. 50, 42,
118-9, 93, 60-1, 82-3.

9.   William Cecil Dampier, <u>A</u> <u>History</u> <u>of</u> <u>Science</u>
(Cambridge University Press, 1966), pp. 82, 84,
90-1, 64.

10. A. Rupert Hall and Marie Boas Hall, <u>A</u> <u>Brief</u>
<u>History</u> <u>of</u> <u>Science</u> (New York: Signet Books, 1964),
p. 55.

11. The reader may be surprised that I refer to
the seventeenth century (and sometimes to the
eighteenth and even the early nineteenth) in the
context of the Middle Ages: these centuries are
far later than customary historical classifications place the Middle Ages. My treatment is not
due to naivete; it is because, despite all of the
changes brought by onrushing modernity, a major
portion of the medieval mix--social hierarchy,
authoritarian mental processes, towering religion,
guilds, feudal traits, etc.-- remained as late as
the middle of the nineteenth century. It only
requires, for example, a reading of a history of
the French Revolution to see how much medievalism
there was still to be overcome in the late
eighteenth century.

12. G. F. Young, <u>The</u> <u>Medici</u> (New York: Modern
Library, 1930), pp. 672-3, 668.

13. L. T. Woodward, <u>The</u> <u>History</u> <u>of</u> <u>Surgery</u> (Derby,
Conn.: Monarch Books, Inc., 1963), pp. 26, 28,
29.

14. Arturo Castiglioni, <u>A</u> <u>History</u> <u>of</u> <u>Medicine</u> (New

York: Alfred A. Knopf, 1958), pp. 357, 360, 256, 309, 245, 250, 385-7, 329.

15. Lynn Thorndike, The History of Medieval Europe (Boston: Houghton Mifflin Company, 3d ed., 1949), p. 60.

16. Rene Taton, History of Science (New York: Basic Books, Inc., 1963), pp. 511, 481, 475, 487.

17. Herodotus, The Histories (Baltimore: Penguin Books, 1954), p. 102.

18. It is illustrative of my point that the Middle Ages in many respects continued into the eighteenth and nineteenth centuries that Rousseau, writing in 1762, still believed in the Ptolemaic theory that the sun revolves around the earth. It is really quite a parody on his own theory of education when in Emile he says of his pupil "Let him not be taught science, let him discover it" and then shows the level of "commonsense" scientific knowledge this method had given Rousseau himself: "Since the sun revolves round the earth it describes a circle, and every circle must have a center; that we know already. This center is invisible, it is in the middle of the earth, but we can mark out two opposite points on the earth's surface which correspond to it. A skewer passed through the three points and prolonged to the sky at either end would represent the earth's axis and the sun's daily course." Jean Jacques Rousseau, Emile (New York: J. M. Dent & Sons, Ltd., 1911), pp. 131, 133.

19. Edwin P. Hoyt, A Short History of Science (New York: John Day Company, 1965), Vol. I, pp. 223, 227.

20. José Ortega y Gasset, Man and Crisis (New York: W.W. Norton & Co., Inc., 1962), pp. 134, 132.

21. Saint Augustine, Confessions (New York: Modern Library, 1949), pp. 16, 189, 154, 9, 231-3.

6

THE IMPACT OF IMMATURITY

My main purpose in the preceding chapters for
discussing what I have called "man's cosmic immaturity" and the non-paradigmatic nature of earlier
social systems has been to lay a foundation for
understanding the divisions within modern civilization. These bring us to see that we could hardly
expect modern man to have arrived at a consensus
or to behave in a thoroughly mature fashion.
Since my purpose has been to lay this foundation,
I have not been discussing the immaturity and lack
of paradigm for their own sakes.

They are, however, interesting enough in
themselves that I hope the reader will forgive me
for dwelling on them for just a while longer. It
is worthwhile, I think, now that we have the background of the preceding chapters in mind, to notice how very greatly human immaturity and incapacity have affected each of the major social philosophies. Each philosophy strains, after its own
lights, to make the best of an imperfect humanity.
And each, in turn, is rendered problematical by
the fact that its aspirations and expectations
will in all likelihood be frustrated by the diverse
and seemingly obstinate nature of mankind.

Classical Liberalism

Classical liberalism is the social philosophy
which favors capitalism and limited government.
Broadly speaking, its approach toward the problem
of human incapacity is to establish a "free floating" system. Within this system, individuals are
to rise and fall according to their respective
capabilities. A factual supposition of classical
liberal thought is that people are for the most
part capable of handling their own affairs. But

there is also a moral postulate: a "moral imperative" that they make themselves capable. The upshot is that classical liberals generally think
it ultimately more beneficial to human well-being
not to treat weakness with overweening solicitude.
This is so even though many favor placing a floor
under at least the "deserving poor."

The summary I have just given masks, though,
a number of subtleties.

If we focus first on the capacity of the
average man to participate in public affairs (as
distinguished from running his own personal business),
we see that historically classical liberals have
differed among themselves about it. On the continent of Europe during the eighteenth and nineteenth
centuries, most classical liberals doubted the
ability of the ordinary man to sustain a democracy
which would be compatible with individual liberty.
In Germany, France and Russia, this led them to
see the most effective liberal course to be in
"enlightened despotism." Bastiat and Tocqueville
wrote in a somewhat more democratic vein than this
would suggest, but even they were deeply concerned
about the ultimate compatibility of democracy with
liberty.

The tendency in England, though, was to feel
considerably more trust in the average man -- especially when the possibility of perfecting men
through education was taken into account. John
Stuart Mill valued freedom mainly as an educative
process. John Bright devoted the second half of
his political life to universal manhood suffrage.
And in the United States the party of Jefferson
and Jackson combined a devout classical liberalism
with an abiding faith in the common man.

In neither case, of course, did classical
liberals feel confident about an unlimited majority
rule. "If men were angels," Madison wrote, "no
government would be necessary."[1] He was quick to
add that there is no reason to suppose government

110

officials more angelic than the rest.

Personally, I think this is a wholesome distrust. When we consider the mixed condition of
mankind -- in which good and evil, the social and
the antisocial, the strong and the weak compete in
perpetual tension --, the classical liberal hesitation seems quite realistic. It has the advantage
of avoiding the naive supposition that governments
will be dependably benevolent. And unlike the
usual socialist, a classical liberal doesn't assume
that someone sharing his values will always be in
control. Instead, he knows that "power corrupts."

The second aspect of capability has to do with
each man's capacity for handling his own individual
concerns. As I have indicated, classical liberals
believe, as a factual matter, that most men really
are able to handle their own affairs. They sense
that men are tough and not dumb when it comes to
their own interests. This doesn't, of course,
preclude some naivete when people are dealing with
something that is unfamiliar to them. But it is
amazing how "savvy" the average person is about
things that really touch him. The result of the
classical liberal's appreciation of the average
person's ability is that in his political philosophy the classical liberal is not going to
interfere with that person's freedom in order to
assist him paternalistically. At the same time,
however, a classical liberal will have reason to
favor such laws and institutions as are helpful
in providing the framework in which the individual
can act. (A statute calling for a uniform method
of disclosing the true rate of interest paid on
a savings account, for example, might facilitate
individual choice, since most people can't be
expected to have, or to gain, sophisticated knowledge about the many ways interest can be computed.

It is precisely because they see men as basically capable that classical liberals value the
voluntary transaction as a valid expression of
freedom. Such transactions are in their system

given social and legal sanction and become the
building blocks, when repeated billions of times,
for the "market economy." The linking of voluntary relationships leads to vast human effort and
to the division of labor.

The Left opposes the market economy by attacking both the presumption of capability and the
voluntary transaction. They argue that millions
of men are trapped by life and that the voluntary
transaction is vitiated by "exploitation." In
this regard, I distinguish between four different
theories of exploitation. An adequate discussion
of them requires considerable space, so I will have
to leave that for my later books on the ideologies
themselves. It is enough right now to say that
classical liberals don't agree with the exploitation theories (although in my writing I have
stressed that there are points raised by two of
the theories which classical liberals ought to
take seriously in the context of their own philosophy).

I mentioned earlier that classical liberalism
imputes a moral imperative over and above the
factual supposition about capability. To the extent men are not capable, their duty as free human
beings is to make themselves so. This is ethical,
not descriptive. It is an ethic of self-reliance
which is fundamentally important to a free society.
If men are not self-reliant, they cannot be left
to their own decisions; nor will they want to be.
The work ethic and the push toward education are
essential parts of individualism. Because of this,
classical liberalism identifies strongly with the
so-called "Protestant" or "middle class" ethic.
(By calling the ethic "Protestant" or "middle class,"
the Left seeks to categorize it in a culturally
relative way to diminish its universality; classical liberal thought posits it as a general ethic
and not simply as the ethic appropriate to a certain religion or class.)

If individuals fall down within a voluntaristic setting, the solutions offered by classical liberalism are consistent with its overall value system. It calls first upon the individual's own energy and pride. Secondly, it will look to private charity as the voluntary form of help. If tax supported relief is still needed, the classical liberal would much prefer to see that relief given on the local level. At the same time, an important desideratum, even though it doesn't appeal to the type of humanitarianism we have heard for so long from the Left, will be to design the relief in such a way that it will encourage those who are on it to get off at the earliest possible time.[2]

It would be erroneous to think that all classical liberals have agreed on the priorities I have just recited. Herbert Spencer, for example, was a man of clear intelligence and very real compassion, but he adopted a Darwinian-type evolutionary rationale and even argued for letting the weak perish.[3] His views in this regard were not representative of the majority of classical liberals.

I happen to think that the mainstream of classical liberal thought deals appropriately with the problem of human weakness. It recognizes both the strengths and weaknesses of people and builds in a pull toward a higher elevation. If the framework of classical liberalism is adequately designed, a free society has many advantages.

A part of my earlier comments, though, was that each of the philosophies is rendered problematical by the problem of weakness. This is certainly true with classical liberalism. The movement away from it in the past century suggests that, among other things, classical liberalism is "out of keeping" with the actual spiritual and intellectual condition of mankind.

We often remark that the Welfare State reduces initiative. The relationship, however, almost

113

certainly runs the other way, too, with human
weakness contributing to the demand for the Welfare
State. Classical liberalism today represents a
higher aspiration than many people are willing to
accept.

It may even be that this is a profound disparity; it may be too much to expect men at our present evolutionary level to sustain a system based
heavily on self-reliance. If this is true, it
militates strongly against the realization of
classical liberal values at this point in history.

But this is by no means clear. It is still
problematical because of two factors which have
been so influential that they have kept the past
century from being a clear test of the average
man's aptitude for freedom. Because we cannot
isolate the factors, we cannot know how much our
recent reliance on the Welfare State is due to
these factors and how much is due to innate weakness.

The first factor is the alienation of the intellectual subculture from bourgeois society
(this, in fact, is the main subject I will discuss
later in this book). When deep alienation exists
in men who have the cultural leverage which intellectuals exercise, it isn't surprising that the
society will move away from classical liberalism.
This is especially true because the intellectual
has consistently sought an alliance with the
have-nots, which in turn has led him to champion
their cause as he perceives it. Thus, the root of
the Welfare State and of egalitarian socialism
may be more in the ail of the intellectual than
in the mediocrity of the average man. This obscures the situation, keeping us from getting a
clear reading of how well classical liberalism com-
ports to the underlying human condition.

The second complication has to do with the
hedonistic, pragmatic, unprincipled characteristics
of modern life. These qualities lead men away

114

from classical liberalism. It may, however, be too early to tell whether spoiledness is unavoidable under affluence. If it is, classical liberalism will be inherently unstable; such men will be impatient toward the responsibilities it imposes.

Egalitarian Ideology

Not all types of socialist theory are egalitarian, but most do involve a far-reaching egalitarianism. In this context, "equality" does not mean "equality under the law" or "equality of rights." It refers to an unequal treatment of unequals to produce an equal result.

Socialism and the Welfare State seek this type of equality through the state or some other collective. Because of the Left's perception of humanity as largely trapped and exploited, the state is seen not simply as an equalizing but also as a liberating mechanism. The state becomes the "next friend" of the weak.

This trust in the state raises problems, though, which relate directly to the nature of man. It invokes coercive power as a principal instrument. This recalls a famous exchange in which Friedrich Hayek argued in The Road to Serfdom that because of its use of coercive power even democratic socialism possesses a tendency toward totalitarianism, and in which Herman Finer responded in The Road to Reaction that types of socialism differ and that democratic socialism has no such inherent tendency. For my part, I agree with Hayek in the weight of his concern, even though I don't agree with his thesis that the tendency is irresistible. Lord Acton seems to me to have been correct when he wrote that "power corrupts"; and Parkinson was perceptive when he noted the tendency of bureaucracy to grow. Great power also serves as a magnet to demagoguery and opportunism. All classical liberals consider the problem of power of profound concern. In shrugging off the danger, democratic socialists

115

have failed to take sufficient account of human nature.

But there are still other factors that make the socialist solution dangerous. The Spanish philosopher José Ortega y Gasset diagnosed the spiritual condition of modern man fifty years ago in The Revolt of the Masses. He took a pessimistic view of the average man, whom he described as spiritually self-satisfied and inert. He said that such men demand nothing of themselves; they are persons "for whom to live is to be every moment what they already are, without imposing on themselves any effort toward perfection."[4] Such a man possesses a "spoiled child mentality"; he wants the benefits of a developed social order while at the same time his nature keeps him from appreciating the round-about, orderly processes by which that social order is maintained. Civilized men, Ortega wrote, make force the last, not the first, resort, but the "mass man" reverses this because of his "direct action" tantrum mentality. This use of force has its final social expression in statism, which institutionalizes the psychology of the predominant type of man.

Much of what Ortega ascribes to the "mass man" I would attribute to the broader category of human immaturity in general. I would place his views in perspective by pointing out that "direct action" techniques are by no means the invention of the modern "mass man." The history of almost any epoch is, in fact, a wearying recital of their use. Nevertheless, both his view and my broadening of it point to spiritual factors which make any reliance on a powerful state very dangerous.

The strong tendency of the intelligentsia to use the state for elitist and essentially theocratic purposes also points toward abuse. The intellectual's sensitivities and his normal self-serving aspirations often cause him to want to use the state as a church -- i.e., as an instrument to remold men. The modern era has seen no real separa-

116

tion between the church and state, since secular
social religion has attached itself to the state.
The result has been a tendency toward intolerant
uses of the state to carry out the values of the
intellectual elite. This is obscured by the intellectuals' alliance with the have-nots; the
alliance's emphasis on majority rule and a levelling egalitarianism masks the elitism.

We should note that each of the factors that
lead to serious abuse of socialism are also factors which make socialism unstable. Neither democratic socialism nor the Welfare State can give
assurance that it will not be just a transitional
phase.

A levelling egalitarianism has serious defects,
though, even if the danger of abuses isn't considered. A part of its ideology is to refuse to
make "bourgeois" moral distinctions. The moral
imperative toward decency and capability which is
stressed by classical liberalism is deliberately
omitted and even attacked. I recall Morris Cohen's
comment a few years ago in the New Republic that
"it is the Puritanic feeling of responsibility
which has blighted our art and philosophy and has
made us as a people unskilled in the art of enjoying life."[5] When the intellectual allies himself
with the have-not to gain weight in his rivalry
with the acting man, he can no longer champion
moral excellence, since moral excellence has little
appeal to the have-nots. Nor does the intellectual
want to affirm the same ideals espoused by his rivals in the business culture. Art, music and
literature accordingly become immersed in an "anti-
hero" theme, while at the same time there is a
reliance on the collective rather than on the individual as the moral agency of society. The abdica-
tion of leadership toward individual responsibility
reinforces the other factors which have tended to
remove the preconditions for a classically liberal
society. The continuing immaturity of man is
accented. And men are encouraged by socialist doctrine to be the inert, malleable matter which Bas-

117

tiat observed socialists would like them to be.[6]
Above a race of pygmy men, the state stands like
a colossus.

An awareness of the underlying elitism of the
intellectual subculture, though, can justify a
projection not of a levelled sameness, but of a
new domination by an intellectual priesthood. The
result will probably be more like the intellectual
despotism desired by Auguste Comte than like the
mild leadership hoped for by John Stuart Mill. It
is despotism rather than an educated self-reliance
that the diminished man will be best suited for.
Socialists often assume that everyone will become
an intellectual in such a society -- that men will
not remain diminished, but will blossom into self-
fulfilled individuals within a high culture. Thus,
the New Left author Robert Theobald projected that
"life will essentially be learning."[7] And I am reminded of the socialist utopia fantasized almost
a century ago by Edward Bellamy in Looking Backward
in which socialism supported vibrant individuals
who filled their lives with music, literature and
the arts.[8] Such an assumption reflects an intention to remake men. This is based both on a
thorough-going dislike for man as he is and on a
naive Rousseauistic optimism about man's residual
potentialities.

Burkean Conservatism

Until the middle of the nineteenth century,
the worldview which in a broad sense I refer to
as "Burkean conservatism" was the main force in
Western civilization, even though by that time it
had long been under attack. It has a number of
extremely literate advocates even today.

The contemporary Burkean authors Wilmoore
Kendall and George Carey have summarized the position by referring to five main points: a principled morality as distinguished from a relativistic
view; social hierarchy; historic, evolved rights

as against a rationalistic "rights of man"; tradition as opposed to "the will of the present generation"; and, finally, religion versus secularism.
In making a separate list, Russell Kirk emphasized
the same points: belief in divine intent, affec-
tion for traditional life, a "conviction that
civilized society requires orders and classes,"
support for private property, control over man's
will and appetite, and a distrust of change for
change's sake.

    In the twentieth century this outlook is
championed mainly by a group of Catholic thinkers.
Its name is derived from Edmund Burke, who in the
eighteenth century expressed its values in his
critique of the French Revolution.[10] This can
be misleading, though; Burkean conservatism embodies a view of man and of institutions which is
far larger than any one group of thinkers. The
organic view of a society headed by landed aristocracy and morally directed by organized religion
was the Roman ideal of the mos maiorum. It was
the central conception of the Middle Ages. As
late as the nineteenth century it was articulated
by such figures as Samuel Coleridge, Thomas
Carlyle, John Ruskin and Matthew Arnold.

    An aristocratic philosophy is acutely aware
of human weakness. Russell Kirk spoke of "the
doctrine of human depravity," which he said is
broader even than Augustinian Christianity.[11]
Richard Weaver based his analysis on the Catholic
doctrine of original sin.[12] For the Burkean, human will, appetite and reason are very much suspect. He hopes to overcome these by integrating
the individual into a social order founded on
hierarchy, faith and religion. This is just the
opposite of Rousseau's optimism; it is also different from the classical liberal's mixed view of
men. Historically, the aristocratic view has not
favored individual liberty as a general system
which would involve countless individuals pursuing
their own ends and happiness.

119

Burkean conservatism deals with weakness by incorporating the individual into an organic whole. The leadership of society is placed in the hands of people who are leisured, cultured and educated -- ideally a good hedge against the incapability of ordinary men. Many thoughtful people have favored this out of a sincere regard for the welfare of humanity. Samuel Johnson was one of them; he said that "I am a friend to subordination, as most conducive to the happiness of society. There is a reciprocal pleasure in governing and being governed." He added that "I consider myself as acting a part in the great system of society."[13] His good will was evidenced by his statement that "an adequate provision for the poor is the test of every civilization." The Burkean system, seen as an ideal, is not intended to be harsh and malevolent. Its supporters think of it as embodying profound truths about man and his relation to God. They also believe it has advantages arising from a sense of community, from an ethic of chivalry and civility, and from the virtues of humility, piety and discipline.

I will hasten to add, though, that I cannot agree with this idealization of it. Although I agree with John Stuart Mill's belief that Burkean philosophy captures some important truths (Mill saw an important half of the truth in Coleridge's writing[14]), I don't view Burkean conservatism as correct either in general or as a way of dealing with the problem of weakness.

The intellectual humility fundamental to classical liberalism precludes any feeling that a given religious view ought to be made the foundation of civil society. It also precludes any designation of who shall and shall not be the aristocrats in society, especially if that station is to be passed on by inheritance. Even to select an aristocracy of merit presupposes an exercise of judgment which the mentality of freedom finds repugnant. The Burkeans will answer that they don't intend these to result from rational

selection by a planner, but despite their protests
to the contrary their philosophy does involve a
preconceived model. But even if such social patterns were set upon spontaneously, they would be
untenable for other reasons. The organic conception of society offers, for example, no solution
to the problem of the abuse of power. History
shows that such a regime cannot be counted on to
remain benevolent; a status system is often
characterized by a type of mental death and rigidi-
ty and oppression. This abuse of power would be
especially predictable if the Burkean's own
postulates about evil are correct, but it is predictable even under the more optimistic mixed view
of human nature held by classical liberals.

There are two additional points I would make
about the Burkean solution. The first is that a
solution which would divide mankind into those who
are capable and those who are not would tend
strongly to solidify the incapable in their weakness.

The second is that it would act to reverse
the tendency toward increased compassion which
has occurred during the modern period. More people
participate in society today and are the objects
of concern by others for their rights and well-
being. Julien Benda wrote that this compassion is
mainly the residual of the eighteenth century and
that that is a moral capital we are rapidly losing;
but I can't fully agree with him on it.[15] The increased compassion does have important origins in
that century which have been weakened, but it is
also the product of our increased affluence and of
the "age of the common man." Even though this
compassion may be shallow and incomplete, any
shift back toward aristocratic, status principles
would be a serious loss of progress already made.

With regard to the other philosophies, I have
concluded by commenting on their instability. The
instability within Burkean conservatism resides
in the tendencies toward abuse inherent within it

121

and toward reaction against that abuse. Each
status society has had a built-in class struggle
as the lower orders have fought their way free.
It cannot be a permanently acceptable paradigm.

Radical Versus Conservative Method

Each social philosophy is concerned with the
question of means. Each forms an attitude toward
change and toward the methods which are available
to promote change. In the present context, it is
worth noting that man's immaturity has an important
bearing on this question.

The immaturity says, in effect, that men are
neither perfect nor readily perfectible. In turn,
this suggests an anti-radical conclusion: that
we ought not to want to destroy much that is
valuable to make way for anyone's projected utopia.
We have good reason to believe a utopian prospect
chimerical. We can hardly base social policy on
an assumption of man's perfection when we know
that it will take a long evolutionary cycle before
he will drop (if he ever will) his many childlike
traits.

The restraint this suggests isn't the same
thing as a purely resigned acceptance of the status
quo. There are things we won't tolerate; and
yet our willingness to use drastic means is
tempered when we consider that the abuses we abhor
are not entirely remediable under any circumstances;
the fundamental imperfections of a childlike humanity will continue in one form or another. It
will never be worthwhile, certainly, to tear down
civilized society to pursue a utopia. When the
Russian nihilist Nechayev called for the destruction of all existing order as necessary for a
transition to a socialist utopia, his deep alienation had caused him to lose all sense of a balance
of values.[16] He was devaluing the existing society
far below what it deserved and was valuing the
utopia far too highly.

My point is a repudiation of the Rousseauistic
vision which has been repeated so many thousands
of times during the past two and a half centuries.
Rousseau thought that social improvement was largely a matter of clearing away debris so that the
pure gold of a pristine human nature could shine
through from underneath. This idea was picked up
by Marx when he predicted that men would reach a
perfected condition as soon as the dialectical
process had obliterated private property and the
class struggle. Recently the New Left philosopher
Herbert Marcuse has looked forward to a utopia
based on a technological horn-of-plenty after the
current society has been smashed; and Theodore
Roszak wants to undercut civilization so much as
to revert to man's primitive origins.[17] Such views
as these appear profound in their radicalism; but
they are actually simplistic, not nearly radical
enough. By catching on to scapegoats and illusions of perfectibility, they produce anti-civilizational theories. Indeed, the alienation of the
intellectual has made him the most destructive
element in modern civilization. He will remain so
until he sees that the problem is far more profound
than he has conceived it.

NOTES

1. James Madison, The Federalist, No. 51.

2. The classical liberal desire to encourage people
to get off welfare was reflected in the report of
the royal commission in England in 1832 which embodied the Poor Law Amendments which were subse-
quently enacted in 1834. The report said: "The
first and most essential of all conditions . . .
is that his situation on the whole shall not be
made really or apparently so eligible (i.e.,
desirable) as the situation of the independent
laborer of the lowest class." Henry Hazlitt,
The Conquest of Poverty (New Rochelle: Arlington
House, 1973), p. 79.

3. Herbert Spencer, _Social Statics_ and _Man Versus the State_ (New York: D. Appleton and Company, 1897), p. 99; _Man Versus the State_ (Baltimore: Pelican Books, 1969), pp. 139-141. Spencer's compassion is apparent when he asks "What would you do if placed in the position of the laborer? How would these virtues of yours stand the wear and tear of poverty?" It is worth noticing that Spencer did not stand consistently behind his endorsement of letting the weak perish; he was willing to admit the validity of private charity because of its voluntary nature.

4. José Ortega y Gasset, _The Revolt of the Masses_ (New York: W. W. Norton & Company, Inc., 1957), p. 15.

5. As quoted in Henry May, _The Discontent of the Intellectuals_: _A Problem of the Twenties_ (Chicago: Rand McNally & Company, 1963), p. 23.

6. Frederic Bastiat, _The Law_ (Irvington-on-Hudson: Foundation for Economic Education, 1964), p. 34.

7. Robert Theobald, _An Alternative Future for America_ (Chicago: Swallow Press, Inc., 1968), p. 53.

8. Edward Bellamy, _Looking Backward_ (New York: Modern Library, 1942).

9. As quoted in Jeffrey Hart, _The American Dissent_: _A Decade of Modern Conservatism_ (Garden City: Doubleday & Company, Inc., 1966), pp. 192-3.

10. Edmund Burke, _Reflections on the Revolution in France_ (New York: Liberal Arts Press, 1955).

11. Russell Kirk, _Enemies of the Permanent Things_ (New Rochelle: Arlington House, 1969), pp. 146-7; _The Conservative Mind_ (Chicago: Henry Regnery Company, 1953), pp. 7, 8.

12. Richard Weaver, _Ideas Have Consequences_ (Chicago:

124

Phoenix Books, 1948), p. 4.

13. James Boswell, The Life of Samuel Johnson
(New York: Modern Library, 1952), p. 122; same
(Everyman edition, Vol. I), p. 396.

14. John Stuart Mill, On Bentham and Coleridge
(New York: Academy Library, 1950).

15. Julien Benda, The Betrayal of the Intellectuals
(Boston: The Beacon Press, 1930), p. 160.

16. Robert Payne, The Terrorists (New York: Funk
and Wagnalls Company, 1957), p. 24.

17. Herbert Marcuse, An Essay on Liberation (Boston: Beacon Press, 1969); Theodore Roszak, Where
the Wasteland Ends (Garden City: Doubleday &
Company, 1972).

PART II:

THE MODERN CRISIS

7

WE REACH THE MODERN CRISIS

In Chapter 2, I said that I would be looking at the modern predicament on three different levels. These would, in turn, place it in the broadest possible historic context, define its specific elements and look at the respective "worldviews" which have reflected the divisions within modern society.

The first aspect was the overall phenomenon of human immaturity, which carries over into our own day framing much that we do, but which needed to be seen in long-term historic continuity if we were to avoid blaming it provincially upon ourselves. This has been the subject of the first several chapters.

The second level referred to the divisions which have existed during the past two hundred years. We entered modern Western civilization richly fertilized from the past. But we have faced the problem of immaturity in a unique way: the old aristocratic elites have been knocked out and there has been a spectacular rise of the average man into participation and predominance since the eighteenth century. The fact that this is a problematical basis for a civilization is reflected in the scepticism voiced by so many modern thinkers. Still further, our civilization has had to "find itself" after emerging from an age of theology and status; and it has had to do so even in the absence of satisfactory paradigms suggested by the past. The result has been existential uncertainty, if not crisis. Both as a result of this uncertainty and as an exacerbation of it, there has been a profound socio-ideological division between the major social groups in modern society. The intellectual has long been bitterly alienated from the broad middle class; from there, he has

gone on to form an ideological alliance with society's have-nots. The consequence has been a
uniquely bifurcated civilization with built-in tensions and a dynamic toward change in a certain
direction. The void of existential uncertainty
and social division has been filled with flaming
passions or by the apathy of meaninglessness.

Our civilization, then, is not a settled
fact, a final Being. It is a Becoming, a complex
and moving system of forces and interactions.
These aspects are what I will want to explore during the middle chapters of this volume, and I will
want to go into as much depth as I can about them.
Then in the final chapters we will take up several
of the situations which have resulted from them
in modern history, to illustrate the actual ways
they have appeared.

The third aspect was on a still more ontolo-
gical level. It has to do with the fact that there
is no consensus about what the modern social reality really is; that there is a welter of conflicting
perceptions. These perceptions are not isolated;
they are organized into competing systems of
interpretation, ideologies, worldviews, each seeking to put together a mediated reality which is
comprehensible. They interpret reality, but at
the same time constitute a major part of the reality they seek to understand.

In subsequent volumes I will review each of
the major worldviews. As I do so, they should be
seen not just as bodies of thought, but also as
both a major part of and a product of the modern
predicament. In large measure they spring from
the divisions. At the same time, they deepen the
predicament because their conflicting presence
means that modern men are divided profoundly in
their perception of social reality; which is to
say that they are divided as profoundly as if they
were divided over matters of religion.

8

THE RISE OF THE MULTITUDES

As we approach the twenty-first century we seem far removed from the age of aristocracy. It is hard for us to realize that until quite recently man's story has not been the story of the many, but of the few. Historically, the great bulk of humanity existed in a submerged condition in which they were committed socially, intellectually, economically and politically to a life outside the limelight. The chimney sweep and the charwoman were there as givens; they were the mute and inert matter of mankind, playing their roles quietly -- supportive and unsung.

We don't need to favor a dogmatic Marxist interpretation of history to realize that dominant groups and classes have stood above the main body of the human race. No modern historian would want to overlook the underlying demographic factors and other sociologically important aspects of a past society, but for the most part the active, educated, directive part of each society was found in its aristocracy.

The period since the end of the eighteenth century, however, has seen the death of aristocracy. Men have come fully into an age of general participation. We have our wealthy, our jet-setters, our prominent personalities and statesmen, our famous entertainers, but we having nothing comparable to the aristocrats of old in the sense of their being a cohesive social class elevated well above the rest of mankind and strongly differentiated from it.

Many philosophers have remarked that what we have instead is what Ortega described as "the revolt of the masses." Europe and America have witnessed two simultaneous and related phenomena:

an enormous increase in the numbers of average
people, and the elevation of their participation in
society to the point at which the tone of almost
all activity -- in fact, of the civilization -- is
established by their presence.

Ortega noted fifty years ago that "it is more
life than all previous existence."[1] He pointed
to the amazing statistical fact that during the
twelve centuries between the sixth century and the
beginning of the nineteenth Europe had never ex-
ceeded 180 million people in its population, and
that during the period of slightly more than a
century between 1800 and 1914 the population had
increased from the base of 180 million to as much
as 460 million!

Despite this statistic, those of us who are
alive fifty years later are inclined to think of
the "population explosion" as just now taking
place -- or as something that will occur mainly in
the future. We forget that the explosion was well
underway in the nineteenth century. Ortega points
out that this brought with it a fundamental change
in society.

The increase has not been an increase in
aristocrats. The aristocracies had no such proli-
fic potential. There was instead a magnification
of the previously submerged corpus of mankind. It
has been an explosion precisely of the average man.

This numerical increase was accompanied by
the rise of the "multitudes" to a culturally predominant role. Ortega wrote from the perspective
of an aristocrat, but we don't have to share that
viewpoint with him to agree with him that "the
characteristic of the hour is that the commonplace
mind, knowing itself to be commonplace, has the
assurance to proclaim the rights of the commonplace
and to impose them wherever it will." As a mere
physical presence, the average man pervades our
times: such men fill the highways with their
campers, crowd the ski slopes with their families,

stand in line to be served at restaurants. Average
humanity is no longer backstage; it is in the
forefront, "occupying all places." It is to this
average humanity that the mass market makes its
appeal, and it is this average humanity which makes
its tastes felt in music, literature, conversation
and entertainments -- i.e., in every aspect of
life.

We may identify ourselves with these multitudes or try to distinguish ourselves from them as
men of aristocratic bent have sought to; but this
makes no difference; the fact remains as one of
the more significant of the modern period.

This enormous increase in numbers would once
have provoked a Malthusean prediction of famine
and misery, but just the same there has been a
continuing improvement in the average man's standard of living. Even though there are different
degrees of well-being, we live in an age of affluence. Compared to anything before, it is a time
of immense affluence.

The problem of human weakness hasn't been
abolished; pockets of enervation exist even within
our society, perhaps nourished by the very policies
that seek to help them. But the comparison with
the past is notable if, for example, we read John
Bright's diary about conditions in Portugal and
Turkey in the 1830's. His description of Portugal
wouldn't be an accurate picture of Europe or America today: "About the streets are great numbers of
dogs. They are without exception the dirtiest,
lousiest, most emaciated, forlorn-looking creatures I ever beheld . . . The streets are filthy,
owing chiefly to the habit of emptying everything
from the windows at night."[2] Our own civilization
is so dynamic that we have to be reminded that
stagnation is possible for peoples and cultures;
we see such stagnation in Bright's description of
Turkey: "Property and even life being insecure,
no inducement is held out to the people to march
on the road to civilization. There exists no spirit

133

of emulation amongst them, and they drag on their
existence as nearly as possible in the same list-
less and apathetic manner in which their fathers
have done before them."

The pace of change is so rapid with us that
we adapt quickly to even the most striking changes.
We take it for granted that the average person
should participate as a full member of the community. But it is surprising to me, as I read back
over the history of Europe during the nineteenth
century, how recently the average man's rise
occurred. It was almost yesterday in the history
of Western civilization.

It was only two hundred years ago that Adam
Smith was able to write of "that drowsy stupidity,
which, in a civilized society, seems to benumb the
understanding of almost all the inferior ranks of
people."[3] Speaking of the situation in the first
half of the nineteenth century in England, Trevelyan referred to "the illiteracy of a large part of
the working classes," which he says caused such a
reformer as Cobden to be anxious to teach them to
read before giving them the vote.[4]

Even the predominance of the middle class came
quite late. In his Principles of Political Economy,
John Stuart Mill spoke of the landowners, not the
middle class, as "the masters of the legislation
of England, to say the least since 1688."[5] It
wasn't the middle class that came into power in
1688; it was aristocracy. Trevelyan notes that in
the 1840's "Peel has realized that under the existing franchise the House of Commons did not represent the lower classes at all, or the middle
classes more than a little." He points out that
even "the Reform Act of 1832 had left half the
middle class unenfranchised and the rest insufficiently represented under the arbitrary system by
which the seats were distributed in favour of the
landed interest." Richard Cobden argued the case
of the middle class to Peel by asserting that the
Reform and Corn bills had established the founda-

tions for middle class government.[6] This was in
the middle of the nineteenth century! And although
some victories were won to move Britain away from
aristocratic government, we sense in Cobden's life
a continuing frustration, as though even after
those victories his voice remained a cry in the
wilderness.

In the 1820's the Philosophical Radicals felt
that the main task was to oppose the aristocratic
domination of England's political life. Joseph
Hamburger says that "in their view the important
thing was to achieve total political victory, i.e.,
to destroy aristocratic power."[7] John Stuart Mill
was still able to speak of "the two principles
which divide the world, the aristocratic principle
and the democratic." Hamburger reports that even
"by 1839, far from having merged into an aristocratic party, the Whigs and Tories were poised against
one another in a fairly even struggle for power.
The two aristocratic factions that James Mill had
opposed twenty years before continued to dominate
the political scene." Along the same lines, John
Morley wrote in his life of Cobden of the need for
the mercantile and manufacturing classes to counter-
act "the feudal governing class of this country"
in the first half of the nineteenth century.[8]

During those years, indeed, the emphasis was
not on a struggle between capitalism and socialism,
but between capitalism (mainly represented by the
Free Trade movement), the middle class and growing democracy, on the one hand, and the continuing
carry-over of aristocracy, on the other. This was
especially true on the continent, where there was
a renewal of monarchical institutions after the
Napoleonic Wars while at the same time there was
growing bourgeois participation.

During all this, there was constant pressure
from below toward an enormous uplift. The many,
including the middle class, were expanding and
rising. In England this culminated in the reform
of 1867, extended in 1884-1885. D.C. Johnson says

135

these reforms "extended the household suffrage to
all constituencies, in counties as well as in
towns," with the result that "roughly speaking,
England enjoyed universal male suffrage after
these bills."[9] And this was just a short century
ago!

It was common to think of the multitudes both
as rising and as badly in need of improvement.
The rejoicing was tainted by doubt. John Stuart
Mill, for example, felt great sympathy for the
"masses," but he regarded them with a reserve
which was inseparable from his own elitism. He
saw the multitudes as having come culturally into
their own; he described this somewhat balefully
in On Liberty: "The general tendency of things
throughout the world is to render mediocrity the
ascendant power among mankind . . . At present individuals are lost in the crowd . . . The only
power deserving the name is that of masses, and
of governments while they make themselves the
organ of the tendencies and instincts of masses."
He quickly added that "I am not complaining of all
this. I do not assert that anything better is
compatible, as a general rule, with the present
low state of the human mind."[10] Just the same, he
wasn't pleased; he pointed to the mediocre thinking of the "masses," to their mutual conformity
and to their total absorption in business.

What we see is that at the time the final
political battles were being fought with aristocracy, the multitudes were absorbing everything
into themselves.

This bears heavily on the unique problems of
modern Western civilization. In an aristocratic
society we are concerned with the special problems
of an elite. The quality of the aristocracy can
vary from high nobility to extreme decadence. But
in modern society a great deal turns on the qualities of the average man. Here there is a direct
picking up, without a selective process, of the
ordinary foibles of an immature humanity. In an

age of the common man the infant nature of mankind
has a direct bearing which is partially deflected
or transformed in an aristocratic society.

The passing of aristocracy and the rise of
the multitudes obviously raises the importance of
the multitudes, but an additional point is that
the intellectual has also been rendered more pivotal. Ortega has viewed the "masses" as overwhelmingly powerful in their own right. For many purposes, this is correct; but I agree with Ludwig
von Mises when he says that even in a mass culture
the role of the intellectual is often central:
"The main error of this widespread pessimism is
the belief that the destructionist ideas and
policies of our age sprang from the proletarians
and are a 'revolt of the masses.' In fact, the
masses, precisely because they are not creative
and do not develop philosophies of their own, follow the leaders. The ideologies which produced
all the mischiefs and catastrophies of our century
are not an achievement of the mob. They are the
feat of pseudo-scholars and pseudo-intellectuals
. . . What is needed to turn the flood is to
change the mentality of the intellectuals. Then
the masses will follow suit."[11]

Modern life cannot be understood without appreciating the leading role of the intellectual.
Much of my discussion in later chapters will deal
with that fact. But the intellectual community
does not operate in the modern period on a monarchy or an aristocracy or an established church;
it operates, instead, within the milieu created by
the explosion of the multitudes. The vacuum left
by the demise of traditional institutions is important in giving the intellectuals' leadership
particular weight. The intellectual has always
been significant, but he is especially so today --
although I am no more willing to make the role of
intellectual a "one shot" explanation of history,
including modern history, than I am with any other
factor. Things are too complicated for that, as
I am sure Mises himself would be quick to point out.

An Assessment of Quality

Those who write about the spiritual problems
that come from the "massness" of the modern period
often write as though the problem of human quality
were a new one springing from the specific conditions of the nineteenth and twentieth centuries.
We get this impression especially from Ortega's
The Revolt of the Masses.

But it isn't that people have deteriorated
during modern times. In fact, the opposite is
true. The average person in Europe and America
today will compare very favorably with the wretched illiterates of two centuries ago.[12] Massness
and the problem of quality simply continue the
much larger problem of human immaturity. People
have never been perfect; they aren't perfect today.
What we have witnessed is not a fall, but a continuation of the older problem in a new form.
Because of this, a critical look at contemporary
man should not be understood to suggest praise of
some earlier condition. It is worth keeping this
in mind as we review the analysis Ortega made in
The Revolt of the Masses.

Ortega noted the numerical expansion of what
he and so many others have called the "masses,"
but he went on to distinguish between two types
of men. He said that humanity is divided radically into two types of people, according to the demands that they make upon themselves. He called
the type of person who makes continual demands
upon himself, seeking always to be better than he
has previously been and never being contented with
what he is, a "noble man." The other type of
person -- the type who reclines back with self-
satisfaction at what he already is, seeks no perfection and makes no special demands upon himself
-- is what he meant by "mass man."

He continued his analysis by observing that
it is precisely this second type of man -- the mass
man -- who predominates during our time, overwhelm-

ing even groups that have heretofore always been selective. He was careful to make it clear that the type of man he defined as "mass" had little to do with social classes. Mass men were found at all levels, as were noble men. But Ortega saw the immense predominance of the mass man as having a suffocating effect. Such men insisted upon, and succeeded in imposing, the "rights of the commonplace" in every aspect of life.

He was candid to say that he held to a "radically aristocratic" view of history in the sense that human society has no choice but to be aristocratic. To the extent, he said, that a society stops being aristocratic, it stops being a society. It is only a society to the extent that selectivity is one of its characteristics. He sensed, accordingly, a "palpitating danger" under the surface of our times, an "element of terror."

Chapters three and four of The Revolt of the Masses were no doubt intended to show Ortega's appreciation for the affirmative potential of the rise of the multitudes, but even here his concern over the dangers came through as the main emphasis. (The book was written during the years between the world wars.)

To Ortega, the mass man is the typical man of our age; and this man takes on the aspect of a "primitive" who has come to exist ironically in the midst of a long-developing civilization. He said such men had proved uneducable in everything except the techniques of modern gadgetry. At the same time, they are rootless, having no real respect for the highly civilized culture they have inherited. They take that civilization for granted in the same way they take everything for granted. Ortega considered them to have two basic psychological traits, both of which are attributes of spoiledness: one was a "free expansion of his vital desires," with a perception of endless possibilities; the other was a "radical ingratitude" toward everything that the mass man had inherited

from the culture of the past and that made his
life easy. Ortega made the analogy to the "psychology of the spoilt child."

Ortega observed that the mass man jumps to
opinions without effort. Not only is this mental
inertia destructive of intellectual values, but it
has untold significance in political life. He
said that the Syndicalist and Fascist movements
were the first sign in Europe of a kind of person
who "does not want to give reasons or to be right,"
but who is simply determined to "impose his
opinions." This mentality reverses the usual posture of true civilization: instead of force's
being made the final resort, it is elevated to the
first or even the only resort. "Direct action" --
the leaping to results without regard for the
civilities of an ordered society -- became the by-
word, as it did with Sorel. "Direct action" finds
the state an easily available tool, since the
state most possesses the means for immediate gratifications. The relationship of this to modern
totalitarianism is easily evident. The mass does
not limit itself individually or collectively; nor
does a state representing the masses feel the need
to do so.

In another area, the extreme specialization
which has developed in modern thought has a similar effect on intellectuals and scientists.
"A mass of technicians" exist who are essentially
rootless outside their own specialties, and who
have no "intimate solidarity with the future of
science." These technicians may be quite intelligent, but they share the lack of attachment to
civilization in its fuller meaning. "Specialism
begins to dislodge integral culture from the individual scientist," and, going on, Ortega said
that "the specialist 'knows' very well his own tiny
corner of the universe; he is radically ignorant
of all the rest."

The greatest danger, according to Ortega, is
the state. He referred to the Romans from the
time of the Antonines, and anticipated that "the

140

state (will) overbear society with its anti-vital supremacy. Society begins to be enslaved, to be unable to live except in the service of the State."

I have given so much time to Ortega's analysis because I see it as inescapably true in light of our own contemporary experience, at least as to its main observations. His description of the spiritual and mental qualities of the typical person of our times is borne out both in everyday life and in public events. We can hardly understand contemporary life without taking into account the rootlessness, the spoiledness, the shallowness, the spiritual inertia, the uncivil grabbing, the continuing infantilism which are normal to it. "The postulate that men are rational beings," Herbert Spencer said, "continually leads one to draw inferences which prove to be extremely wide of the mark."

Despite everything, Ortega was still able to say that there is a more optimistic side to the predominance of the masses, since it means "an all-round rise in the historic level." The life of the average person is now on a "higher altitude" than previously. Even though he said that man today has no vision of "what to create," he preceded this with the observation that during our period of history people think of themselves as "fabulously capable of creation." As a result, modern life has a "programme of possibilities" which is "superior to all others known to history."

There is an intrinsically valuable and at the same time infinitely promising aspect in the increased well-being of mankind's overall membership -- and in its advancement into full participativeness. There are problems, even immense problems, but mankind stands at a new scale and even at something of a culmination of its wildest dreams. For men in general, our present condition, especially in Europe and America, is clearly preferrable to any earlier condition.

141

If modern man's faults bring a total destruction of his civilization, hindsight will tell us that the promising aspects should have been disregarded. But this is a hindsight we can't anticipate. We have no reason to overlook the immense potential which is present.

An aspect of this hopefulness appears in the continuing tendency of people to lower the threshold of compassion, including more and more people within the scope of sensibility. Coining a phrase, I have sometimes called this the "decline of the fish principle." Sportsmen do not hold trout above the threshold of their sensibility; the trout are sufficiently differentiated from them psychologically that they have no felt awareness of their suffering. Men can make the same psychological differentiation from other men, placing them below the threshold. In ancient civilization, the people of other cities were excluded from sensibility. If they were defeated they were usually either killed or pressed into slavery. The crucifixion of Spartacus and seven thousand of his followers illustrates an aspect of ancient man which we view with horror today. We can say this despite the horrors of the twentieth century; despite their immensity they have not obliterated the general truth that our compassion knows much wider limits today than it did among the ancients.[13] There has been a "decline of the fish principle," a decline of the psychological truncation of feeling. Such a truncation has continued to exist in National Socialism's treatment of the Jews, in the Stalinist herding of millions into slave labor camps, in the terrors of Communist China and elsewhere; and the impersonality of war has permitted us Dresden and Nagasaki; so we see that the growth of compassion should not be thought of as a uniform cultural phenomenon. But even with these horrors, countless billions of man-years of beneficent life have been lived in the twentieth century in which the amenities of modern society have been enjoyed by average humanity.

142

Earlier, I indicated my disagreement with Julien Benda's view that this sensibility is entirely an inheritance we enjoy from the eighteenth century -- an inheritance which, he said, we are rapidly losing. In his The Betrayal of the Intellectuals, he argued -- after a long review of the savagery of a great deal of modern thought as reflected by, among others, Nietzsche, Barres and Sorel -- that although "the historian . . . is amazed at the transformation of a species which only four centuries ago roasted prisoners of war in bakers' ovens, and, only two centuries ago forbade the workers to establish a pension fund for their aged members," he must nevertheless "point out that these improvements cannot be credited to the present age. They are the results of the teachings of the eighteenth century, against which the 'masters of modern thought' are in complete revolt."[14]

Of course, there is much truth in Benda's view. Modern thought has enjoyed no real consensus about the preconditions of an advanced and satisfactory civilization, and in this conflict there have been many positions taken which involve an intensely anti-civilizational aspect. Karl Popper has counted Karl Marx as standing on the side of genuine humanitarianism,[15] but from a different perspective I would place Marx clearly among the more destructive thinkers. This illustrates the inevitable difference of assessment which would be present in any attempt to classify the many voices which have been heard since the eighteenth century. But whatever our classification in a given case, we may agree that in many ways the ideals of the Enlightenment have been eroded (though in others they have been fulfilled).

This is not the entire picture, though. When we speak of increased compassion we do not mean merely an ideological expression of compassion; we may speak of compassion in fact. Several non-ideational factors have been at work since the eighteenth century to lower the threshold of compassion, despite all that the Nietzsche's have said. One of these has been the self-interest of the multitudes themselves; much of our pity or empathy comes from our identification with the victim: "there, but for the grace of God, go I." The vulnerable appreciate vulnerability.[16] Another factor has been our affluence. It is easier to be concerned for others when we ourselves have enough; someone starving in Europe will hardly be concerned with the starving in India.

We can accept Marshall McLuhan's suggestion (without necessarily agreeing with his entire emphasis) that a third factor comes from the extension of our modern awareness through the media.[17] Our nervous systems are almost literally extended by television, photography, films and the press to feel pain wherever it occurs (just as the same media permit us to share the beauty of the Canadian ballet). We often comment, as Thoreau did, on the extent to which this outreach is prostituted; we have become the playthings of every sentiment. This extension of our senses is played upon by politicians, ideologues and interest groups. But this does not invalidate the fact that we are not as insulated as we once were: the threshold has actually been lowered.

These factors lead me to agree with the observation made by Edward Alexander in his book on Arnold and Mill. "Even in the seventeenth century, Tocqueville argued, sympathy extended so little beyond class boundaries that a humane and civilized person like Mme de Sevigne could descend to jocularity about the fate of galley slaves. But in democratic society imaginative sympathy had been immeasurably extended by a social revolution. The democratic man, feeling himself equal to all his fellow men, and in some sense actually being so, could with his imagination, enter into sympathy with the most wretched of his fellow men."[18]

There are other massive and yet subtle developments which should be noticed, but this lowering

144

of the threshold is itself one of major importance
and one which relates intimately to the "rise of
the multitudes." I take a favorable view of it --
even though its ultimate consequences can't be
foretold. Herbert Spencer might have deprecated
this compassion as running counter to the continuing selectivity which he considered important to
the ultimate well-being of the human race. And he
may have been right. But I value the broadened
humaneness for its own sake; it is one of the ends
toward which I would hope evolution would be taking us. It is an end in itself -- although if it
is premature it may ultimately prove harmful.

In the following sections I will discuss
several of the character or spiritual problems
present in modern life. Since we will be focusing
on problems, it is worth keeping in mind that they
cannot themselves tell the whole story; otherwise,
we would not be able to maintain the advanced civilization that we have.

Spoiledness. Several factors -- the continuing immaturity of mankind, the affluence of the
modern age with its comforts and the expansion of
possibilities, the mental structure of rationalism,
and the inertia which so many people have which
negates any real will to culture or understanding
or appreciation -- contribute to one of the main
facts about the contemporary spirit: the aspect of
spoiledness.

Ortega's view of the spoiledness of contemporary man was central to his analysis. Richard
Weaver expressed a similar perception in Ideas
Have Consequences. Weaver referred to "the spoil-
ed-child psychology of the urban masses." He explained that "the spoiled child has not been made
to see the relationship between effort and reward.
He wants things, but he regards payment as an imposition or as an expression of malice by those who
withhold for it. His solution, as we shall see, is
to abuse those who do not gratify him."[19]

Weaver saw this quality as having broad im-

plications in the modern man's worldview: "He has
been given the notion that progress is automatic,
and hence he is not prepared to understand impedi-
ments; and the right to pursue happiness he has
not unnaturally translated into a right to have
happiness, like a right to the franchise. If all
this had been couched in terms of spiritual insight, the case would be different, but when he
is taught that happiness is obtainable in a world
limited to surfaces, he is being prepared for that
disillusionment and resentment which lay behind
the mass psychosis of fascism."

But what is the psychology of the spoiled
child? It is illustrated by a child who hears
the music of an approaching ice cream truck on a
summer's day. If the child's mother knows the
child has already eaten enough sweets for that
day and denies the child's request, a spoiled child
will be resentful and maybe throw a tantrum.

This includes several psychological elements:

• There is a knowledge of the possibilities.
The far-away music communicates a possibility --
in this case of eating ice cream.

• At the same time, there is a wide expansion
of desire. Ice cream may not have been in the
mind of the child earlier, but the desire for gratification is now overwhelming.

• The child is not concerned about either the
effort that has been needed to acquire the means
which make the gratification possible, or about
the long-term consequences of receiving the gratification. The spoiled child doesn't understand
the meaning of the money; he takes its value and
presence for granted. Nor is he thinking of obe-
sity or rotting teeth -- which are the mother's
concerns.

• The child has an unquestioned feeling of
having a right to the gratification. The child
will feel the denial of the cone as the denial of

something to which he is entitled, as though the mother were acting out of bad faith.

• There is a willingness to use a "direct action technique" to get the gratification. A tantrum-throwing child has no regard for civility or for round-about methods.

• Finally, there is little appreciation for the cone even if the mother gives in. This characteristic follows easily from the others -- from the sense of entitlement, from the lack of appreciation of the effort required to gain the means, from the general lack of regard for the feelings of others and from the preoccupation with self that inheres in the entire complex.

Our immaturity is certainly a factor in the presence of this psychology among adults in modern society. The immaturity can easily dull any of the elements of a broader, more civilized comprehension, taking away the appreciation of values, the regard for consequences and the willingness to abjure socially unsatisfactory methods. Each of these things require a person to stand back, to be willing out of mental discipline to back off momentarily from the immediacy of his felt needs. But immaturity makes this less possible. In fact, we could define immaturity as its absence.

At the same time, we can easily see the role of modern affluence. The ancients often felt an austere awareness of the uses of self-denial and rigorous discipline; we saw this among the Spartans and in the Athenian stress on disciplined competitiveness, the philosophies of the Stoics, the Epicureans and the early Christian ascetics. The ancients accordingly commented frequently about the unfavorable moral consequences of a comfortable life. Polybius, for example, saw a "deterioration" when Rome, "after warding off many great dangers . . . . arrived at a high pitch of prosperity and undisputed power."[20] Affluence brought effeminacy, weakness and loss of discipline.

A knowledge of possibilities and an expansion of desires are inherent in affluence. People are also less willing to tolerate delay in gratification, since delay is less imperative. The connection of affluence with a failure to take a larger view is less readily apparent, but is present just the same: the press of other contingencies is less urgent; values mean less, since it costs less to acquire them; consequences are more easily remedied; and there is a habit of gratification which by itself will diminish the force of more remote considerations.

Taking the causes a step further, I am struck by the parallel, at least to a certain point, between the psychology of spoiledness and the rationalist mentality (to which I myself subscribe and which is so characteristic of science and secular modes of thought).

Secular knowledge deals with the visible matters of this world, especially as those matters relate to the so-called "practical" aspects of life. It inherently involves a concern about "possibilities" in the sense in which I have used the word in the illustration of the spoiled child. The growth of technique provides the basis for a continuing expansion of desires: what previously was not even thought of becomes possible, and most people will reach out for it. It is not satiation that seems to occur most, but a constant outreach -- though this is a human reaction which is vigorously criticized by social commentators who see it as a blind process that involves very real costs for the human beings who are kept psychologically pressed by their own ever-expanding "needs."

Where technique is highly refined and is developing, there are few inhibitions to slow a desire for immediate gratification. An example is that if we have the "know-how" to go to the moon, we are not prepared to put it off for long. This is why I have felt that the slow-down on the exploration of space after the initial Apollo flights

148

was atypical; we will hardly deny ourselves for very long a full exploration to the outer limits of our capabilities. (Nor should we, in my opinion.) Those who have means and an awareness of possibilities in any area will in the absence of serious counterweights be drawn to use those means.

So far, the analogy between spoiledness and rationalism has held up well. It becomes doubtful, though, when we get into the psychological elements that pertain to appreciation and depth of understanding. These are pivotal elements as to whether a person is "spoiled" or not. There is no inherent reason why rationalism should involve this lack of breadth and appreciation. Accordingly, it is not rationalism per se which we must condemn. But this lack can come from other sources and merge with rationalism, at which time spoiledness and rationalism can become mutually supportive. At the same time, though, rationalism can help overcome spoiledness to the extent it creates an awareness of consequences and values.

This interplay of factors is important today in the relationship between the sexes. It would be well for marriage counselors to understand it. The mental habits of both a general spoiledness and rationalism accustom a male, perhaps not without justification, to think about sexual possibilities: both from the bombardment of sexual enticements he receives from the culture and from his own mental make-up he is aware of the potential. Whatever he may do in his behavior, there is at least psychically an expansion of desire; except to the extent other considerations make him repress this desire, he will have a psychic impulse to live sexually as much as any man can. He will see no reason to exclude himself from the democracy, so to speak, of sexual fulfillment; not accustomed to denying himself anything unless a valid reason compells him to, he will feel entitled to fulfill these possibilities as a matter of right.

149

As with rationalism, the process may stop
there. He may put the expanded desires aside out
of an appreciation for a balance of other values.
But this requires some discipline, some ability to
stand back and take a look at things. Such psychic
restraint will not occur if spoiledness and shallowness prevail, or if cultural restraints are
weak. But even where these are strong, his rationalism will cause him to demand reasonable jus-
tifications for any denial of desire. An unrea-
sonable denial will seem intolerable (and we need
to realize that he is not entirely an objective
observer as he judges its reasonableness). It is
for this reason that the male today has a particularly strong psychic need for sexual variety
within marriage. A wife who does not satisfy this
need will find her husband psychically unsatisfied.

I have been told recently by a lawyer who
specializes in divorce that with the current emphasis on "women's liberation" he has had several
women clients who have experienced this same
psychic need -- so it may not be the special province of the male.

Hedonistic orientation. Secularism, affluence and spoiledness, together with still other
qualities of people today, lead to a preoccupation
with hedonistic values -- comfort and enjoyable
diversions. Weaver commented unfavorably that
"certainly there is no more innocent-seeming form
of debauchery than the worship of comfort; and,
when it is accompanied by a high degree of technical resourcefulness, the difficulty of getting
people not to renounce it but merely to see its
consequences is staggering. The task is bound up,
of course, with that of getting principles accepted again, for, where everything ministers to
desire, there can be no rebuke to comfort." He
added that "absorption in ease is one of the most
reliable signs of present or impending decay."

The preoccupation with pleasure is connected
with cultural mediocrity. This is important to

150

realize for its own sake, but it also touches some related issues: it is one of the reasons for the deep cultural alienation of the intellectual; it contributes to the apathy and modulation which so often typify the "middle class" in politics and public issues; and the hedonism was itself a major ingredient in the "hippie lifestyle" of the "counter-culture" of the 1960's and 1970's in the United States.

Intellectual shallowness; the arrogance of uniformed opinion. When I read one of Richard Cobden's diary entries written in 1847 in which he told of his trip to Russia, I was struck by his frustration over an absence of intellectuality which we in America would take for granted today: "They rise from table as soon as they have swallowed their dinner, and proceed to the card-table, billiards, or skittles. There is no intellectual society, no topic of general interest to be discussed -- an un-idea'd party."[21]

Such non-intellectual social relations struck Cobden as unusual in his day, but they are virtually universal in contemporary American culture. In middle class society today it is rare to enter into serious intellectual conversation with guests. We wouldn't think to complain about rising from dinner and going, say, to a bridge table. The "un-idea'd" quality of almost all social contacts is thought to be natural. But we should see in this the actual unnaturalness of our situation: intellectual relations should be integral to the lives of intelligent people. We have suffered a decline from Cobden's standard.

This is something about which Wilhelm Röpke commented in A Humane Economy. "Thought is becoming shallow, uniform, derivative, herdlike, and tritely mediocre." He wrote of "the growing predominance of the semi-educated . . . and the presumption with which this homo insipiens gregarius sets himself up as the norm and chokes everything that is finer or deeper."[22] This process has

151

taken place so comfortably that most of us hardly realize it.

Röpke also spoke of the literary limitations imposed by such a culture when he referred to "the tight corner into which books really worth reading are driven, together with serious periodicals not catering to mass tastes." This reminds me of Nietzsche's lament: "Would it be permissible for me to confess what books are read today? Accursed instinct of mediocrity!" It is reminiscent, too, of Henry David Thoreau's anguish in Walden almost a century and a half ago in the United States about the lack of good reading and conversation.[23]

This seems to be a general characteristic of the rise of the multitudes. John Stuart Mill complained of a "general indifference to those kinds of knowledge and mental culture which cannot be immediately converted into pounds, shillings, and pence." He thought that English society in general as he knew it was "thoroughly insipid," involving a "low moral tone" and an "absence of high feelings." In Germany at the time, Jacob Burckhardt saw the same thing. In an introduction to an edition of Burckhardt's Force and Freedom James Hastings Nichols has summarized Burckhardt's feelings: "Men of education, tradition, and character were suspected and hated by the traditionless, rootless masses, even if not actually ostracized in Athenian fashion."[24]

An aspect of this commonplace mentality which has often attracted the unfavorable comment of intellectuals has been the self-assurance of the commonplace mind in insisting dogmatically on the validity of opinions formed without effort. Ortega complained of this in readers who would reject his thesis out of hand: "Many of those dissentient readers have never given five minutes' thought to this complex matter. How are they going to think as I do? But by believing that they have a right to an opinion on the matter without

152

previous effort to work one out for themselves, they prove patently that they belong to that absurd type of human being which I have called the 'rebel mass.' It is precisely what I mean by having one's soul obliterated, hermetically closed." In a book about Matthew Arnold and John Stuart Mill, Edward Alexander has commented in the same vein that "in such an age, the layman was convinced that his opinion, blind and uninformed as it might be, on any particular subject, was as good as that of anyone else." This phenomenon can be seen at the typical American university today under the regime of open admissions: many "students" are impatient with any learning beyond the catchwords of the conventional intellectual fashion.

Uneducability; effect on education. These considerations shade imperceptibly into still another: that education, the hope of Jefferson, Mill and others, has not ennobled the average man to anything near the level of culture for which they hoped. Mediocrity has in the main conquered education, not education mediocrity. The anxious hopefulness of sincere democrats of the nineteenth century has been largely disappointed. "The typical college graduate," according to Russell Kirk, "reads little or nothing except ephemera and the selections of one of the gigantic book clubs. Popular fiction reeks of the brothel."[25] Weaver has commented that "they read mostly that which debauches them." He has pointed to the prevailing desire to use education only to "enable one to acquire enough wealth to live on the plane of the bourgeoisie," and he has added that this falls far short of instilling higher values. Burckhardt complained that as his most talented students were drained off into business, they found it necessary to count on others to supply them with intellectual culture, just as I have noticed in university teaching that my better students have avoided academic careers to go into practical professions -- a process which is justified by practical considerations in a given case, but which drains the society of intellect. This in turn leaves the

academy to those with a temperament less adapted
to the active world. This is all a part of cultural emphasis, and the emphasis among the multitudes is not on intellectual culture.

The effect on academic life is extreme.
Students are graduated in large numbers from
colleges of business, say, in our state universities who cannot even spell "business" and who in
general possess the literacy of a third grader.
A college junior -- after sixteen years in American public education -- told me that the New Deal
was Herbert Hoover's program. The ignorance and
militant know-nothingism of so many in our universities, including even some among the faculty,
merits more than quiet acceptance. It means, in
effect, that the most extensive educational effort
in history, an effort backed by resources surpass-
ing even the imagination of earlier generations,
is often unable to instill even the slightest
intellectual culture. This partly reflects the
low level of inherent educability of the so-called
"mass man"; it also reflects a cultural emphasis
which at some future time, under other circumstances, will almost certainly be different.

Ortega observed that the average man of his
time "leaves the impression of a primitive man
suddenly risen in the midst of a very old civilization. In the schools, which were such a source of
pride to the last century, it has been impossible
to do more than instruct the masses in the technique of modern life; it has been found impossible
to educate them."

Rootlessness. Modern man is cut off from the
roots of past society. The social cements which
these intellectual, moral, spiritual, culture underpinnings could provide are greatly weakened.
This shallowness in turn strengthens the tendencies
toward relativism, the relaxation of morals and
manners, the ebbing and flowing of fads, the decline
of loyalties -- and toward a loss of identity in
an existentially indeterminate present. It involv-

es, as well, a loss which we can afford only on the assumption that the experience of past generations really has nothing important to tell us -- an assumption which the great majority of "practical men" at all levels implicitly accept.

The same thinkers who have commented on the other aspects of modern character have also addressed this subject. Burckhardt observed that Americans "have to a great extent foregone history, i.e., spiritual continuity, and wish to share in the enjoyment of art and poetry merely as forms of Luxury." Röpke spoke of "rootlessness" and said that "the sense of continuity and of our links with history as a living part of knowledge is declining more and more widely." Those who observed the "counter-culture" of the 1960's will appreciate his perception that "there is not as much conformism in tradition as there is willful eccentricity; it goes with disorientation and discontinuity, with disdain of anything conventional, time tested, or normal." Weaver adds that "today over the entire world there are dangerous signs that culture, as such, is marked for attack because its formal requirements stand in the way of expression of the natural man." I particularly enjoy his comment that "it has been well said that the chief trouble with the contemporary generation is that it has not read the minutes of the last meeting." Kirk speaks of "what Burke called the flies of summer, unable to link with dead generations or those yet unborn, lacking memories or high hope." And again Ortega states the problem eloquently: "The meaning is that the type of man dominant today is a primitive one, a Naturmensch rising up in the midst of a civilized world. The world is a civilized one, its inhabitant is not: he does not see the civilization of the world around him, but he uses it as if it were a natural force."

Lack of shared belief. Weaver has commented that modern men "no longer have the same ideas about the most fundamental things," and contrasts this with an "age of shared belief." Although I do not accept his suggestions about what the shared belief of mankind ought to be, he is accurately describing the contemporary predicament. Modern Western civilization would involve a Babble of conflicting beliefs even if the qualities we have just discussed were not present to exacerbate the lack of consensus. This is so because secular, rationalistic society, as distinguished from an age of faith and accepted ideas, has never settled the main questions in philosophy or lifestyles or economics or politics or religion. These are up in the air as an aspect of our cosmic immaturity. The ancients bequeathed us no consensus on them, and as we have picked up the threads of disputation as we have emerged from the Middle Ages we have unavoidably renewed countless avenues of contra-dictory thought. A succession of modern thinkers -- Hegel, Marx, Spencer, Nietzsche, Bentham, the Mills, Coleridge, Carlyle, Comte, Proudhon, and countless others -- show the variety of views which modern humanity has been implored to adopt. This will be pertinent when in later volumes I review the major ideologies: while in important ways each ideology involves a pecular adaptation to modern social cleavages, each also carries on ideas which have found supporters for thousands of years.

Secularism. Our civilization is now over-whelmingly secular. This has serious implications with regard to the loss of prior belief. But I am one who on epistemological grounds sees no acceptable substitute for secularism, which I wel-come as an advance. This is not to say that con-temporary man does not face severe spiritual needs for which he desperately needs secular solutions. The decline of theistic religion leaves man exis-tentially adrift, and genuine answers to the mean-ing of life are fully as essential as they were before.

The spiritual void within the modern psyche is apparent even in the everyday life of prosper-ing society, where it is an element in the hedonism and spoiledness. But it becomes most apparent when

156

things are not so comfortable, as in Germany after
World War I. The yearning for something larger,
something ultimately more significant, than the
ordinary is an important factor in the totalitarian
social religions of this century.

This yearning has been expressed by several
thinkers. It has often taken the form of a condemnation of peaceable, productive life, and has
glorified war. Some men feel boredom and ennui
within an ordered system. This appears in Hitler's
anguish in Mein Kampf about not having been born
in time for the Wars of Liberation against Napoleon,
"when a man, even without a business, was really
worth something."[26] It is in Burckhardt's praise
of "an atmosphere of danger" and of the uses of
war, and in Nietzsche's statement that "it is the
good war that hallows any cause," a comment which
he followed with the reflection that "one has renounced the great life when one renounces war."

Anyone familiar with the literature of the
last two centuries knows how common such feelings
have been, but anyone who is not may be surprised
by them, since these feelings so greatly contradict the increased compassion and love of comfort
today. This surprise, though, shouldn't obscure
the fact that such yearnings are important ingredients in modern life. Viktor Frankl wrote that
"the existential vacuum is a widespread phenomenon
of the twentieth century . . . This existential
vacuum manifests itself mainly in a state of boredom."[27] Existentialist authors have commented
about this at considerable length.

The declining sense of nobility. Our age
is secular, rationalistic and democratic. Superficially, then, we should be able to match the
spirit of the Greeks. But manifestly we do not.
What is missing? Probably more than anything else
an agreement on a standard of heroic emulation.
We have nothing which compares with the Greek
areté in any of its forms, and we have no shared
religion similar to the Greeks' which gives us an

157

Olympian standard. The feelings of ennui and emptiness exist, but our behavior in overcoming those feelings is scattered: sometimes into totalitarian movements, sometimes into the distractions of entertainment and _libido_, sometimes into personal commitment. We lack a common striving after a vision of what is considered the most ideal in human life.

For a time the "middle class" carried on some of the cultural values of the old aristocracy, but this patrician code has been dying within my lifetime: it was palpably held by my grandparents, existed in shallow form among my parents, and is hardly perceptible today. We may, of course, applaud this as an increase in democracy; but the patrician values contained much more than mere snobbishness. They embodied a view of man, an aspiration, which was by no means totally divorced from that of the Greeks. Without the elevated sensibility either of the Greeks or of our earlier European aristocracy, our democracy lacks an essential breath of spirit and style. It is qualitatively below an appropriate standard for mankind.

The omnipotence of power. I was about to write "the omnipotence of majorities," but it is a broader phenomenon than that. Those who exercise power without being a majority seem willing even without the majority to exercise power as omnipotently as they can. I have a few times been placed in extraordinary situations in which naked power speaks on its own terms, admitting the irrelevance of argument or reasons, and simply asserting its will. At such times, the Machiavellian underpinnings of many human relationships show through. This is something Machiavelli himself would have taken as natural, but Ortega would say it must be reversed and culturally, morally inhibited if true civilization is to exist.

During the past century, majorities have most often possessed this unchecked power. The question has been whether these majorities would acknowledge

158

restraints upon themselves. This has been thoroughly problematical. The loss of roots has entailed the loss of appreciation for restraints imposed at an earlier time. A case in point would be the United States Constitution; such attitudes and the dominant ideology have made it a freely floating document.

Herbert Spencer and Alexis de Tocqueville each predicted this lack of majority restraint with foreboding. In The Man Versus the State, Spencer wrote that "the great political superstition of the past was the divine right of kings. The great political superstition of the present is the divine right of parliaments." He added that "the divine right of parliaments means the divine right of majorities." He noted that "the function of Liberalism in the past was that of putting a limit to the powers of kings. The function of true Liberalism in the future will be that of putting a limit to the powers of Parliaments."[28]

This is no mean task. The problem is only partly political and legal. Far more, it is cultural and spiritual and intellectual. This makes it much less amenable to quick reform. Ortega would have felt the problem so inherent in the quality of modern man that it is wishful thinking to expect any really satisfactory solution. Tocqueville's observations were also directed to culture and to the ubiquitous power of the majority. "In America the majority raises formidable barriers around the liberty of opinion; within these barriers an author may write what he pleases, but woe to him if he goes beyond them . . . The ruling power in the United States is not to be made game of. The smallest reproach irritates its sensibility." He warned that "absolute monarchies had dishonored despotism; let us beware lest democratic republics should reinstate it and render it less odious . . ." He made the interesting comment that "the Inquisition has never been able to prevent a vast number of anti-religious books from

159

circulating in Spain. The empire of the majority
succeeds much better in the United States, since
it actually removes any wish to publish them."[29]
I would have us complicate this picture by taking
into account the role of the intellectual subculture, but Tocqueville's observations are certainly correct with regard to the culture at large.

Man diminished; the state raised. "Only
where the state ends," Nietzsche wrote, "there
begins the human being who is not superfluous."
Ortega added that "This is the greatest danger
that today threatens civilization: State intervention; the absorption of all spontaneous social
effort by the State, that is to say, of spontaneous
historical action, which in the long run sustains,
nourishes, and impels human destinies. When the
mass suffers any ill-fortune or simply feels some
strong appetite, its great temptation is that
permanent, sure possibility of obtaining everything
-- without effort, struggle, doubt, or risk --
merely by touching a button and setting the mighty
machine in motion." Richard Weaver reflected that
"an ancient axiom of politics teaches that a spoiled people invite despotic control." Röpke spoke of
modern man as an "aborted form of Homo sapiens
created by a largely technical civilization, a
race of spiritual and moral pygmies lending itself
willingly -- indeed gladly, because that way lies
redemption -- to use as raw materials for the
modern collectivist and totalitarian mass state."

Socialism and the Welfare State are often
thought to corrupt men, and I have no doubt that
this is true, but it may be more important to
appreciate that a diminished type of man -- who is
undermining in countless ways the moral, intellectual, spiritual, cultural, and hence political and
legal, prerequisites of a free society -- leads to
the enhanced state. Here the causation is the
other way around. The Welfare State in America
may reduce the vitality of millions, but it is
also noteworthy that reduced vitality has (along
with many other factors) produced the Welfare
State. The collectivism of the twentieth century

have not, for the most part, been imposed on a reluctant people; the collectivism reflects their inner condition. When combined with the constant thrust of the intellectual subculture to use the state as a church to remold mankind in its own image, this mediocrity negates the ideas and values which support self-reliance, individuality and a minimum of coercive impingement on the individual.

Spencer saw the effects of a decline in self-discipline when he noted that "the diminution of external restraint can take place only at the same rate as the increase of internal restraint. Conduct has to be ruled either from without or from within . . . The degree of freedom in their institutions which any given people can bear, will be proportionate to the diffusion of this moral sense among them." Elsewhere, he pointed out that "it is the national character that decides . . . Similarly with the institution maker. If the people with whom he has to deal are not of the requisite quality, no cleverness in his contrivance will avail anything. Let us not forget that institutions are made of men, and that frame them together as we may, it is their nature which must finally determine whether the institutions can stand." He commented perceptively about law that "judicial protection is vitiated by the depravity of the age."

It was because of such things that Lord Acton felt compelled to write that "liberty has lost its spell; and democracy maintains itself by the promise of substantial gifts to the masses of the people."[30]

And yet an explosion of technique. It would be a mistake to end the discussion without observing again that despite all of these things we live in a civilization which is unbelievably dynamic and which possesses a number of virtues that correspond to its vices.

161

Consider, for example, the men who live in a typical middle class American neighborhood. All of the factors I have mentioned have a bearing on their lives. But those things are not a complete portrait. The men work hard and often their wives are employed to help provide the standard of living they both desire. Their homes are well built and clean, the lawns nicely maintained. The men keep busy with the uses of their mechanical expertise. There is a vast multiplication of hobbies, sports, club activities and night classes, so that personal enervation is almost unheard of. The picture is one of bustle, pleasantness, good neighborliness -- of a common humanity with all its foibles living comfortably, gregariously and, by its own standards, well. Only an observer applying other standards, even though they are standards of major importance to human culture, comments upon the emptiness.

This dynamic has carried us on and on, with a multiplier. Quite nonrationalistically, it is moving to its own as yet unforeseen consequences. That it is doing so is one of the frustrations for the type of social critic who would like to remold this culture in some other image. The culture has ignored his criticism and simply continued on. This is one of the conservative dimensions in modern society, since it resists the importunities of the intellectual sub-culture. At the same time, it embodies its own radical dimension by containing processes of rapid change which are clearly carrying us into new vistas.

Innumerable thinkers have reflected pessimistically about modern life. It would be hard not to see the bases for that pessimism. The voids within modern civilization loom so large that the whole undertaking is problematical. But there is no plausible substitute for the predominance of the multitude. We couldn't return to aristocracy if we tried, and that wouldn't be desirable in any case. We have no choice but to ride the roller coaster out. The destiny of these masses is in

162

their own hands, and we should not allow ourselves
to become so engrossed that we fail to appreciate
how exciting the experiment really is. Those who
see the problems can strive to elevate, to build
and to lead; but forces far beyond our control
will determine whether that is successful. The
major problem within modern society, given these
constraints, is to "civilize the intellectual" so
that the multitudes can have the benefit of a
mild "clerisy" to play a crucial directive role.
But that puts us ahead of our story.

NOTES

1. José Ortega y Gasset, The Revolt of the Masses
(New York: W. W. Norton & Company, Inc., 1960),
pp. 47, 50, 18, 70, 15, 16, 108, 20, 21, 51, 58,
73, 75, 120, 87, 111, 121, 28, 44, 47, 68, 51, 82,
120.

2. R. A. J. Walling (ed.), The Diaries of John
Bright (New York: William Morrow and Company,
1931), pp. 21, 41.

3. Adam Smith, The Wealth of Nations (New York:
Modern Library, 1937), p. 735.

4. George Macaulay Trevelyan, The Life of John
Bright (Boston: Houghton Mifflin Company, 1913),
pp. 60, 145, 365.

5. John Stuart Mill, Principles of Political
Economy (Toronto: University of Toronto Press,
1965), Vol. II, p. 885.

6. John Morley, The Life of Richard Cobden (London: Chapmen and Hall, Ltd., 1881), Vol. I, pp.
395, 458; Vol. II, p. 396.

7. Joseph Hamburger, Intellectuals in Politics --
John Stuart Mill and the Philosophic Radicals

8. Morley, Cobden, Vol. II, p. 396.

9. D. C. Johnson, Pioneers of Reform (New York: Burt Franklin, 1968), p. 159.

10. Edwin A. Burtt (ed.), The English Philosophers from Bacon to Mill (New York: Modern Library, 1939), pp. 1000-1001.

11. Ludwig von Mises, Planning for Freedom (South Holland, Ill,: Libertarian Press, 1952), p. 171.

12. Ortega himself does not paint a uniformly unfavorable picture of the "mass man." He observed that "it is not a question of the mass-man being a fool. On the contrary, today he is more clever, has more capacity of understanding than his fellow of any previous period." He recognized that this man is on a higher plane than before.

13. Arnold J. Toynbee, Civilization on Trial (New York: Oxford University Press, 1948), pp. 150-151: "Our world has risen to an unprecedented degree of humanitarian feeling. There is now a recognition of the human rights of people of all classes, nations, and races; yet at the same time we have sunk to perhaps the unheard-of depths of class warefare, nationalism, and racialism. These bad passions find vent in cold-blooded, scientifically planned cruelties; and the two incompatible states of mind and standards of conduct are to be seen today, side by side, not merely in the same world, but sometimes in the same country and even in the same soul."

14. Julien Benda, The Betrayal of the Intellectuals (Boston: The Beacon Press, 1930), p. 160.

15. Karl R. Popper, The Open Society and Its Enemies (Princeton: Princeton University Press, 1950), p. 275.

16. Friedrich Nietzsche, The Portable Nietzsche, trans. Walter Kaufmann (New York: Viking Press,

1968), pp. 516, 539, 506, 159, 489, 163. Nietzsche spoke of "the mob aspiration for generous
feelings" and later expanded his analysis: "I
take the liberty of raising the question whether
we have really become more moral. That all the
world believes this to be the case merely constitutes an objection. We modern men, very tender,
very easily hurt, and offering as well as receiving consideration a hundred-fold, really have the
conceit that this tender humanity which we represent, this attained unanimity in sympathetic regard, in readiness to help, in mutual trust, represents positive progress and that in this
respect we are far above the men of the Renaissance. But that is how every age thinks, how it
must think . . . another, later constitution, one
which is weaker, frailer, more easily hurt, and
which necessarily generates a morality rich in
consideration. Were we to think away our frailty
and lateness, our physiological senescence, then
our morality of 'humanization' would immediately
lose its value too."

17. Marshall McLuhan, Understanding Media: The
Extensions of Man (New York: Signet Books, 1964).

18. Edward Alexander, Matthew Arnold and John
Stuart Mill (New York: Columbia University Press,
1965), pp. 169, 38.

19. Richard M. Weaver, Ideas Have Consequences
(Chicago: University of Chicago Press, 1948),
pp. 113, 114, 116, 117, 14, 49, 25, 176, 92, 91.

20. Polybius, The Histories of Polybius, trans.
Evelyn S. Shuckburgh (London: Macmillan and Co.,
1889), Vol. I, p. 507.

21. Morley, Cobden, Vol. I, p. 458.

22. Wilhelm Röpke, A Humane Economy: The Social
Framework of the Free Market (Chicago: Henry
Regnery Company, 1960), pp. 54, 58, 63, 12.

23. Henry David Thoreau, _Walden -- Essay on Civil Disobedience_ (New York: Airmont Publishing Company, 1965), pp. 80, 81.

24. Jacob Burckhardt, _Force and Freedom_ (New York: Pantheon Books, 1943), pp. 34, 43, 152, 290.

25. Russell Kirk, _Enemies of the Permanent Things_ (New Rochelle: Arlington House, 1969) pp. 141, 54.

26. Adolf Hitler, _Mein Kampf_, trans. Ralph Manheim (Boston: Houghton Mifflin Company, 1943), p. 157.

27. Viktor E. Frankl, _Man's Search for Meaning_ (New York: Clarion Books, 1962), p. 108.

28. Herbert Spencer, _The Man Versus the State_ (Baltimore: Penguin Books, 1969), pp. 141, 151, 155, 183; _Social Statics and The Man Versus the State_ (New York: D. Appleton and Company, 1897), p. 106.

29. Alexis de Tocqueville, _Democracy in America_ (New York: Vintage Books, 1954), Vol. I, pp. 274, 275.

30. John Emerich Edward Dalberg-Acton, _The History of Freedom and Other Essays_ (Freeport, N.Y.: Books for Libraries Press, 1967), p. 93.

9

EXISTENTIAL PROBLEMS IN A COMMERCIAL CULTURE

The three chapters which follow this one will go into considerable detail about the alienation of the modern intellectual from the bourgeoisie. It is worth noticing, though, that the immediately preceding chapter talked about the multitudes in general. It did not deal narrowly with the "bourgeoisie." In it, we saw quite a lot of intellectual dissatisfaction with the multitudes themselves. The breadth of the dissatisfaction suggests, in fact, that the alienation of the intellectual is not so much with the middle class per se as it is with modern man in general. The breadth takes it far beyond the middle class as such. This is a fact which has been obscured by the politics and rhetoric which have resulted from the alliance which the intellectual subculture has for so long formed with the "have nots" in society. Despite the broad democratic thrust and the championing of the position of the underprivileged, modern literature makes it clear that the intellectuals' loathing has been for the culture at large.

These thoughts are important as we begin an analysis of the spiritual difficulties associated with the commercial aspects of our culture, since it would be misleading to accept the notion that these difficulties are attributable solely to that commercialism. Such an interpretation is too narrow. The problems are as much problems of a mass culture as of a commercial one.

In chapter eleven I will review the causes of the intellectuals' alienation. The existential problems which I will discuss in the present chapter will be important at that time. We will see that when the existential problems are combined with the mediocrities of mass culture, there are strong substantive reasons for sensitive men to be dissatisfied. It would be a mistake to think the alienation is caused entirely by the neuroses of the intellectuals themselves. Real causes do exist. To overlook them would be to ignore some of the genuine problems in our society. This is true, in my opinion, even though in weighing the causes I have concluded that the alienation is mainly caused by the nonsubstantive factors. This conclusion does not deny that the substantive problems are at least major contributing causes. They are also important as the grievances upon which the alienation focuses as it articulates its dissatisfaction.

There have been many existentialist analyses of our modern lifestyle. These have almost always been unfavorable. Instead of repeating someone else's analysis, I can express more meaningfully the problems as I have felt them in my own experience.

Those who have read my book Emergent Man will notice that I will simply be saying in a more structured way what I said more passionately there. That earlier discussion will also need to be supplemented by our seeing the relationship of the spiritual defects to the divisions within modern society.

An Existential Split

The radical solitude. In a certain sense, a human's consciousness is entirely personal. It can never be directly experienced by another person; it is fully the possession of the person whose consciousness it is. Although two consciousnesses can come in touch, with each making an impression on the other, it is ontologically true that each knows only itself, even though it is its altered self.

Ortega observed that "human life . . . is essentially solitude, radical solitude" and added

168

that "what is most radically human in man (is) his radical solitude."[1] The fact that each person contains a "soul," so to speak, knowable only to himself means that he is, in an ultimate sense, alone within himself.

This final personalism of life is especially evident in such cases as when a person suffers from mental illness or color blindness or actual blindness or a severe headache. He bears his own reality, and this isn't directly experienced even by those close to him. Even if there is a person with him who is living through identically the same subjective reality, his experience is still personal to himself. This is certainly true with someone who is dying: we can feel sorry for him and try to comfort him, but we can't share his experience of dying.

This ultimate solitude is not, however, just at a time of crisis. It is an inherent part of individuality. When, for example, I as a professor meet a class, I and the students share a classroom for a period of time. "Objective reality" shows us there together, all pretty much alike. But subjectively there are great personal differences. Each person brings to the class a consciousness which has its own existential reality and carries its own history and content. It becomes obvious how different I am subjectively from the others when I tell them even so superficial a thing as where I have lived: Tucson, Miami, Mexico City, Guadalajara, Denver, San Diego, New York City, Colorado Springs, Wichita. Each suggests its own memories and associations. This means I am no longer just another person; subjectively, I am sui generis, and so is each of the students. Even if I were to act as though I were on a psychiatrist's couch and tell my memories for hundreds of hours, I couldn't transfer my consciousness directly to those who listened.

Only a reproduction of this subjective existence can be communicated -- and only part of the

169

whole, at that. A substratum remains that is in-
communicable. This was the basis on which Ortega
made an existentialist analysis of love: "From
this substrate of radical solitude that is irreme-
diably our life, we constantly emerge with a no
less radical longing for companionship. Could we
but find one whose life would wholly fuse with,
would interpenetrate ours! . . . Genuine love is
nothing but the attempt to exchange two solitudes."

For what follows, it is important to note
that for anything really to mean anything to us
and to take on profound significance for us, it
must touch us in this personal inner life. If it
does not affect us in what we are there, its
meaning to us is shallow. And it is in this
radical solitude that meaning, once attained, will
reside to serve as the judge of all else.

The extroverted outer reality. Much in life
and among people has little vital touch in this
vibrant center, but passes off without affecting
it deeply. There is an "outer flow" among human
beings which could relate closely to what is important inside each man's solitude, but which is
usually preoccupied with the mediocre and the trivial. This is overwhelmingly present if a culture
turns away from mental and emotional cultivation
and prefers the commonplace.

This empty outer flow is an "extroverted outer
reality." Although it can vary in content from
one culture to another, in a commercial society it
almost unavoidably possesses a gregarious, amicable
structure, since a gentle friendliness is most
typical of the sales relationships cultivated by a
seller with his customers. Years ago, I noticed a
sharp difference in this outer flow between life in
the Marine Corps, where few people thought it was
necessary to be pleasant, and civilian life, where
people are almost invariably pleasant. There is
much to be said for that friendliness. Because of
this, we usually speak favorably of "extroversion."
It is the introvert who is most often suspect.

However, an extreme shallowness characterizes this gregariousness -- and it is in this shallowness that the spiritual problems find their root. In _Emergent Man_ I illustrated this shallowness by telling an example of a man who drove into a service station to have his gas tank filled.[2] The driver was a member of the Federal Reserve Board on his way to a meeting which would have to face an international monetary crisis. As he drove to the meeting, his mind was filled with the many aspects of the crisis itself, of the upcoming meeting, and even of his years of experience and study which were about to reach a culmination. When suddenly he noticed his car was low on gas, he drove into the station, where a young man came out to greet him. For his part, the young man also had been filled with a subjective world of his own. He was eagerly looking forward to the end of the day and to a date with his girl, a prospect which in his mind had created a rich tapestry of possibilities.

When two such men meet at a gas pump, what will their contact amount to with each other? Will it intimately touch the really vital existence of either? For the most functional of reasons the contact between them will almost certainly avoid anything but the most superficial involvement with the emotional or intellectual life of either. After the economist peremptorily tells the attendant the kind and amount of gas he wants, the two men will probably talk briefly about the weather and sports. For a minute or two while the gas is being pumped they may hold the liveliest conversation about the football game they saw on television the night before. Then they will go their separate ways. Each will return to the radical solitude which he has not revealed to the other.

Anything else would be dysfunctional. The economist might be temporarily amused if the attendant poured out his romantic feelings, but after one or two such occasions he would probably

171

go to another station. For his part, the attendant may have no background for or interest in the
issues involved in the monetary crisis. In any
case, the brevity of their contact forbids anything
but the most cursory exploration of any subject.
It is trivia which is most functional to them
both in this situation.

     Now if we multiply the gas station example by
several billion, which is the number of such contacts which take place every day in our society,
we can easily see the extent to which our commercial system involves the built-in repetition of
trivia. Even though there are many other things
going on at the same time, there is also this
never-ending reiteration of human contacts focused
on an emotionally and intellectually meaningless
content. The extent of such contacts will tend
strongly to set the tone for human intercourse in
the society.

     This trivia can absorb men existentially, be-
coming their lifestyle. Our subjective existence
consists of what fills our consciousnesses through
a succession of moments. The greater our preoccupation with an extroversive outer flow, the
more we are defined existentially by it. Many individuals can come to think this flow so natural
that it becomes the center of their lives, negating
any deeper radical solitude in which they cultivate
independent emotions or intellect. Although this
will rarely occur totally, a lifestyle in which a
person's time is absorbed more or less continuously by extroversive contacts over a bridge table,
or at a cocktail party, or watching television
will center very largely on matters which, while
pleasant, do not grab him up vitally. I think of
this as an "absorption effect." It is possible
for a person's subjective life to be sucked out
and filled with trivial content.

     I recall the sharp contrast after several
months in the Marine Corps' boot camp and combat
training. These months were spent in total ab-

sorption with group life. I was crowded in with
a number of other men with only a minimal chance
to cultivate my own subjectivity. Finally on a
Sunday four or five months after my enlistment I
had time to wander a few hundred yards into the
hills away from the cinder block barracks of Camp
Pendleton. I sat down under a tree alone and
found the silence beautiful. Almost physically,
I sensed an entire untapped contemplative world
which I had almost forgotten. It broke my absorption in the neurotic bustle of the barracks.

The lives of our contemporaries and the tone
of our culture consist of this gregariousness.
Trivialized sociability is considered the rightful
expression of our humanity. We hardly think anything else even possible. This is a phenomenon
which relates to the rise of the multitudes and it
relates, too, to the commercial setting. When
Cobden complained about the lack of serious conversation among the Russians, who got up from the
table to play billiards, he voiced a complaint
which would carry substantially greater force today.

Whatever the beneficial values of the extroversion, the lifestyle it involves tends strongly
to suffocate the truly vital soul of a man. The
radical solitude -- the portion of a man's consciousness which is seriously concerned and sensitive -- is hidden away. It only rarely finds expression outside itself in such a milieu. The
meaningful things of life are pressed underground
and forgotten so far as the outer contacts among
people are concerned, and in the existential
makeup of the men whose content is defined by the
trivia.

Family relationships should be cited as an
exception. Even when they consist of purely
extroversive activities, they are meaningful in the
radical solitude of the people involved. To see
a child bubbling with happiness and taking his
first step is a sight which reverberates deeply,
not trivially, within a parent. The same is true

173

to a lesser degree about extroversive contacts in
general if they are with people we like. An evening of bridge may, for example, involve almost
nothing of the intellect or deeper emotions of the
people playing, but just the same it can glow from
the simple companionship. And, too, any of the
activities people adopt in a gregarious, hedonistic
culture -- skiing, bowling, cards, gadgetry, boat-
ing, traveling and the like -- can develop a deeper meaning if those doing them will raise them to
a level of pride and achievement so that they will
touch more than the surface of the players' lives.
Any human activity, if done well, can lose its
trivial nature.

There is a continuum rather than a sharp
polarity. Contemporary culture, however, is manifestly toward the shallower end. The trivialization remains perhaps the most important fact in
any discussion in which we attempt to describe the
existential problems of people today.

With this in mind, we come to the crucial
questions: Is there anything which is really
meaningful and important to human beings in life?
If so, does it find any really satisfying expression in this outer flow?

I won't attempt at this juncture to define
what the meaningful things are. Different people
will offer a variety of answers. It is enough to
say that many people do feel that there are important things about human existence, that our lives
in one way or another do have significance, and
that there are meaningful answers to the questions
of "Why are we here?" and "What are we hoping to
accomplish before we die?" This isn't to deny
that many others will seem content to go through
life with only minimal reference to such concerns,
but to many people such ultimate questions are
deeply relevant.

174

Problems Related to the
Trivialized Outer Reality

Whatever our personal answer to these questions may be, if we take them seriously we immediately see how little our answer to them is
served by the trivialization of life. It is as
though the sacred is always forced to seek expression through the profane. Whenever matters of
ultimate personal significance are suffocated
under a human nexus which denies their existence
and offers them no catharsis, there will be
serious spiritual problems. The common thread
which runs among them is that the deeper intellectual and emotional subjectivity of the human being
is given no real place in the person's relations
with others. There is in each the profound split,
exacerbated in our culture, between the inner and
outer realities.

Denial of a higher vision. Many thinkers
have denounced the secularization of modern life
because the secularization takes our eyes off of
the truer realities, which are spiritual. Whatever the merits of this critique, there is a
counterpart to it in the fact that a preoccupation
with trivia has a definite effect on an individual.
Such a preoccupation fills the mind with itself
and necessarily forecloses, to the extent it is
present, a subjective emphasis in other areas.
The absorption in trivia is analogous to emphysema
of the lungs: it fills the spaces and denies entry
to anything else.

This is a disaster for human beings if intellectual and emotional concerns are important to
the human spirit. Countless people have found
that, notwithstanding its pleasantries, a gregarious, hedonistic life is essentially unfulfilling.
Its amiability and human warmth are very real and
the diversions it offers are enjoyable, but there
comes a time when mere enjoyableness isn't enough.
The pleasure does not provide significance, attainment, creation, pride, satisfaction.

175

I think of this as a "suffocation of a higher vision." It invokes a Gresham's Law of the spirit, by which the shallow drives out a deeper cultivation. When men are trivialized, they are reduced. Although many people pass through life without any apparent difficulty over this (at least superficially; their sensing of it often shows up in countless personal ways without their even being conscious of it), for others life hardly seems worthwhile without a religious meaning. (In my thinking, "religious" includes a type of secular religiousness, since the secular man is as confronted by the question of significance as anyone else.)

Lostness and withdrawal. We should differentiate the different types of spiritual crises through which people can pass as a result of these things. A crisis may be felt in several ways. In my own case, as a young man I never lost my bearings because of the trivialization. Although there were times of intellectual crisis because I was grappling with difficult and fundamental issues, they were not due to the emptiness of my contacts with others. What I did feel, though, and often intensely, was a sense of lostness within the insanities of an unreal milieu. I didn't lose sight of my own values and convictions, but it was as though my intellectual and emotional reality -- my radical solitude -- were a bouy floating in an alien sea. The unexplainable emptiness, the vacuity and lack of concern, the cravenness and pettiness -- all of these were very cutting, since I hadn't developed a defense against them or even an understanding of them. This form of crisis doesn't disappear; it stays on because it is rooted in the social reality of the individual. Personal adjustments -- particularly marriage and a family -- lessen its impact, but otherwise we can hardly escape the effects of it on our social reality.

There can be another type of crisis, probably far more gripping. This is if the emptiness causes

176

the person to lose or perhaps never to gain his inner bearings, even though he may have a spiritual yearning for them. There could be no end to the turns and twists his soul could take. It could continue until he finds his bearings and works out his own way of adjusting them to the world.

Those who undergo the first type of crisis -- the type I have experienced myself -- develop a natural tendency toward withdrawal. The thoughtful and sensitive man must withdraw; he can't permit himself to be defined existentially by the trivia. His values demand an inner cultivation which can't be gained by preoccupation with the outer flow. Emerson captured the essence of it a century and a half ago: "It is when your facts and persons grow unreal and fantastic by too much falsehood, that the scholar flies for refuge to the world of ideas, and aims to recruit and replenish nature from that source."[3] Such a man uses books, art and music to enjoy contact with other souls who have poured out the deepest expression of their own solitudes in ways which the trivial milieu can never know. He joins the dialogue which exists among expressive men over the ages -- and, far from being without human sustenance, experiences the finest companionship with other men like himself, many of whom are long dead.

Later we will discuss directly the causes of the alienation of the intellectual from contemporary culture. At that time, we will refer back to the present discussion. I will make the point that this split between the inner and outer realities, and the intellectual's necessary withdrawal into himself to cultivate his own meaning, are one of the major substantive explanations for the alienation. The present analysis is given for a double purpose: for its own sake, and for its bearing on that later discussion.

Loss of "vital touch." A tragic consequence of this existential split lies in the extent to which it separates people. Gregariousness

177

superficially seems to bring people together, but spiritually they are strangers if they don't share their deeper sensibilities and concerns.

My wife and I have known a couple for several years and have met with them socially many times. Despite our seeming closeness to them, we never knew they were having marital difficulties. When they separated and were divorced, it came as a shock to us. With hindsight, it is evident that we had hardly known them. Our friendship was superficial and didn't touch the real essence of their lives.

For a number of years, I saw a cousin regularly during the summer. Through our separate routes, we each came to spend some time in the Colorado mountains; then we went our own ways during the rest of the year. We talked, went on hikes and occasionally camped out together. Then four or five years intervened during which I didn't see him; we were both grown and the regularities of childhood could no longer be counted on. At the end of this time, my mother thought to ask me, "Did you hear about Johnny?" She then told me he had gotten married, but had soon discovered he had cancer and had died.

I wanted to write a note to my aunt, his mother, expressing my sadness. But the note was peculiarly difficult to write. I could write the usual sentiments, and they would be true enough; but I wanted to say more. But I couldn't, and the reason was that I realized that I really didn't know the meaningful things about him. I knew only the surface of his life. Did the tragedy lie mainly in the fact that a boy I had known -- a likeable, friendly, shining human being -- had died? Or was it instead in the fact that a person of unique worth, of developed intellect and sensibility, of a whole complex of aspirations and strivings, had left us, mostly unfulfilled? There is a world of difference between these two, and suddenly I realized that I knew absolutely nothing about him

in this second sense. I knew nothing about the
depths of his mind and soul, not even so superficial a thing as the type of career he had pursued.
To write a letter speaking only of the one, as
though that counted most, was in effect to deny
the importance of the other. For better or for
worse, I never wrote the note.

D. H. Lawrence built much of his philosophy
around an awareness of this loss of vital human
connection. His "philosophy of touch" stresses
the existential remoteness between human beings
and the spiritual need for them to share the deeper aspects of their lives.[4] He shared Ortega's
existentialist perception, which I noted earlier,
that "genuine love is nothing but the attempt to
exchange two solitudes." Many modern voices have
expressed the same need. I believe it is the main
explanation underlying the various centers of
"touch therapy" which have sprung up in recent
years and which seem so esoteric from our ordinary
perspective. Outside commercial culture in the
precincts of far-flung and often alienated intellectuality, people have sought to do something
about this spiritual separation. Although I am
not now discussing the steps which could be taken
to overcome this gulf, it is worthwhile to point
out that the gulf is a problem which bourgeois
culture ought to take seriously. At such time as
the supporters of our culture are able to move
from a strictly defensive posture, this should be
among their concerns.

All becomes politics. We easily recognize
that inner sensibilities require cultivation. We
don't necessarily realize, though, that the outer
flow becomes an art of its own. The absorption
of people in trivia isn't just a passive process;
it is also active. The extroversion requires
skills of its own. Many people master these skills
by adopting completely the style and values of the
extroversion.

On one occasion a few years ago I sat among

a circle of college professors and graduate students who were visiting in a home near the Princeton University campus. I was a graduate student in economics at New York University; one of the men was employed by a writing project and had recently been the editor of a newspaper; another had just returned from a mathematics conference in India. But instead of leading to a probing conversation springing from our studies and experience, the evening centered around the expert garrulousness of two college girls. They held center stage for two or three hours, sitting on the floor in the middle of the room, and were remarkably good at a banter which had no content outside the art of gregariousness. I could give this as an example of the split between the two realities, but it also illustrates the skill that extroversion involves. The girls possessed this skill far more than any of the others present, despite the others' education and experience.

This has more significance than appears, though, from an example involving just one evening. Extroversive skills and values have become the primary way of life among acting men. This involves an approach to life that is very different from the approach made by the sincere man of ideas.

In 1966 I was a candidate for district judge in Colorado Springs. At the same time, two proposed state constitutional amendments were on the ballot. One was to abolish the death penalty; the other was to establish an appointive system for judges which in practice would mean a life tenure. I opposed both of them for reasons which we won't pause to discuss. Occasionally I was asked to speak on the amendments at service club meetings, and this included a couple of debates. This seemed natural, and I went and presented my views. But then in a conversation over lunch with a popular young attorney he told me something which put my activity in a wholly different light. He told me how unhappy he was that his wife had told someone his views on one of the amendments.

180

He didn't want anyone to know.

There was a stark difference between his view of life, of the mind and of himself, and my own. His highest values didn't include reason, openness and the give and take of ideas. Instead, he gave top priority to popularity and success.

"All life is selling youself," a speaker once told an audience of business students. I winced as I recalled the countless times that sincere, open men have commented in literature on the spiritual and intellectual disparity between this philosophy of life and their own. If all life is salesmanship, the gregarious facade becomes supreme. But what then becomes of the inner reality of the mind and the spirit?

The opponents of a society based on individual freedom and the market economy have given this a lot of attention. It is one of the reasons for their alienation. It is time the friends of such a society became sensitive to these things, too. If a free society means spiritual, intellectual emptiness, it is its own worst enemy. Freedom must be seen as a plateau which makes it possible for men to rise higher -- not to become sunk in a semi-conscious denial of the spirit. I would support freedom in any case because no person or group is perfect enough to be given extensive power over others, but this does not mean that I should be an apologist for a cultural mediocrity which deflects the finest possibilities of freedom. Those who love liberty most should be the severest critics of such a cultural tone.

The supporters of freedom take pride in the fact that in a free society a man's success depends upon his ability. Ludwig von Mises was, of course, one of the leading classical liberals of our time; he spoke of "the sway of the principle, to each according to his accomplishments."5 This is essentially true in a competitive system, since no amount of gregariousness will entirely mask a shoddy

181

service or commodity. But this doesn't fully
describe the process; "who you know, not what you
know" is quite important. There are two tendencies, which are opposing and yet in some ways
complementary: competition within the profit and
loss system demands accomplishment; the cultural
tone of extroversive trivia demands that ideas
and attainments be smothered. To the extent that
the latter is at work, all tends to become politics
in the broadest sense of the word.

In the late 1960's violence and ideological
tension struck American university campuses.
Many people were surprised at the spinelessness
of the great majority of college administrators.
But this should not have been surprising; for many
years it had been the man who cultivated the art
of "not making enemies" who had gone up the ladder
in administrative positions. This isn't the same
thing as to say that such men were not capable;
the gregarious art requires as much ability in its
own way as any other. But it is an art which ill-
prepares men for conviction and character. This
is the primary art in our society both in and out
of business. It isn't accidental that it is
closely associated with weakness of character.

This helps explain many of the apparent
irrationalitities of behavior today. In Chapter 2
I mentioned my experience with a college faculty
when eight professors who had strongly opposed a
department chairman's action in declaring a "slow-
down" actually voted to support it when it came to
a vote at a faculty meeting. This otherwise
incomprehensible turn-about becomes intelligible
if we take into account the mechanism culturally
which "turns all into politics." Each professor
was right in thinking that his academic career
would be smoother if he voted with the department
chairman.

The problem of integrity. We come now to a
problem which is as old as humanity, but which is
made worse by the existence culturally of a tri-

182

vialized outer flow: the problem of integrity. I
define integrity in its usual sense -- as the correspondence between a person's inner being, especially his principles and values, and his actual
life. If the correspondence is high, he is a man
of integrity; if it is low, he is not. Again we
are dealing with something which involves a continuum rather than an absolute polarity. Most men
are somewhere between the extremes.

The problem of integrity has been so difficult for serious men at all times in history that
those who have sought something close to complete
integrity have usually found it necessary to withdraw into a personal religious shell. They have
been forced to understand that any connection with
the world of men would make them vulnerable. The
result has been the religious asceticism and withdrawal into self which was so much a part of Epicurean and Stoic thought, as well as of countless
other philosophical and religious schools. This
has been most urgently necessary for sensitive men
when the life around them has been inane and brutish.

The extroversive outer flow with its functional imperative toward the meaningless entails,
by its very nature, a suffocation of concern over
each individual's principles, values or system of
convictions. If he lives within that flow in
keeping with its expectations, there will be little
place for his deeper concerns. No real hearing
will be given to any objections he may have. The
commonplace just isn't interested. It considers
the individual's convictions an eccentricity.

This is one of the more important factors to
be taken into account in business ethics. The
"ways of the world" try to extend themselves into
all corners. They insist on their own norms and
develop their own rationale. A person with higher
values than the average will not ordinarily find
himself honored for his ethics. More often, he
will be denigrated as naive and impractical. I

183

remember an instance in which a young lawyer was
called into a senior partner's office and was told
to see a judge to have a client's traffic ticket
fixed. It happened that the "fixing" could no
longer be accomplished, although at an earlier
time the judges would dismiss tickets if asked to
do so by attorneys. The young lawyer tried, but
the best he could do was to get a reduction in the
fine.

What might have happened if the young lawyer
had refused to make such an effort? What if he
had said that he felt an ethical scruple against
it? Let's assume he mentioned this with the utmost tact, in the most inoffensive possible way.
If so, he might have gotten away with it, at least
once. But as he left the senior partner's office,
is it likely that the older lawyer would say to
himself "He's a fine young man. He has ethics!"
If anyone thinks so, his experience has been different in life than mine. Far more likely, the
older lawyer has his own ethically mediocre position fully rationalized: "That young man is still
wet behind the ears. They don't send them out of
law school understanding what's practical. We
have to serve our clients just as aggressively as
any other lawyer. Damn it, I'll have to run the
ticket over to the courthouse myself!"

The ethical denominator of the two men is
very different. One is deeply concerned with a
system of convictions and scruples; the other has
rationalized expediency. This can occur in any
culture, but a cultural tone which makes people
unaccustomed to hearing personal convictions
strongly reinforces it. When "all has become
politics," a person does not politic best by raising irritating obstacles in the form of principled
objections.

In such a milieu, a person who acts with un-
compromised integrity will soon "burn his bridges."
Those who withdraw from human contact -- such as
the religious hermit, the ascetic or the intellec-

tual who by Emerson's description "flies for refuge to the world of ideas" -- are taking the only
position consistent with complete integrity.
Those who choose to remain among men, though (and
for my part I think this is by far the better
choice), find that the daily problem is how to make
their stands where they will count most. They
have to optimize their most important principles
while being careful not to burn all the bridges.

Colorado law has voiced a "strong public
policy" against gambling, and the state Supreme
Court has long declared this in high moral tones.
I was in court one time when the sheriff brought
in several slot machines he had confiscated from
clubs over the weekend. The judge solemnly ordered them smashed. But every year while I was
attending law school and practicing as a young
lawyer in Denver the local bar assocation sponsored an annual summer buffet for its members.
Several times after the dinner was finished the
dinner tables were cleared away and gambling
tables were brought in. Money piled high as lawyers gambled.

I have no particular opposition to a person's
gambling if he wishes. I would be inclined to
leave it to his own choice. But I was bothered by
the hypocrisy. I wrote a letter to the president
of the bar association about it. The scruple
came to nothing: the event was held exactly the
same way the next year. The only gain was in
ill-will. The question is whether it was worth it
to have burned that bridge. For the man who
doesn't withdraw, it is necessary to ask whether
he could do more good, by having more influence,
by not raising a given point.

The world needs its Savonarola's -- those
irritating men who serve as thorns in its side to
remind it of important truths. But the argument
for becoming a Savonarola isn't clear-cut. There
are costs, and these are not just to one's position
in life. They are also costs to one's effective-

185

ness, and costs in terms of frustration and alienation. Anyone who chooses to live in the world
must select his priorities to optimize his values.
I should emphasize that this is very different
from ignoring important values and simply joining
the parade of "getting on." It has the danger,
of course, of degenerating through a process of
continuing rationalization, and that would have to
be guarded against.

The mask of hypocrisy. We can see from the
preceding two sections that a lifestyle which
trivializes human relations tends to involve a
high degree of hypocrisy. Those who develop the
art of extroversion and shy away from living a
cultivated personal reality will often be hypocritical in the ordinary sense of thinking one
thing and doing another; even this blatant form
of hypocrisy will be widespread. But a more subtle hypocrisy will also be pervasive because of
the operation of two additional mechanisms.

First, there are many people who never cultivate their own deep values. Technically, then,
they are not splitting their actions from their
thoughts. Strictly speaking, they are not engaged
in hypocrisy. But the effect is much the same.

Second, a culture which persistently trivializes things will distort its perception of reality.
To a man who takes reality, or some part of it,
seriously, this trivialization looks like a lie.
A good example arises out of the same faculty
fight I have mentioned about the department chairman's declaration of a slow-down. The fight was
taken seriously by everybody involved and left
scars for years. But three or four years later
the dean made a passing reference to it in an
after-dinner speech. The reference was amiable and
minimized the incident almost to the point of denying that it ever occurred. This extroverted trivialization of it seemed a falsification to those
who still felt the pain. No doubt it could be
thought of as hypocritical. The dean's reference

186

to it was functional in an after-dinner speech,
just as the outer flow is generally functional.
My point, though, is that there is a split between
such a functional reference and the truth of what
happened.

It is interesting that Burkean conservatives
argue the benefits of hypocrisy. They are not
committed philosophically to a piercing rationalism.
Because of this, they are ideally situated to see
how functional hypocrisy often is, both as a healing balm and as a protection for the mythology
that holds a society together.

In light of this, the case against hypocrisy
may not be indisputable. But men live largely by
reference to reality. Ayn Rand has stressed the
opposite of what the Burkean observes; she has
emphasized the need for men to grasp reality ra-
tionally. A culture which enhances hypocrisy obscures and denies the concern for truth which
exists in the radical solitudes of individuals as
they seek to understand and deal with the world.

A lowered intellectual level. It should
hardly be necessary now to mention the effect the
trivialization has on the intellectual, moral and
aesthetic tone of our society. Intellectuals
have been criticizing our culture on precisely
this ground for a century and a half. We will review these criticism in detail in Chapter 10 when
we trace the history of the alienation of the intellectual. Sinclair Lewis didn't make up George
Babbitt out of whole cloth; we can acknowledge
this even if on the whole we disagree strongly
with Lewis' overall position.

I mentioned earlier that the mediocrity within
our culture is by no means entirely caused by the
society's commercial emphasis and the resulting
extroversive preoccupation. It is even more a
result of the sudden rise of the multitudes. It
is a mistake to blame this mediocrity on capitalism
per se, unless we are also willing to credit

187

capitalism with the "accession of the masses" and
then make a negative judgment about that, too.
The literary, aesthetic, moral tastes of the
average human being of past ages were not so high
that we were bequeathed a paradigm from which we
have fallen. The collapse of aristocracy in the
nineteenth century raised the importance of the
average man and his values.

Perhaps most important is the fact that the
alienated intellectual has failed to raise an
exalted standard. This is probably because of his
alliance with the "have nots" and the entire
ideology he cultivated to fit that alliance. In
literature, morals and the arts he has championed
the "anti-hero"; and he has proclaimed a carping
"poverty of the soul." He has often indulged a
relativistic nihilism. This deprives civilization
of essential leadership. It must be corrected
before our society can fully regain its bearings.

NOTES

1. José Ortega y Gasset, Man and People (New York:
W. W. Norton & Company, Inc., 1957), pp. 46, 50.

2. Dwight D. Murphey, Emergent Man (Denver:
Bradford-Robinson, 1962), pp. 4, 5.

3. Ralph Waldo Emerson, The Portable Emerson
(Viking Press, 1946), p. 70.

4. Mark Spilka, The Love Ethic of D. H. Lawrence
(Bloomington: Indiana University Press, 1957).

10

THE ALIENATION OF THE INTELLECTUAL

We have heard a lot about "alienation" during recent years. Since the term is used wherever there is dissatisfaction or hostility, it is not without ambiguity. "Alienation" is sometimes used, with or without Marxian overtones, to mean a man's dissatisfaction with his work. Not long ago I was on a television panel with two other professors discussing "The Roots of Dissent." Both spoke at length about the hostility an employee may feel toward his job and, in a broader context, about the frustration a person may feel when he is unable readily to influence the activities of a large organization. These uses are valid enough, but they are different than I will be using in this book.

The term is also sometimes applied to a separation between a person and his potential -- as that potential is perceived by the speaker. Several years ago I heard a lecture in which the theme was that "we are born into a world of alienation from ourselves." "Humanity," the lecturer said, "is estranged from its potential."[1] He did not make his intellectual sources explicit, but there were clear reverberations from Rousseau, Veblen, Freud, Marcuse, and Maslow, each a thinker who has seen a wide gap between contemporary man and what he could be if he were to "self-actualize" his "basic human nature."

At other times, "alienation" may refer to a specific conflict, such as the "alienation between the sexes" or between "parent and child."

The different uses of the term were brought home to me a few years ago by a conversation I had with Professor Stephen Tonsor of the University of Michigan while we were both attending a meeting of

the Philadelphia Society. When I remarked that
Emerson had been deeply alienated (without saying
from whom or from what), Tonsor denied it in his
delightfully animated way. The meeting began
before he could explain his denial. The conversation was renewed several years later on a train
and at that time he agreed that Emerson was alienated and was surprised that he had ever said otherwise. I suspect that the initial difference was
caused by my not having made clear the object of
Emerson's alienation.

In this chapter I will discuss the alienation
of the modern intellectual from the great middle
class -- the "bourgeoisie." This type of alienation has been of particular importance during the
past two and a half centuries, if we date it from
Rousseau. There has been an enormous tension between the intellectual subculture and the predominant type of man within the larger culture. This
tension must be understood if we are to grasp the
competing value systems and "systems of interpretation" within our society.

There is, of course, some embarrassment when
we are asked to define the word "intellectual,"
even though this term is central to "the alienation
of the intellectual." Nor is there absolute clari-
ty in speaking of the "bourgeoisie."

We will have to bear with these embarrassments
and avoid any attempt at precise definition. The
historic phenomenon with which I will be concerned
is palpable enough that we need not delineate it
closely at the edges. I will often refer to the
"intellectual" in a sympathetic sense as the
"thoughtful and sensitive" man, the man of "tender
conscience" in Emerson's phrase, whose life involves an emphasis on contemplation and theory and
a sincere concern for ideas. This is the man of
books and words, often the academic man, who is
removed from active life within the cloister of a
protected, cerebral existence. And I will use the
term in a broad sense to include a variety of men

and not just the giants of thought (who in their independence are probably less involved in the mass alienation than are lesser intellectuals). In doing so, I will be departing from Aquinas' usage.

It is also worth noting that when I will speak of the "alienation of the intellectual" I will be making a generalization which has many exceptions. By no means have all modern intellectuals shared the alienation. Many have devoted their lives to opposing it, although for many years these have been in the minority. And there are many outside the mainstream of articulated social thought who would not want to be numbered among the alienates: intellectuals, for example, in business, the professions, or in colleges of business, engineering, etc. These may even compose the majority numerically on a campus, although in terms of articulated social commentary they are a very silent minority.

Still further, there is a problem from the snobbery inherent in the word "intellectual." It isn't just the bookish man who thinks. Intelligent businessmen sometimes take offense at the entire concept of an "alienated intellectuality," since they are not willing to admit that the alienated group has a corner on intellectuality. Ayn Rand has championed this viewpoint by stressing the extent to which the acting man brings intelligence to bear on reality.

I agree with this criticism, but in another sense I demur from it. We need some term to reflect the difference between someone who devotes himself to ideas and sensibilities and others who do not. Each deserves credit, but they are not the same. If we can use "intellectual" without belittling others, it seems the appropriate term to connote sustained effort in abstract ideas.

Even after these qualificiations, we come to yet another difficulty. When intellectuality goes

191

beyond individual effort and becomes a group phenomenon, the "intelligentsia" becomes a subculture.
But many who assume the lifestyle and accoutre-
ments of that subculture are in no real sense
"intellectuals" in the more favorable meaning of
that term. Some are mere camp followers. Not
everyone in Greenwich Village has been an intellectual in the fullest sense, but even those who are
not are still part of the subculture. The same
is true of the "counterculture" of the 1960's.
It isn't too much to say that even in universities
not all faculty members are "intellectuals" in the
fullest sense. Or if we must say they are, we see
how much alloy the word is permitted.

As to the concept of the "bourgeoisie," I
have already mentioned the difficulty which comes
from the fact that the intellectual actually seems
to have been alienated from the entire spectrum
of contemporary men. Even where he has allied with
the have-nots, he intends their ultimate reformation. The word "bourgeoisie" is too narrow to
denote the true object of the alienation. If it
serves at all, it must be to mean everyone who
stands within the predominant culture. It will
not do, at least in this century, to narrow the
meaning to a smaller group with specific characteristics. Even the substitute term "middle
class" isn't fully adequate, since the alienation
also runs against any so-called "upper class" and
reaches in the other direction to include, say,
the blue collar worker. The alienation has been
so extensive that it is an alienation against modern
Western civilization itself. But we will be justified in speaking of the alienation as being
against the middle class or bourgeoisie -- both to
remain consistent with the usual way in which it
is expressed and because the "middle class" is
so broad today as virtually to cover our entire
society anyway. The ideology expressing the alienation has cast itself in anti-capitalist terms,
stressing its conflict especially with the bourgeoisie.

Alienation in History

In the beginning chapters I mentioned that a thoughtful and sensitive person might feel very acutely the insanities of his own time. It may be that alienation is almost an inseparable companion to sensibility. Sensitive men have felt unhappiness with the men around them many times over the centuries.

There could hardly have been a more bitter commentary on human beings that Johnathan Swift's story of Gulliver's visit to the country of the Houyhnmnms.[2] This was the most biting of his satires. He told the story of Gulliver's landing on an island and then meeting a horse (a "Houyhnmnm") who turned out to be quite intelligent and civilized. For his part, the horse was amazed that Gulliver (a "Yahoo") was civilized. Gulliver was taken into the Houyhnmnm's family as a pet, where Gulliver soon observed the barbarity of the other nearby Yahoos. These were described prophetically by Swift almost as though he had been in the twentieth century to see some of the more extreme examples of the old German Youth Movement or the American hippie movement. Eventually the Houyhnmnm parliament became concerned over a family's having a Yahoo as a pet, and ordered Gulliver sent back to England. Amusingly but bitterly, Swift had Gulliver comment at the end that although he had been back in England for five years he still found it distasteful even to touch the hand of his wife.

If Swift meant to say anything seriously by this story, it was to comment on the insanities around him. We would have to classify him, without derogatory implication, as an alienated intellectual. The same would be true of Moliere and Stendhal, who at different times commented on the corrosive hypocrisy of French society. We can even go back almost two thousand years to the Roman historian Tacitus, who in the age of the Antonines complained passionately of the "utter poverty of thought" around him.[3] The theme of my

preceding chapter is reflected in his lament that
"a liking for actors and a passion for gladiators
and horses, are all but conceived in the mother's
womb. When these occupy and possess the mind, how
little room has it left for worthy attainments!
Few indeed are to be found who talk of any other
subjects in their homes, and whenever we enter a
classroom, what else is the conversation of the
youths." A great deal of ancient philosophy attempted to deal with the individual's relationship
with an unsatisfactory world.

The alienation has been intense in modern
European thought. This lends further support to
the observation that the sensitive man may be
alienated in almost any context. The European
alienation is also something which we need to
appreciate as background for my discussion of
American intellectual history in the final part of
this chapter. I will be tracing the alienation
as it has occurred in American history, but the
feeling in America has related closely to the
alienation in Europe.

In later books I will discuss Burkean conservatism and the Left. At that time we will see
aspects of their thought which will give us a
structured insight into much of the alienation
in modern Europe. For the present, we need to
realize that many intellectuals continued to support the value system of the Middle Ages even
after Europe had emerged from that system. Such
men have raised serious objections to commercial
culture, industrialism, secularism, rationalism,
individualism and the rise of the multitudes. As
with all other broad viewpoints, this position has
had a variety of attitudes within it; but the
aristocratic and faith-oriented critique was necessarily hostile to the culture of the New Philistines. This has been one of the main sources of
European alienation, especially among the monarchical thinkers on the continent. This will stand
out as we review various of the nineteenth century
German authors. It is also apparent in Burkean

conservatism, even though the English Burkean has usually been much more mild.

The alienation within the Left in Europe has overlapped with aristocratic thought. Modern socialism has important origins in the alienation of the aristocrat against commercial culture. This apart, the Left can virtually be defined as a hostile critique based on an alliance of the intellectual with the have-nots. This alliance has put the Left in the position of seldom being in the position to perceive sympathetically even the strengths of modern society. For example, in Herbert Marcuse's writing the strengths and beneficent aspects of bourgeois society are interpreted as merely soporifics which are designed manipulatively to cause people to overlook the shortcomings.[4] Socialism, anarchism and fascism were all built around a hostile critique of middle class, commercial culture.

In modern Europe. It would take quite an enormous book to illustrate adequately the full range of alienation in modern European thought. The reader will need to understand that my references here are the barest sample.

Julien Benda's well known book The Betrayal of the Intellectuals, which was written early in our century, is an example of both alienation and opposition to alienation. Benda himself held to an aristocratic critique of modern man, which means that he was alienated in his own way: he was deeply hostile to secularism, to the multitudes and the bourgeoisie; and his own values, although not directly spelled out in the book, were medievalist. He could speak of "the common herd";[5] and although he made perceptive criticisms of modern thought, he laid the causes of the vicious tone of much contemporary thinking at the feet precisely of the bourgeoisie and the multitudes. This is evident in his observation that "these causes arise from certain phenomena which are most profoundly and generally characteristic

195

of the present age. The political realism of the
'clerks' (the intellectuals), far from being a
superficial fact due to the caprice of an order of
men, seems to me bound up with the very essence
of the modern world." When I speak of him as
alienated, I don't mean that his criticisms don't
have a lot to them. His criticisms have much in
common with the analysis I have made in the preceding chapters. But I would have us note his
alienation and that it is different from my own.
It arose out of a perspective which does not
affirm the present age; I basically value contemporary culture, while at the same time wanting us
to heal its divisions and fill its voids.

Benda's alienation is not, however, the main
thing about his book. It has much to say about
the alienation and neuroses within modern intellectuality. "For twenty centuries," he says,
"the 'clerks' preached to the world that the State
should be just; now they proclaim that the State
should be strong and should care nothing about
being just . . . This denunciation of liberalism,
notably by the vast majority of contemporary men
of letters, will be one of the things in this age
most astonishing to History, especially on the
part of the French." (Emphasis added) In the
modern intellectual "the soul of Greece has given
place to the soul of Prussia among the educators
of mankind." He noted "the cult of success," by
which "I mean the teaching which says that when a
will is successful that fact alone gives it a
moral tone . . . This philosophy . . . is professed
by many a modern teacher in political life (it may
be said, by all in Germany since Hegel, and by a
large number in France since de Maistre)." He
spoke particularly of Nietzsche, Barres, Peguy and
Sorel.

Benda's account shows that there has been a
welter of confused voices. Instead of affirming
liberal values, many have exalted medievalism,
antirationalism and aristocracy (in the next volume
we will see that there are among them many who,

196

as supporters of Burkean conservatism, have done
so with high intelligence and gracious civility).
Many have preached power and the State within a
context of "might-makes-right." Many have cried
out for nationalism or racialism or class warfare.
And many have constructed a socialist critique.
In the midst of this welter, it has been difficult
to find voices who have affirmed our civilization
and have sought sympathetically to serve it. The
main exceptions have been classical and neo-clas-
sical economics, which have made up the largest
part of classical liberalism.

In The Open Society and Its Enemies, Karl
Popper discussed important parts of this alienation. Picking up a phrase from Schopenhauer, he
referred to an "age of dishonesty."[6] It was Hegel,
he said, who mainly originated the mentality
"controlled by the magic of high-sounding words,
and by the power of jargon." Hegel "became the
first official philosopher of Prussianism." From
Hegel came a left wing which "replaces the war of
nations which appears in Hegel's historicist scheme
by a war of classes" and an extreme right wing
which "replaces it by the war of the races."
Popper further illustrated the point Benda made
about an anti-liberal exaltation of power when he
quoted Hegel to the effect that "the State is the
Divine Idea as it exists on earth . . . We must
therefore worship the State . . . " This led Hegel
to juridical positivism -- "the doctrine that
might is right."

It is far too superficial to assign the tendencies of an age to just one man, but in Hegel
we can see an intellectual root for the totalitarianisms which have so greatly embodied the intellectual and social pathologies of the nineteenth
and twentieth centuries. And, too, there are important inputs into Nazism in Nietzsche's writing,
despite many insights scattered like gems within
his writing. Nietzsche denounced liberalism as
mere "herd-animalization"[7] and saw democracy as a
"form of decline in organizing power." He spoke

of "the contemptible type of well-being dreamed of by shopkeepers, Christians, cows, females, Englishmen, and other democrats." He exalted the "will to power" and in The Antichrist he defined as good "everything that heightens the feeling of power in man, the will to power, power itself" and as bad "everything that is born of weakness." He exposed the depth of his alienation when he wrote that "there are days when I am afflicted with a feeling blacker than the blackest melancholy -- contempt of man. And to leave no doubt concerning what I despise: it is the man of today." (His emphasis) He was passionately aristocratic, and affirmed "the order of castes, the order of rank," which he said "merely formulates the highest law of life."

Nietzsche's work contains many valuable insights; the open-minded John Stuart Mill would almost certainly have acknowledged that Nietzsche knew his own corners of the truth. But there should be little trouble in recognizing the monstrous nihilism Nietzsche also represented. Although many authors downplay the notion, I see little reason to hesitate in confirming the connection between his thought and that which later moved Hitler.

In Mein Kampf, Hitler echoed the anti-bourgeois alienation: "As a young scamp in my wild years, nothing had so grieved me as having been born at a time which obviously erected its Halls of Fame only to shopkeepers and government officials . . . This development seemed not only to endure but was expected in time (as was universally recommended) to remodel the whole world into one big department store in whose vestibules the busts of the shrewdest profiteers and the most lamblike administrative officials would be garnered for all eternity . . . Why couldn't I have been born a hundred years earlier? Say at the time of the Wars of Liberation when a man, even without a 'business,' was really worth something?! Thus I had often indulged in angry thoughts concerning my earthly pilgrimage."[8]

In Germany the "Storm and Stress" movement
a century earlier had been followed by the Romantic movement. Each was a reaction against the Enlightenment. Reinhold Aris has written an illuminating history of German thought from the beginning of the French Revolution to 1815, and
it is worth noting the direction the thinking was
taking. Of the Romantics, he says that "all
these thinkers were anti-bourgeois"[9] and he tells
us that they were deeply opposed to modern rationalism. He says that "no one clung to the ancient
order of society so uncompromisingly" as Justus
Moser; "no one turned against new ideas more re-
solutely than he." Despite the superlative applied to Moser, he says about Herder that "there is
no other thinker of the period in whose works
anti-rational tendencies found such strong expression as in his." He traced Herder's rejection of
the Enlightenment into the thinking of Fichte,
Schelling, F. Schlegel and Hegel, where it fertilized both nationalism and historicism. Alienated
against modern society, Herder was one of the
first to seek a rehabilitated view of the Middle
Ages.

Aris next tells us of de Maistre, who "lost
himself in mystical speculation and in a passionate
attempt to re-establish the superiority of the
highest medieval power in Europe, the Pope." He
is followed in Aris' account by Novalis, "the
most important thinker amongst the early Romantics,"
who was a "mystic impressionist" and who joined in
the flight from the Enlightenment. Novalis joined
many others in exalting the State. This was a
theme picked up by Schlegel; and a certain refrain
becomes monotonous in the history: "Here again
we meet that distrust of capitalism which is one
of the characteristics of Romantic thought."
Schleiermacher in his turn deprecated the bourgeois
"desire for personal happiness" and stressed that
"to give oneself to the community becomes an ethical duty." It is with foreboding that I read Aris'
comment that in Schleiermacher we see "the first
traces of the modern racial theory."

Aris' narrative is a good one, but the unavoidable redundancy of its subject matter is apparent as he goes on to Adam Muller, who again was "carried away by an unbridled mysticism, in which the State becomes the 'totality of life.'" This constantly reiterated theme shows that modern European thought experienced an explosion of philosophies hostile to the main body of the civilization. The thinkers have often been mystical, aristocratic, statist; and their writing has run like rivulets into later thought which has continued the hostility. From a distance it is difficult to tell the mystical and aristocratic views from much socialist thought, except that the various socialist models, both Left and Right, have differed from a purely aristocratic view by seeking mass support. All of them have been profoundly alienated.

I hardly need to illustrate this with regard to the Left in modern Europe. The depth of its alienation is so well known that it may be assumed as a given. It is enough to say that from Rousseau through Babeuf and Saint-Simon and Fourier and Comte and Proudhon and Marx and Bakunin and Kropotkin and Sorel and the Webbs and the Coles and Lenin and Trotsky and Che Guevara--to mention only a few--the alienation has blazed ominously. These thinkers have not formed a homogeneous group, of course; they have had many differences both about the particular socialist model that should be put in the place of capitalism and about method. But they have held in common an abiding conviction that modern society is sick and that in one way or another it must be set right by collectivist solution.

In his well known speech about the relationship between the white and black races in America, Booker T. Washington used the metaphor of the hand. He said that for some purposes the races were as separate as the fingers and that for others they were as united as the palm.[10] The same could be said about the many forms of anti-bourgeois

thought since Rousseau. They have been separate
in concrete ideology, but they have shared a common impulse. This is well illustrated in Ludwig
von Mises' account of the intellectual migration
of Sombart, who in succession belonged passionately to the anti-capitalist German Historical School,
the Marxists and the Nazis. "The straight line
that leads from the work of the Historical School
to Nazism cannot be shown in sketching the evolution of one of the founders of the School," Mises
wrote, "for the protagonists of the Methodenstreit
era had finished the course of their lives before
the defeat of 1918 and the rise of Hitler. But
the life of the outstanding man among the School's
second generation illustrates all the phases of
German university economics in the period from
Bismarck to Hitler. Werner Sombart was by far
the most gifted of Schmoller's students. He was
only twenty-five when his master . . . entrusted
him with the job of reviewing and annihilating
Wieser's book, Der naturliche Wert . . . Twenty
years later Sombart boasted that he had dedicated
a good part of his life to fighting for Marx.
When the war broke out in 1914, Sombart published
a book, Handler und Helden (Hucksters and Heroes).
There, in uncouth and foul language, he rejected
everything British or Anglo-Saxon, but above all
British philosophy and economics, as a manifestation of a mean jobber mentality. After the war,
Sombart revised his book on socialism . . . While
the pre-war editions had praised Marxism, the
tenth edition fanatically attacked it, especially
on account of its 'proletarian' character and its
lack of patriotism and nationalism . . . Then,
when the Nazis seized power, he crowned a literary
career of forty-five years by a book on German
Socialism. The guiding idea of this work was that
the Fuhrer gets his orders from God."[11]

American Alienation

The Revolutionary generation. The generation
of the "Founding Fathers" in the United States does

201

not seem to have been touched by deep cultural alienation. If such a feeling existed, I do not know of it. It will have occurred outside the intellectual mainstream. There is nothing in the writings of Jefferson or Madison or Hamilton or Franklin or Adams that is akin to the alienation we have just reviewed--or which we will see in the rest of American history. They argued heatedly among themselves, showing fierce political partisanship, and they reflected diverse philosophical approaches; but there was no hostility to the main cultural environment.

American "liberalism" has often tried to debunk those years, since the legend which has surrounded them in the public mind has been a major support for classical liberalism.[12] I certainly don't wish to join in that debunking. But if we are to understand the rest of American history it is important to take into account the fact that there was considerable division within Americans at that time. It wasn't the kind of division that involves cultural alienation, but neither was there a thorough-going consensus. The foundation wasn't really there to justify Thomas Paine's ecstatic feeling that Americans could make a completely new beginning: "We have every opportunity and every encouragement before us, to form the noblest purest constitution on the face of the earth. We have it in our power to begin the world over again."[13]

The immense achievement of George Washington was that by sheer doggedness he was able to succeed despite the apathy and mediocrity of many of his contemporaries. Beveridge said in his Life of John Marshall that "throughout the (Revolutionary) war, the neglect and ineffectiveness of the States, even more than the humiliating powerlessness of Congress, time and again all but lost the American Cause."[14] He reported that in a letter to his nephew Washington wrote sadly about "great bodies of military in pay that never were in camp; . . . immense quantitites of provisions drawn by

202

men that never rendered . . . one hour's service
. . . I am wearied to death all day . . . at the
conduct of the militia, whose behavior and want
of discipline has done great injury to the other
troops." Washington complained of Pennsylvania's
poor support of the war: "It is a matter of
astonishment to every part of the continent, to
hear that Pennsylvania, the most opulent and popu-
lous of all the States, has but twelve hundred
militia in the field, at a time when the enemy are
endeavoring to make themselves completely masters
of, and to fix their winter quarters in, her capital." He wrote that the people of that state gave
him little assistance and were either "totally disaffected or in a kind of Lethargy." We see from
all this that the success of the Revolution was
not caused by the equal industry and devotion of
all Americans alive at that time.

Even during the years of constructive work
after the Revolution there were bitter personal
animosities and a rising party factionalism. The
pamphlets and newspapers of the early years were
virulent in their attacks on public men. Violent
disputes sprang up between such men as Hamilton
and Jefferson. We know, of course, that Hamilton
was killed in a duel with Aaron Burr. Burr himself, although he almost won the Presidency in
1800, was later tried for treason. The Whiskey
Rebellion challenged the new government; foreign
interests tried to embroil the United States in
the war in Europe on the side of France; the Alien
and Sedition Act produced widespread anger; and
during the War of 1812 there was significant anti-
war agitation.

This fragmentation is relevant when we ask why
there was not to be an overpowering classical liberal consensus which would deflect an incipient
cultural alienation and would point toward solutions to the emerging national issues. But at
least we do not see during the years of the Founding Fathers the type of cultural dissatisfaction
we see later. Benjamin Franklin was older than

the rest of the Founding Fathers, but he is an
excellent example of the rough-and-tumble, non-
alienated orientation of the leading men of the
eighteenth century. Franklin was an intellectual
of the first rank; he was proclaimed in Europe as
one of the leading scientists of the time. But
he felt no sharp sensitivity and no proclivity toward being easily bruised. He lived in an imperfect world, but he took it in stride and dished
out as much as he took. This is clear in his
Autobiography, which should be read in contrast
immediately before or after reading Thoreau's Walden or Emerson's essays. Franklin makes clear
his own free-wheeling spirit when he tells of having constantly jeopardized his health by consort-
ing with "low women."[15] He exhibits no bruises
as he tells of friends who borrowed money and
never repaid it, or about his abortive arrangements
with Governor William Keith that stranded him
in England without any of the promised letters of
credit or of introduction. Unlike many a later
intellectual, he did not spend his time in England
writing a bitter existential novel; he simply enjoyed himself to the hilt and worked to earn
enough to buy his passage home. I am amused when
he tells of his courtship of a girl and his refu-
sal to marry her when her parents wouldn't mort-
gage their house to get money to pay off the debts
on his printing business. He also tells how he
persuaded the legislature to establish a system of
paper money and how he then got the contract to
print that money. Benjamin Franklin is one of history's best examples of a type of unalienated
intellectual who is both in the world and of it
and who feels no separation from his fellows. To
a somewhat lesser degree perhaps, this was true of
the other leading men of his time, most of whom
were also intellectuals.

No doubt these men were "alienated" from
George III. They did, after all, conduct a revolution. And it may be pertinent that they were
something of an aristocracy, despite all their re-
publicanism. Still further, they did not yet face

fully the "rise of the multitudes." But despite these things, the fact remains that the "alienation of the intellectual" did not yet exist in America.

The generation of Emerson and Thoreau. Within in a few years a startling change occurred in American intellectuality. An abiding unhappiness set in. Before the new Republic had been given a chance, men with a new and tender sort of sensitivity began to declare it and the culture upon which it was based sick. The "soldiery of dissent" came into being.

Henry David Thoreau cultivated beans and his "radical solitude" beside Walden Pond outside Concord. Just a few years after the shot was fired which was "heard around the world," Thoreau looked out upon Concord society and commented darkly that "most men, even in this comparatively free country, through mere ignorance and mistake, are so occupied with the factitious cares and superfluously coarse labors of life that its finer fruits cannot be plucked by them . . . He has no time to be anything but a machine."[16] We hear a very different voice from Franklin's when the deeply sensitive Thoreau speaks of a world of " . . . lying, flattering, voting, contracting yourselves into a nutshell of civility, or dilating into an atmosphere of thin and vaporous generosity, that you may persuade your neighbor to let you make his shoes, or his hat, or his coat, or his carriage, or import his groceries for him; making yourselves sick, that you may lay up something against a sick day, something to be tucked away in an old chest, or in a stocking behind the plastering or, more safely, in a brick bank; no matter where, no matter how much or how little. I sometimes wonder that we can be so frivolous." He said that "the mass of men lead lives of quiet desperation."

Accordingly, Thoreau was alienated against the cultural tone of his time. "What does our Concord culture amount to?" he asked. "There is

205

in this town, with a very few exceptions, no taste
for the best or for very good books even in
English literature . . . Even the college-bred
and so-called liberally educated men here and
elsewhere have really little or no acquaintanceship with the English classics." After commenting
in question form that "one who has just come from
reading perhaps one of the best English books will
find how many with whom he can converse about it?"
he adds an observation strikingly similar to the
lament I quoted earlier from Tacitus: "Our reading, our conversation and thinking, are all on a
very low level, worthy only of pygmies and manikins."

There is something very different in Thoreau
from the generation of Franklin and the Founding
Fathers. He stands apart, a spectator to the
people among whom he lives, profoundly unhappy with
his fellows. By his solitary life at Walden Pond
he has withdrawn into a world of his own. This
isn't to say that his is not a valuable world, a
world of perceptions and of love of life and of
nature which has been an inspiration to countless
readers since. But it is a world in which his
radical solitude senses agonizingly the trivialization of life around him.

He did not formulate an ideological critique
expressing a theory which embodied the alienation.
This came later in American intellectual history.
He was neither a socialist nor a twentieth-century
"liberal." This is apparent in his statements
about philanthropy and poverty which show that he
had struck no alliance with the have-not and had
not undergone a change in values to accommodate
such an alliance. Unlike a later socialist or modern liberal, he was able to write that "if I knew
for a certainty that a man was coming to my house
with the conscious design of doing me good, I should
run for my life." And he could write of the poor
that "often the poor man is not so cold and
hungry as he is dirty and ragged and gross. It is
partly his taste, and not merely his misfortune.
If you give him money, he will perhaps buy more

rags with it." He could say that "philanthropy is almost the only virtue which is sufficiently appreciated by mankind. Nay, it is greatly overrated; and it is our selfishness which overrates it." He continued: "Do not stay to be an overseer of the poor, but endeavor to become one of the worthies of the world."

Thoreau told of his affinity for "the philosophy of India." Although this would have created a tendency toward alienation from his own culture, his alienation came before any sort of socialist theory. His ideology was not yet anti-capitalist, but the alienation, fed by Thoreau's intellectual origins, led within a generation to an anti-capitalist rationale. This suggests that the substantive problems in our culture which I examined in Chapter 9 and which he stressed in his writing were meaningful contributing causes to alienation and then to the Left, even though in my opinion there have been even more important causes. The alienation came first, then socialism; not socialism and then alienation.

Ralph Waldo Emerson, a slightly older man, shared Thoreau's feelings. Again there is a vast change from Benjamin Franklin's energetic insensitivity. Emerson, like Thoreau, was a man of introversive sensibility. He was far enough removed from the rough-and-tumble to judge life and find it wanting. He had formed no doctrinaire anti-capitalist position yet, either; but nevertheless he saw much that he abhorred: "The young man, on entering life, finds the way to lucrative employments blocked with abuses. The ways of trade are grown selfish to the borders of theft, and supple to the borders (if not beyond the borders) of fraud. The employments of commerce are not intrinsically unfit for a man, or less genial to his faculties; but these are now in their general course so vitiated by derelictions and abuses at which all connive, that it requires more vigor and resources than can be expected of every young man, to right himself in them; he cannot

move hand or foot in them. Has he genius and
virtue? the less does he find them fit for him to
grow in . . . ; he must forget the prayers of
his childhood and must take on him the harness
of routine and obsequiousness . . . The general
system of our trade is a system of selfishness; is
not dictated by the high sentiments of human nature; is not measured by the exact law of recipro-
city, much less by the sentiments of love and
heroism, but is a system of distrust, of concealment, of superior keenness, not of giving but of
taking advantage . . . The sins of our trade belong
to no class, to no individual. One plucks, one
distributes, one eats. Everybody partakes, everybody confesses -- with cap and knee volunteers
his confession, yet none feels himself account-
able."[17]

There is apparent in this passage the same
deep dissatisfaction with the life around him
that we saw in Thoreau but did not see a generation
before. And yet, Emerson has refrained from
"scapegoating" the problem; neither he nor
Thoreau has divided the world into good and bad
or into classes, blaming one and exonerating the
other: the abuses are abuses "at which all connive." Emerson's writing does not yet reflect an
anti-capitalist opposition to commerce as such:
business is "not intrinsically unfit for a man."
He is alienated, but is still far short of Marx
or Rousseau or Proudhon, say, in his formulation
of ideology. This isn't to deny that he had a
deep personal commitment to a philosophy of Christian simplicity and love, and that some of his
passages yearn for the day when "love would rule"
and government would be unnecessary. Emerson,
like Thoreau, had intellectual roots which predisposed him to alienation. But both were pre-
"liberal" and pre-socialist.

Emerson went beyond simply stating the alienation as it affected him. He went on to describe
the broad intellectual movement which felt as he
and Thoreau did. This movement was a reaction by

a good many people who felt the alienation, withdrew into themselves and then came back into
society with "a fertility of projects for the
salvation of the world." The alienation and withdrawal are both apparent in Emerson's statement
that "it is when your facts and persons grow unreal and fantastic by too much falsehood, that the
scholar flies for refuge to the world of ideas,
and aims to recruit and replenish nature from that
source." He said in 1844 that "there was in all
the practical activities of New England for the
last quarter of a century, a gradual withdrawal of
tender consciences from the social organizations.
There is observable throughout, the contest between
mechanical and spiritual methods, but with a steady
tendency of the thoughtful and virtuous to a deeper
belief and reliance on spiritual facts."

We can hardly assign anything hard-and-fast
to this dating, but his reference would take us
back to 1819. It is at that time that he says the
alienation and withdrawal began.

Emerson went on to say that the "man of tender
conscience," having felt the need to withdraw,
came back into American life with a "great activity
of thought and experimenting . . . appearing in
temperance and nonresistance societies; in movements of abolitionists and of socialists; and in
very significant assemblies called Sabbath and
Bible Conventions; composed of ultraists, of seek-
ers, of all the soul of the soldiery of dissent."
He exclaimed: "What a fertility of projects for
the salvation of the world! One apostle thought
all men should go to farming, and another that no
man should buy or sell, that the use of money
was the cardinal evil; another that the mischief
was in our diet, that we eat and drink damnation
. . . Others attacked the system of agriculture,
the use of animal manures in farming, and the
tyranny of man over brute nature; . . . Others
attacked the institution of marriage as the foun-
tain of social evils." Elsewhere he wrote that
"in the history of the world, the doctrine of Re-

209

form had never such scope as at the present hour."

    With regard to almost the same period, C. S.
Griffin cites the wide variety of projects about
which Emerson spoke: "During the years from 1830
to 1860 a host of reformers in a variety of reform
movements together examined and attacked every
American institution, every idea, every conceivable
sin, evil, or burden of suffering." He points to
the movement against slavery and that against the
drinking of liquor; the opposition to prostitution;
the anti-Catholic agitation; the movement to re-
deem criminals and help the mentally incompetent;
the public school movement; various communitarian
socialist societies; the drive for women's rights;
the dietary movement; the opposition to monogamous
marriage; the effort to put a Bible in every home;
and to such "fads and fancies" as "phrenology,
hydropathy, mesmerism, . . . spiritualism, and
free love."18

    All of this was widely varied in its forms,
but it was, in a more general sense, a single
phenomenon. As such, several observations are pertinent to it:

    • This effusion of many viewpoints was, of
course, an expression of liberty. In a free
country, everyone could assert his own point of
view.

    • At the same time, the immense variety shows
how much nineteenth century man lacked an inherited consensus. No paradigm held sway to produce
an agreed-upon understanding of society.

    • It is startling that so strong a movement
of dissent came into existence so soon after the
American Revolution. It is as though the Revolution and Founding Fathers had had no soul to pass
on to the next generation. Classical liberalism
in the form given it by Jefferson and Jackson failed to capture the imagination of the more thoughtful men of the time. This is certainly one of the

most fateful intellectual failures in the history
of the world. For these dissenters, classical
liberalism apparently had no attraction as the
philosophy of a free society. It did not ignite
them by saying "let us unite on a common view of
the free society, assume the many advantages we
enjoy and move on to a more perfected freedom to-
morrow." Such an appeal was present in the speeches of the various Jacksonian Presidents up to
the Civil War, but somehow it did not move the
man of "tender conscience."

• The dissent started in New England and had
Christian and Federalist roots. It represents an
inability of those of an aristocratic and a
faith-oriented bent to accept the individualistic
society which had come to exist in America. As
in German thought, we see the anti-bourgeois continuity which has so often linked aristocratic
values and socialist thought -- except that here
the entities are slightly less identifiable: The
New England elitism leads to alienation from nineteenth century American individualism; this later
bears fruit as modern "liberalism," a movement
which involves an interesting mixture of alienation,
socialist thought, pragmatism and local American
elements.

• An ideology rationalizing the alienation
had not yet come into being.

The development of an ideology. Those who
have felt this alienation have never totally come
together. If we are to refer to them under a
common heading, we have to stress their agreements
without emphasizing their differences. But, of
course, this is a part of acknowledging the existence of any ideology; diversity always remains
despite a number of shared elements. We are justified in speaking of the birth of American
"liberalism" (which I will refer to as "modern
liberalism" to distingiush it from classical liberalism). By the end of the nineteenth century
the intellectual community in the United States had

211

developed a substantial homogeneity which shared the alienation and developed a rationale to express it.

The coalescence toward a "school" which would express the alienation is represented by the letter Henry Adams wrote to his brother, Charles Adams, in 1862: "what we want is a <u>school</u>. We want a national set of young men like ourselves or better, to start new influences not only in politics, but in literature, in law, in society, and throughout the whole social organism of the country -- a national school of our own generation. And that," he continued, revealing his own aliena-tion, "is what America has no power to create . . . It's all random, insulated work, for special and temporary and personal purposes. And we have no means, power or hope of combined action for any unselfish end."[19]

He was wrong, of course. America did have the power to create such a school. The consensus developed rapidly as the years went by. By the 1890's, the classical liberal sociologist William Graham Sumner at Yale felt outnumbered by those who shared the alienation. By this time it had produced a clearly anti-capitalist critique and was going to Europe for its ideas.

The pre-Civil War agitation included several socialist communities. Brook Farm and several other "Fourierist phalanxes . . . sprang up in the 1840's," Griffin says. "In 1851, Josiah Warren and Stephen Pearl Andrews began Modern Times, a community of anarchists on Long Island." Else-where, "the great goal of the Oneida leaders was not merely to create a single happy community, but to convert the world -- or at least the United States -- to social and Christian perfectionism." Hopedale, too, "begun in 1841, was an experiment in Christian socialism."

If we read <u>Uncle</u> <u>Tom's</u> <u>Cabin</u> not just for its story or for its relation to the slavery issue, we

see that Harriet Beecher Stowe expressed through
her characters a number of anti-capitalist comments
(although they did not all necessarily represent
her own view; some, expressed by Southern characters in the story, repeated the argument which
some pro-slavery thinkers were raising against what
they perceived as the "wage slavery" system of the
North). One character said "I've got just as
much conscience as any man in business can afford
to keep, -- just a little, you know, to swear by,
as 'twere." Another commented: "Look at the high
and the low, all the world over, and it's the
same story, -- the lower class used up, body, soul
and spirit, for the good of the upper. It is so
in England; it is so everywhere; and yet all
Christendom stands aghast, with virtuous indignation," the Southerner said, "because we do the
thing in a little different shape from what they
do it." In an exchange between a Northerner and
a Southerner, Stowe has them agree on the fundamental premise. The Southerner said that "the
slave-owner can whip his refractory slave to death,
-- the capitalist can starve him to death." The
Northerner replied that "it's no kind of apology
for slavery, to prove that it isn't worse than
some other bad thing."20

The following passage spoken by one of the
characters in Uncle Tom's Cabin is filled with a
romantic emotion similar to Marx's contemporaneous
outpouring in the Communist Manifesto: "There is
a mustering among the masses, the world over; and
there is a dies irae coming on, sooner or later.
The same thing is working in Europe, in England,
and in this country. My mother used to tell me of
a millennium that was coming, when Christ should
reign, and all men should be free and happy."

Jack London was an American novelist who wrote
The Call of the Wild and many other books. In some
of his writing, the alienation waxed as a violently
revolutionary creed. His novel The Iron Heel looked ahead futuristically to a socialist revolution
that was to occur in the United States in 1912.

213

The revolution was crushed by the "iron heel of
the Plutocracy," but a later revolution succeeded.
The central figure in the novel was a socialist
revolutionary hero who was strikingly similar to
the heroic capitalist figures later portrayed by
Ayn Rand. In describing him, London reflected
the mixture of elitism and democracy which has been
characteristic of the alliance between the intellectual and the have-nots; the description also
illustrates the relationship even of left-wing socialism with Nietzschean superiority: "I have
said that he was afraid of nothing. He was a
natural aristocrat -- and this in spite of the
fact that he was in the camp of the non-aristocrats.
He was a superman, a blond beast such as Nietzsche
has described and in addition he was aflame with
democracy."21

About the same time, Edward Bellamy returned
from a year in Germany to write the classic
Looking Backward, which now appears in the Modern
Library series. Bellamy's book is partly novel,
mainly polemic for a utopian socialist conception.
In it, Bellamy laid the foundation for the Eastern
"Nationalist" wing of the later Populist movement.
This wing espoused socialism and was opposed within Populism by the followers of Henry George,
among others. Bellamy's book tells the story of a
man who goes to sleep in a basement bedroom one
night in 1887 only to awaken in the year 2000.
His house had burned down over him during the night
and his bedroom had been covered by ashes. He
is discovered there over a century later -- a Rip
Van Winkle of socialist literature. Emerging, he
discovers a perfect socialist society in which
communal effort provides for all material needs
and there is a leisured life of the mind. The
intellectual is given the highest honors: "The
highest of all honors in the nation, higher than
the presidency, which calls merely for good sense
and devotion to duty, is the red ribbon awarded by
the vote of the people to the great authors,
artists, engineers, physicians, and inventors of
the generation."22 There is no anti-social beha-

vior, since greed has been made obsolete. Only good will motivates the governors. But looking back, the main character sees by way of comparison the brutish system of the nineteenth century when capitalism prevailed. Bellamy's alienation against his own time is made abundantly clear.

The literature of alienation was growing and expressed a decidedly anti-capitalist, anti-bourgeois rationale. Theodore Dreiser wrote An American Tragedy expressly for the purpose, he said, of demonstrating "the evil of capitalism."[23] Ayn Rand describes it as telling the story of "a rotten little weakling who murders his pregnant sweetheart, a working girl, in order to attempt to marry a rich heiress." The story is well told, but I agree with Rand when she says that the story doesn't make a case against capitalism. And yet, as a link in the intellectual history I am tracing here, it doesn't matter whether it successfully does this or not. It is enough that Dreiser and many others thought it did.

It was also during this period that Thorstein Veblen wrote The Theory of the Leisure Class in which he applied Rousseau's analysis to American culture. The essence of his theory is in the passage which says that "during that primitive phase of social development, when the community is still habitually peaceable, perhaps sedentary, and without a developed system of individual ownership, the efficiency of the individual can be shown chiefly and most consistently in some employment that goes to further the life of the group . . . When the community passes from peaceable savagery to a predatory phase of life . . . (t)he activity of the men more and more takes on the character of exploit; and an invidious comparison of one hunter or warrior with another grows continually easier and more habitual."[24] This, of course, harks back to the idea that man's origins were simple and brotherly, and that he has developed his greed and vanity because of private property and the competitive system. This is pure Rousseau

-- and it has been reiterated tens of thousands of
times by social critics during the past two and a
half centuries. Veblen extends the argument into
a sociological critique that surpasses Rousseau's.
This in turn has been elaborated and rendered even
more subtle by later followers of Rousseau --
as, for example, Charles Reich in The Greening of
America. Veblen took every aspect of our national
life and through his discussion of "invidious comparison" and "conspicuous consumption" demonstrated the impact of competitiveness and social striving. There was, of course, a value-judgment hostile to such a culture implicit in his discussion.
It is interesting by way of comparison to notice
that the classical liberal John Bright drew just
the opposite conclusion. When Bright visited
Turkey in the 1830's and saw the filth and degradation there, he commented unfavorably that
"there exists no spirit of emulation amongst them."[25]
Bright saw emulation as a necessary motivating
force that leads to progress and civilization.
To Veblen, it was the main feature of a warped
value system.

     The climate of opinion intellectually had come
to the point at which in 1894 Henry D. Lloyd was
able to speak of "the host of ills which now form
the staple theme of our novelists and magazinists."[26]
C. M. Destler's American Radicalism 1865-1901 tells
about a variety of anti-capitalist movements, along
with several others which were not as explicitly
favorable to socialism. "During the late eighties
an urban, eastern, American-born socialist movement
attracted interest in the cities and farming areas
of the West. Known as Nationalism, it developed
. . . (from) Edward Bellamy's Looking Backward."
Bellamy's movement took its place as a faction
within populism. Populism involved both socialist
and anti-socialist elements, but on the whole it
was "committed to government intervention in
business and to limited experiments with state
socialism as a means of combating . . . monopoly."
At the same time, a series of cooperative communities continued the striving in that direction

216

which had begun before the Civil War.

The mixed nature of Populism gives the impression that it was a people's movement and that its roots were in earlier Jeffersonian democracy. To a point, these impressions are true: Labor and agrarian elements gave it a democratic base, and Populism picked up on the Jacksonian distrust of financial interests which became so strong when Jackson fought against the re-chartering of the second United States Bank. But in other important ways, the impressions are false: The role of the alienated intellectual was of major importance in Populism; and the distrust of financial interests -- if generalized into a distrust of capitalism and into a call for large-scale governmental intervention -- was a massive departure from the classical liberal commitment of the Jeffersonian-Jacksonian faith.

Strong elitism appeared in the thinking of Burnette Haskell, who tried to make the Knights of Labor a revolutionary force. This is evident in his comments that "we found that the masses of working men were densely ignorant, cowardly and selfish . . . Any pretext will do (when the time comes to strike) that will rouse the people." Such sentiments were not democratic but elitist.

Destler says that Henry Demarest Lloyd, "a Fabian socialist, . . . was the most outstanding intellectual identified with the American labor movement in the early nineties, with the possible exception of Henry George." There were indigenous non-socialist factors in modern liberalism as it developed, but we need to appreciate how much the alienated intellectual interjected an anti-capitalist critique and imported socialist ideology from Europe. This occurred even though many intellectuals chose to work pragmatically within the American political system without declaring themselves socialist in the way the Fabian Society in England was doing.

So far, I have referred to an assortment of individuals. But there was a common "formative experience" taking place which constitutes the most important factor in American intellectual history. This consisted of the migration of several thousand American doctoral candidates to European universities -- mainly in Germany and secondarily in England -- during the last third of the nineteenth century. This migration finalized the coalescence toward a strongly anti-capitalist rationale as an overlay for the already-existing alienation. Because of the influences at work in German education, it led to the decision by a majority of American intellectuals to follow a gradualistic, non-violent and non-Marxist course. These were the attributes of the German Historical School. The Historical School also gave the impulse to the intensely empirical methods which have been followed by American Social Science ever since.

Eric Goldman's Rendezvous With Destiny is an excellent history of modern liberalism. In it, he reports that "by the Nineties a large proportion of the ambitious young academics were seeking their Ph.D's in Europe . . . Some went to England, where the attack on Spencerianism (the classical liberal views of Herbert Spencer) was far more advanced than in the United States. Most went to Germany . . . The leading German scholars were teaching the 'Historical' approach."[27] He mentions that in 1914 "Germany, on its part, was sending 'Historical'-minded Ph.D's back to America by the hundreds," while in England "the sons of men who had been excited by Ruskin and Morris now had available the still more heady wine produced by Graham Wallas, George Bernard Shaw, and, above all, H.G. Wells." In Jurgen Herbst's The German Historical School in American Scholarship these observations are reinforced by the statistic that "between the years 1820 and 1920 nearly nine thousand American students set sail for Europe to enter the lecture halls, seminars, and laboratories of German Universities."[28] The great bulk went

during the ascendancy of the Historical School.
This appears clearly from Herbst's comment that
"soon after 1870 American students of the liberal
arts and the social sciences began going to Germany in large numbers." The migration was especially to the University of Berlin: "It was
the University of Berlin to which the largest
number of Americans came during the nineteenth
century."

Three major intellectual influences were
present in Germany during the last part of the
nineteenth century: the Historical School, Marxism and the Bismarckian program. Each of these
had some influence on American intellectual
development. As to the first, Herbst tells us
that "the extent of the influence of the historical
school on the German-trained social scientist may
be seen in the results of an inquiry conducted by
Professor Farnam of Yale shortly after the turn
of the century . . . Of the more than 80 who
specified what they regarded the most important
influence on their thinking, 30 listed the
historical school, 23 the scientific and historical
method, 15 the 'point of view,' and 8 the theory
of state intervention." He says fourteen "referred
to Professor Bohm-Bawerk's Vienna School" (the
strongly pro-capitalist "Austrian School of
Economics"), but goes on to say that "most of these
stressed its resemblances rather than its contrast to the German school."

I will devote most of my attention to the
Historical School because of the importance of its
influence, but so that we don't lose sight of them
it will be well to consider first the Marxist and
Bismarckian influences. Of the Marxists, Ludwig
von Mises has written that "the only serious ad-
versaries whom the Schmoller School (the Historical
School) had to fight in Germany were the Marxists."
He was referring to "the Marxian party of the
Social-Democrats." Until 1875 German socialism
had been divided between the followers of Marx and
of Lassalle, but in that year the two factions had

219

united in the Social Democratic Party.[29] Schumpeter says that in 1891 the Social-Democrats opted decisively for Marxism.[30] In their anthology of socialist thought, Albert Fried and Ronald Sanders report that "Germany was to become, in the last quarter of the nineteenth century, the virtual headquarters of the worldwide socialist movement."[31] They add -- and this is especially important for the intellectual history we are tracing -- that "the rise of socialism in Germany attracted many intellectuals." Marxism was the most prominent of these socialist elements. It is perhaps significant that before he obtained his doctorate at Harvard the Negro intellectual W. E. B. Dubois studied at the University of Berlin for two years (1892-1894) under Schmoller of the Historical School.[32] He later became a Marxist, as did Sombart, writing Black Reconstruction, which Goldman has described as so strong that it "could have been written in Moscow."

The influence of Bismarck provokes disagreement among those who have studied it as to whether it should be classified as "socialist." Geoffrey Bruun has argued that "the forceful Bismarck . . . had no liking for democracy or socialism" and that he "determined to destroy the Social Democratic Party before it grew strong enough to constitute a menace." Bruun summarized Bismarck's program by saying "his aims were: (1) to cripple the Social Democratic Party by repressive decrees; (2) to placate the discontented workingmen who voted Socialist by introducing legislation which would ease their grievances; and (3) to make the imperial government financially independent of state contributions by erecting a high protective tariff on imports." With regard to the social legislation, Bruun said that "it is not without interest to note that the autocratic and conservative Bismarck anticipated by more than twenty years the social legislation later enacted by the Liberal-Labor coalition in Great Britain and by the Republican-Socialist block in France." Goldman makes a similar assessment when he says that "study in

220

Germany also meant living in a country where Bismarck's anxiety to undermine socialism was bringing about an exciting series of state-sponsored reforms." We should pause, though, even while we note Goldman's interpretation of Bismarck as anti-socialist, to consider that Goldman is almost certainly wrong when he implies that it was an anti-socialist preemption by Bismarck that captured the sympathy of the American scholars studying in Germany. We have already seen the alienation within the American intellectual community. We have also seen that among the German intellectuals, who presumptively had the greatest influence upon the students, the overwhelming majority weren't anti-socialist at all. They were, rather, Historicist, Marxist or Lassallean. It is relevant to notice that Goldman bases his evaluations on a peculiarly narrow definition of "socialism," since he defines it as a program of the direct state ownership of industry.

Ludwig von Mises, on the other hand, looks on Bismarck from a classical liberal perspective. He sees him as essentially socialist. Mises says that "the government of Bismarck began to inaugurate its Sozialpolitik, the system of interventionist measures such as labor legislation, social security, pro-union activities, progressive taxation, protective tarrifs, cartels and dumping" and explains that this was in keeping with Schmoller's thinking. "Schmoller and his friends and disciples advocated what has been called state socialism; i.e., a system of socialism -- planning -- in which the top management would be in the hands of the Junker aristocracy. It was this brand of socialism at which Bismarck and his successors were aiming." The connection between Bismarck's administration and the gradualistic socialism of the Historical School is referred to also by Joseph Schumpeter in <u>Capitalism</u>, <u>Socialism</u>, <u>and Democracy</u> when he reports that "ideas and proposals normally came to the bureaucracy from its teachers at the universities, the 'socialist of the chair.'" These were the professors about

whom Herbst has said that "the members of the
Verein as a whole were close enough to the socialist
program to be tagged Kathedarsocialisten -- professorial socialist -- by friend and foe alike."
He says that a majority of the Verein fur Social-
politik rejected explicit socialism, "preferring
to base their reforms entirely on science," but
that others "worked at developing a theory of
state intervention, and did not hesitate to call
themselves state socialists . . . In the social
legislation of Bismarck they saw their theory put
into practice."

These things make it hard for me to agree with
the idea that Bismarck was an anti-socialist influence, especially with regard to his influence
on the American intellectuals who studied under
the Historical School. When, as Herbst says, "the
new economists in the American Economic Association
echoed the pronouncements of the Verein fur Social-
politik," they echoed a mixture of influences.
All the influences were favorable to a high degree
of state intervention merging into gradualistic
socialism; and all were touched, too, by an underlay of intensely anti-bourgeois feeling. This
combination of elements has continued within American liberalism throughout the twentieth century,
although the implicit socialism and alienation finally surfaced, as an overtly socialist spin-off,
in the New Left.

Our discussion of the first two influences --
Marxism and Bismarck -- has already given us some
awareness of the Historical School itself. The
Historical School was the third and by far the most
important influence on the Americans studying in
Germany. We have just seen the connection between
the Historical School and Bismarck's position as
commented upon by Mises and Schumpeter. We have
seen that many regarded themselves as socialists,
and that all were "close enough" to the socialist
point of view to be called "socialists of the chair."

The Historical School had several additional

aspects:

• Europe lacked paradigms handed down from preceding ages and had lost its faith-centered consensus. Accordingly, the intellectual culture of Europe became engaged in a variety of approaches to what we now call social science and to the methodology of studying human life. There were countless points of view. We see some of the approaches in Herbst's discussion of (1) the "critical method" which arose from Immanuel Kant's philosophy, which combined empirical study with logical analysis; (2) the rise of comparative philology to look into the origins of words and concepts; (3) the concept of Geistes-wissenschaft which "encouraged German scholars to go beyond factual research and rational analysis, and led to the hypothesis of the fundamental unity of all branches of knowledge"; the rise of speculative philosophy, epitomized by Hegel, as a result of this concept; but then the reaction against speculative thinking and the movement "in favor of empirical investigation, verification and induction." There are many others.

The German Historical School took its place in this enormous controversy over method. It "insisted on rigorously defined, specialized subject matter, taught by experts trained in investigation" and "originated the cult of the monograph and the research journal." It established the positivist tone of American social science which continues today. Apart from its intense specialization and empiricism, the School argued that "society was ever in flux, and could not be caught, as it were, in static formulae." This involved a commitment to cultural relativism. The School urged that each epoch, each culture, should be studied in the context of its own mixture of ingredients. It denied that universal laws of economics or sociology are discoverable. At the same time, it believed that laws of cultural change -- of transition from one state of culture to another -- were in fact discoverable.

223

• The result of this cultural relativism was two-fold: the School denied the validity of classical economics and of any attempt to arrive at the "laws of behavior" which most classical economists had thought possible; and the foundation was laid for a variety of later movements which are hardly distinguishable from this view -- pragmatism, Reform Darwinism, sociological jurisprudence and others.

The relativism gave rise to a bitter argument with classical liberalism. If we read James Mill's earlier Essay on Government, we are impressed by how much he believed he was formulating definite truths about human behavior. The same is true of Frederic Bastiat's Harmonies of Political Economy. Herbert Spencer could argue that there is a substratum of realities which legislators should understand before they legislate.33 To each of these classical liberals and to others, including the Austrian School with Menger and Bohm-Bawerk, the laws of life pointed to freedom as the form of social organization compatible with reality. In our own time, Ludwig von Mises, the leading member of the Austrian School in the next generation, and Ayn Rand, who picked up a great deal from Mises, have continued to approach classical liberal theory in this way.

When the German Historical School denied the possibility of an economic science, and especially one leading to laissez-faire capitalism, it did two things: first, it raised some important and for the most part legitimate criticisms of the existing classical liberal methodology; and second, it used its cultural relativism as a debunking instrument. Relativism has often been used by the Left in modern thought as a method of attack. These two aspects are closely associated, but should be carefully distinguished: the modern scientific mentality leads to relativism, and those who view this mentality sympathetically, as I do, see some important truth in the relativism; but there is nothing about relativism which, out-

side the tactical framework of nineteenth and
twentieth century political thought, should any
more support anti-capitalist than pro-capitalist
views. A cynical relativism can be a nihilist tool
equally against capitalism or socialism. A more
constructive relativism simply leaves them stripped
of dogmatism, which in turn makes them debate
values and their implementation.

American scholars studying in Germany picked
up both of these aspects. They adopted a genuinely
scientific approach, even though this has often
been abused, leading to what Hayek has so aptly
described as "scientism." But they have often
used relativism, also, as an ideological ploy.
American relativist movements can only be understood if both aspects are kept in mind. As it has
come down to us from the German Historical School,
American social science has reflected this dualism
of real science and ideology. It is a combination
we have seen in the behavioral sciences in the
recent past. Not long ago, Russell Kirk warned
that behavioral science threatened to become the
new ideology; and I can understand his warning in
the context of this intellectual history and of
the tone of behavioral science in, for example,
the late 1960's.

• The methodological impact on American
social science was profound, but I am more directly interested in the effects which study under the
German Hisotircal School had on American ideology.

It was at this time that modern American
liberalism, which previously had been scattered
among countless movements without a common ideology,
became an intellectual consensus. I don't mean
to suggest that a great many differentiated viewpoints didn't remain within the consensus; but it
is clearly warranted to generalize that modern
liberal ideology made its appearance. The
alienation had coalesced into the "school" for
which Henry Adams had yearned. Up to that time,
the thinking of the country had been mostly classi-

225

cal liberal; but this was reversed, with a modern liberal consensus becoming predominant in the intellectual community. Modern liberals often argue that their ideology is an extension of the philosophy of Jefferson and Jackson; but this is true only to a minor extent. Modern liberalism picked up the Jacksonian hostility to the marriage of government and high finance (although even this continuity is somewhat mixed when we consider the New Nationalism of Theodore Roosevelt and Herbert Croly, which called for a marriage of big business, labor and government). It continued to favor democratic participation (although the alliance of an elitist intellectual group with the common man is much more tenuous than the far more sincerely democratic views of the Jacksonian classical liberals). But despite these continuities, modern liberalism has for the most part involved a direct hostility to the Jeffersonian-Jacksonian outlook. Eric Goldman joins in the facile interpretation of modern liberalism as an off-shoot of classical liberalism, but it is worth noting that he has devoted a chapter to the modern liberal "attack on the steel chain of ideas." This attack involved debunking and destroying every aspect of classical liberalism. Because of this, it makes more sense to trace modern liberalism to the alienation of the intellectual and to its coalescence into an ideology during the last half of the nineteenth century.

The anti-bourgeois emphasis of German Historical School thinking was referred to by Mises when he said that "many of them were firmly convinced that the foremost task of economists was to aid the 'people' in the war of liberation they were waging against the 'exploiters.'" Herbst says John W. Burgess repeated to his students at Amherst the Hegelian doctrine that the State is "the human organ least likely to do wrong." Herbst also quotes Richard T. Ely as having said that "it is a grand thing to serve God in the State." Another Hegelian, Albion Small, used the Hegelian dialectic, Herbst says, to "supersede individualistic

226

moral philosophy." Henry Carter Adams reflected
the Historical School's opposition to classical
economics when he spoke of "the passing of the
laissez-faire dogma of classical economics."
Speaking generally, Herbst says that "for the new
economists the usefulness of statistics only bol-
stered their devotion to social reforms. They
endorsed Wagner's and Engel's commitment to legislative efforts, made their own adaptation of the
German's advocacy of state socialism, and proceed-
ed to give these doctrines concrete application
through the American Economic Association." The
result was that "during the first decade of the
twentieth century the University of Wisconsin
became a truly state-wide laboratory for testing
a German-style union between academic theory and
legislative practice." Herbst says further that
"the American students of the German social
science tended . . . to regard the humanitarian
motives of socialist reformers with approval . . .
(T)hey contrasted the humane impulse upon which
the reformers acted with the indifference to human
suffering they attributed to the 'soulless' cap-
tains of business and industry, and to the economic
and social theorists who defended them."

• If we are to understand twentieth century
American liberalism, it is relevant that the influence of the Historical School was toward a
gradualistic, non-Marxian socialism. This led
directly into the pragmatic Welfare State reformism
of modern liberalism which has had a strong underlay of explicitly socialist thought and alienation,
but which has found it expedient not to label itself as socialist. "Like the Fabians (the Fabian
Socialists in England), they were primarily interested in the work at hand," Schumpeter says
of the German "socialists of the chair." He points
out that "they deprecated class war and revolution."
This corroborates Herbst's observation that "the
German-trained scholars were mainly middle-class
and middle-of-the-road, not at all inclined to
endorse Marxist socialism, anarchism, or any of
the radical doctrines of which they were periodi-

cally accused . . . These men who regarded socialism in its secular, Marxist form as both dangerous
and damnable, were ready to endorse a socialism
defined as voluntary cooperation in the cause of
economic and political reform." Herbst applies
this to the American political scene of a few years
later when he says that "in (Theodore) Roosevelt's
progressivism scholars saw the long-awaited
synthesis of American individualism and German collectivism."

   Early twentieth century liberal alienation.
My purpose isn't to write a complete history of
American liberal ideology. Its elements will be
taken up much more fully in my later book on
modern liberalism. But at this juncture it is
important to notice the direction which the alienation assumed ideologically as the American intellectual community entered the twentieth century.
(1) The alienation itself continued at a high
pitch, repeating the themes which had been so prominent since Emerson and Thoreau. (2) At the same
time, the ideology, adapting itself to the American
political scene, more or less deliberately obscured its relationship even with gradualistic
socialism, even though underneath the surface, in
the literature rather than in the politics, a significant thread of explicit socialism continued.
I hesitate to state this second point, because I
believe John Stuart Mill was right when he gave
magnanimous credit to almost all viewpoints. I
don't doubt the sincerity of those who held
liberal views. Nor do I doubt that they saw an
important part of the truth about American life.
But it is impossible not to conclude that the
ideology put on a mask. It took on an essentially
dishonest posture which continued until the rise
of the New Left in the 1960's.

   The book which was perhaps the most influential during this period was Herbert Croly's The
Promise of American Life. Eric Goldman stresses
its importance in his history of American liberalism
as having exercised a powerful influence over

228

Theodore Roosevelt. It is this book which illustrates the lack of candor better, perhaps, than any other. As I read Croly's book, I had a strong impression that he was stating a socialist theory without doing so openly. To evaluate this, there is no substitute for reading the book in full. In its endless euphemisms and circumlocutions there is little that can be quoted, but cumulatively they convey a consistent pressure toward a collectivist perspective. Typical of both content and vagueness are his statements that business is worthwhile "just in so far as industry (becomes) organized under national control for the public benefit" and that we suffer from "a sterile and demoralizing Americanism -- the Americanism of national irresponsibility and indiscriminate individualism."[34]

Herbst tells us a good deal when he indicates that the new liberal ideology needed "specific suggestions about how in America a collectivist theory could be translated into a program of political action" and says "that task was undertaken in the writings of Herbert Croly , who as a youth had fallen under the spell of the social theories of Auguste Comte . . . The strongest influences on his thought were those of Comte, James, and the new economists and other scholars of the ethical school . . . Thus Croly trained his guns on 'the automatic harmony of the individual and the public interest which is the essence of the Jeffersonian democratic creed.'"

Croly was an excellent writer and an extremely intelligent man. It is correspondingly difficult to suppose that his euphemistic style was not deliberate. This is especially true when we keep in mind that the same lack of ideological candor has been typical of modern liberal writing. We see it, for example, in Dow Votaw's book Modern Corporations when he advocates a clearly collectivist view in the most round-about manner by suggesting passingly that "the great corporation may ultimately itself become a political or electoral unit in a vastly different governmental structure than we know today."[35] Another example is Albert William Levi's chapter in Towle's _Ethics and Standards in American Business_. Levi restates R. H. Tawney's Fabian socialist views almost verbatim _without assigning any credit to Tawney or even footnoting him._[36] This would be impossible to understand if we did not appreciate just how essential it has been, as a tactical expedient in American politics, for modern liberals to avoid any labeling of their doctrines as socialist.

As I glance through my notes from Charles Forcey's _The Crossroads of Liberalism_, I notice two more examples of the dissimulation. Forcey says that "for the moment the _New Republic_ men intended to be the most cautious of Fabians. The actual radicalism of a new liberalism that would give unions a say in management and socialize the railroads was to be broken gently to the magazine's middle-class readers."[37] Somewhat later he points out that "though Lee Simonson saved his socialist writing for the _Masses_, his pieces in the _New Republic_ bravely defended 'cubism,' 'impressionism,' 'futurism,' and most of the other schools of modern art."

It is time now, though, for me to leave this aspect of the history to resume the process of tracing the alienation as a phenomenon in its own right. The profusion of alienated literature continued. The "Muckraking" movement occurred in American journalism mainly between 1903 and 1909, and involved scandalized exposés of a seemingly endless series of corrupt situations in what was presumptively a discreditable American society.

One of the leading authors during the early part of the century was Sinclair Lewis. In _Babbitt_, he established a permanent caricature of the bourgeois businessman as unexciting, spiritually inert and intellectually dull.[38] In doing so, he reiterated themes which are thousands of years old and are often repeated today. And although they do not contain the entire truth, they do contain part of it.

An excellent source which anthologizes the alienation which existed from approximately 1910 to 1935 is Henry May's The Discontent of the Intellectual: A Problem of the Twenties. (I am critical, though, of May's failure, as a specialist, to have a broader contextual understanding of the phenomenon he was studying. He writes with the misapprehension that the alienation was more or less unique to that time.) May breaks the alienation into three categories: "There were three degrees of alienation among the intellectual critics of American society in the mid-twenties. Some merely carried on Mencken's quarrel with the small town and the village, the already defeated rural America of their own youth. Others took on a more dangerous opponent: the business-dominated urban society of their own time. Others went much further still into a wholesale rejection of the values which had dominated American society since the beginning and of the conception of man on which these values had always been based."39

It may be misleading to fragment the alienation in this way, since each of the three types he cites is just part of the general alienation of the intellectual from modern culture. His description illustrates, however, the breadth and intensity of the alienation, and it demonstrates that the alienation continued into the period of American history he discusses. He quotes passages from a great many authors.

• He quotes a writing by Van Wyck Brooks in 1915 to the effect that "economic self-assertion still remains to most Americans a sort of moral obligation . . . (but) self-fulfillment as an ideal can be substituted for self-assertion as an ideal. On the economic plane, this implies socialism; on every other plane it implies something which a majority of Americans in our day certainly do not possess -- an object in living."

231

This is a statement which echoes the one made by
Henry Adams in his letter of 1862, fifty-three
years earlier.

Ezra Pound wrote of a "half-educated, Zoroastrian rabble of 'respectable' people more stupid
and sodden than is to be found even in America."

• The elitism which inherently underlies so
much of the alienation appears in Pound's comment
that "the Lord of the Universe sends into this
world in each generation a few intelligent spirits,
and these ultimately manage the rest." This elitism is not surprising in itself; but it is at
odds with the politics and rhetoric of the Left in
general as the Left pursues its democratizing
alliance with the have-nots.

• Randolph Bourne wrote of a fictional character similar to "Benjamin" in the movie and book
The Graduate. "He has a rather constant mood of
futility . . . There are moments when life seems
quite without sense or purpose . . . Since he left
college eight years ago, he has been through most
of the intellectual and emotional fads of the day
. . . The reputable people and the comfortable
classes who were having all the conventional emotions rather disgusted him." There is also a
passage which is pertinent to the tension in twentieth century American politics about the problem
of disloyalty. "With his groping philosophy of
life, patriotism has merely died as a concept of
significance for him. It is to him merely the
emotion that fills the herd . . . Having no such
images, he has no feeling of patriotism." This
is a good passage to illustrate the connection between the disloyalty issue and the alienation of
the intellectual. I do not mean to say that all
such intellectuals are in fact disloyal. But the
alienation has laid the foundation for what disloyalty there has been and for the suspicions which
have not incorrectly been felt by American conservatives.

232

• Morris Cohen wrote a comment in 1919 which states with unusual directness the cultural and ethical division that has typified the modern ideological conflict. "It is the Puritanic feeling of responsibility which has blighted our art and philosophy and has made us as a people un- skilled in the art of enjoying life." I know of no other statement which is more helpful in under- standing the basis for the "counter-culture" of the 1960's.

• H. L. Mencken, although a thoroughly delightful author, voiced the alienation when he said of a character that "he seemed only a poor clod like those around him, deluded by a childish theology, full of an almost pathological hatred of all learning, all human dignity, all beauty, all fine and noble things."

• Harold Stearns wrote in 1922 that "the most moving and pathetic fact in the social life of America today is emotional and aesthetic star- vation, of which the mania for petty regulation, the driving, regimenting, and drilling, the secret society and its grotesque regalia, the firm grasp on the unessentials of material organization of our pleasures and gaieties are all eloquent stig- mata."

• The prominent author Edmund Wilson spoke of the late twenties and early thirties in a passage which again shows the relation of the alienation to the loyalty issue. "The next month the slump began (in 1929), and as conditions grew worse . . . a darkness seemed to descend. Yet, to the writers and artists of my generation who had grown up in the Big Business era and had always resented its barbarism, its crowding-out of every- thing they cared about, these years were not de- pressing but stimulating. One couldn't help being exhilerated at the sudden unexpected collapse of that stupid gigantic fraud. It gave us a new sense of freedom; and it gave us a new sense of power to find ourselves still carrying on while

233

the bankers, for a change, were taking a beating
. . . (W)e wondered about the survival of republican American institutions; and we became more and
more impressed by the achievements of the Soviet
Union . . . ."

    <u>Alienation</u> <u>in</u> <u>the</u> <u>recent</u> <u>past</u>. To anyone who
has been at all conversant with the academic com-
munity during the past thirty or forty years, it
is self-evident that the alienation continued
through the thirties, forties and fifties. I was
an undergraduate in the early 1950's and found the
alienation intense at the University of Colorado.
To expedite my tracing of the alienation, however,
I will skip ahead to the last fifteen years. This
recent alienation has been so prominent a part of
our national life that, again, it hardly seems
necessary to speak of it -- other than for the
purpose of completing the record. Alienation has
been one of the central themes in motion pictures.
In <u>The Graduate</u> the story was about a "lost young
man" who had just graduated from college but who
considered the world around him sick and empty.
In <u>Catch 22</u> the world at large was presented as
wildly inane. Only the central character was normal (although it is significant that he was more
an anti-hero than a noble set-off against the inanity). In <u>Reflections in a Golden Eye</u> the characters were either extremely neurotic or pathological. As to books, college bookstores usually display hundreds of socialist tracts, many of them
revolutionary. Charles Reich's bestselling <u>The
Greening of America</u> began by summarizing the
alienation: "America is dealing death, not only
to people in other lands, but to its own people.
So say the most thoughtful and passionate of our
youth, from California to Connecticut. This realization is not limited to the new generation."[40]
He went on to say that "the present crisis is an
organic one . . . (that) arises out of the basic
premises by which we live . . ." and then he listed "disorder, corruption, hypocrisy, war . . .
poverty, disordered priorities, and law-making by
private power . . . uncontrolled technology and

234

the destruction of environment . . . decline of
democracy and liberty; powerlessness . . . the ar-
tificiality of work and culture . . . absence of
community . . . loss of self . . . ."

On the flypage of Robert Theobald's An Alternative Future for America, the editors have written
that "all current initiatives within the realm of
the possible appear to be failing" and Theobald
himself has added a few pages later that "we have
something like six to nine months (the book was
published in 1968) to make visible the beginning
of a change from a society of coercive authority
to a society of shared power. If conditions continue along present lines, if trends continue to
develop as they are presently developing, we will
move into a fascist police state in this country."[41]

In 1969, the main philosopher of the revolutionary New Left, Herbert Marcuse, summarized his
alienation in the following passage from his book
An Essay on Liberation: He referred to American
society as "a society which.compels the vast
majority of the population to 'earn' their living
in stupid, inhuman, and unnecessary jobs . which
conducts its booming business on the back of
ghettos, slums, and internal and external colo-
nialism, .which is infested with violence and re-
pression, .which, in order to sustain the profitable productivity on which its hierarchy depends,
utilizes its vast resources for waste, destruction,
and an ever more methodical creation of conformist
needs and satisfactions."[42]

The following year, even a justice on the
U. S. Supreme Court, William O. Douglas, wrote that
"we must realize that today's Establishment is the
new George III. Whether it will continue to
adhere to his tactics, we do not know. If it does,
the redress, honored in tradition, is also revolution."[43]

The Environmental Handbook published in time
for "Earth Day" in the spring of 1970 contained

235

articles which said that "america (sic.) . . . is dying because of the greed and money lust of a thousand little kings who slashed the timber all to hell and would not be controlled"; "a year is about one-fifth of the time we have left if we are going to preserve any kind of quality in our world"; " . . . the country's present industrial arrogance"; ". . . the worms of capitalism and totalitarianism."[44]

Theodore Roszak, the author of The Making of a Counter Culture, has argued in Where the Wasteland Ends that "we should undertake to repeal urban-industrialism as the world's dominant style of life" and for a mystical, pacifist, anarchist "visionary commonwealth."[45] He has gone further than anyone I have read in repudiating modern culture, since he argues for a return to pre-Christian animism. There is one point at which he even argues that man has lost touch with real values since rising up off all fours; the erect posture has made us unduly cerebral, so that we have lost contact with nature and sensuous life. We need, of course, to be aware of the genuine human problems to which Roszak and so many others have pointed. A sterile cerebration does involve a spiritual difficulty. This is something I discussed in the preceding chapter in connection with D. H. Lawrence. But at the present time I am concerned only that we see the alienation as a fact in its own right.

Its expression slackened in the United States and elsewhere during the 1970's, but an advantage of the long-term perspective we have gained is that we can see how improbable it is that it will have withered away. It responds in the virulence of its expression to current stimuli and to the fad-orientation of the culture in which it exists, so a moment of slackening does not tell us very much. Only the hindsight of several decades will permit us to say whether a fundamental change is taking place.

236

Alienation of the intellectual has been a pre-eminent phenomenon in the history of Western civilization since the early eighteenth century. I do not mean to say that it has been the sole explanation of the events and ideology of the modern period; there are necessarily countless other elements. I am persuaded, though, that the alienation has been of critical importance and that it has been insufficiently understood. It defines the nature of our age. Only when it is transcended will our civilization be able to resolve the tensions within itself and to have appropriate leadership and thought.

NOTES

1. Dr. Dan Costley, speech on "An Image of Man and Its Implications for the Future," Wichita State University, February, 1968.

2. Johanthan Swift, Gulliver's Travels (New York: Modern Library, 1931), pp. 251-337.

3. Tacitus, The Complete Works of Tacitus (New York: Modern Library, 1942), pp. 761, 758.

4. Herbert Marcuse, essay on "Repressive Tolerance," A Critique of Pure Tolerance (Boston: Beacon Press, 1969).

5. Julien Benda, The Betrayal of the Intellectuals (Boston: The Beacon Press, 1930), pp. 135, 142, 81, 93, 116, 119.

6. Karl R. Popper, The Open Society and Its Enemies (Princeton: Princeton University Press, 1950), pp. 224, 225, 227, 236.

7. Friedrich Nietzsche, The Portable Nietzsche, Walter Kaufman trans. (New York: Viking Press, 1968), pp. 541, 543, 542, 570, 610, 646.

8. Adolf Hitler, *Mein Kampf* (Boston: Houghton Mifflin Company, 1943), pp. 157-8.

9. Reinhold Aris, *History of Political Thought in Germany from 1789-1815* (London: George Allen and Unwin Ltd., 1936), pp. 217, 222, 234, 235, 239, 257, 266, 273, 285, 300, 302, 310.

10. Booker T. Washington, *Up From Slavery* (New York: Bantam Books, 1901), p. 156: "In all things that are purely social we can be as separate as the fingers, yet one as the hand in all things essential to mutual progress."

11. Ludwig von Mises, *The Historical Setting of the Austrian School of Economics* (New Rochelle: Arlington House, 1969), pp. 33, 34, 31-2.

12. Eric F. Goldman, *Rendezvous With Destiny* (New York: Vintage Books, year not given), pp. 66-81. The chapter's title is "Dissolving the Steel Chain of Ideas." Goldman talks candidly about the aspect of modern American liberalism which has had to do with debunking every position held by classical liberalism. The modern liberal considered those interrelated positions a "steel chain" which needed dissolving.

13. Thomas Paine, *Common Sense and The Crisis* (Garden City: Doubleday & Company, Inc., 1960), p. 59.

14. Albert J. Beveridge, *The Life of John Marshall* (Boston: Houghton Mifflin Company, 1916), Vol. I, pp. 83, 84, 85.

15. Benjamin Franklin, *Autobiography* (New York: Books, Inc., year not given), pp. 112, 85-87, 111, 109.

16. Henry David Thoreau, *Walden and Essay on Civil Disobedience* (New York: Airmont Publishing Company, Inc., 1965), pp. 13, 14, 80, 81, 58, 9, 60, 61, 49.

17. Ralph Waldo Emerson, The Portable Emerson (Viking Press, 1946), pp. 71-73, 199-204, 70, 112, 110, 111.

18. C. S. Griffin, The Ferment of Reform, 1830-1860 (New York: Thomas Y. Crowell Company, 1967), pp. 1, 2-8, 56, 71, 72, 73.

19. Henry May (ed.), The Discontent of the Intellectuals: A Problem of the Twenties (Chicago: Rand McNally & Company, 1963), p. 42.

20. Harriet Beecher Stowe, Uncle Tom's Cabin (New York: Washington Square Press, 1962), pp. 2, 218, 235, 238.

21. Jack London, The Iron Heel (New York: Arcadia House, 1950), p. 6.

22. Edward Bellamy, Looking Backward (New York: Modern Library, 1942), p. 132.

23. As quoted in Ayn Rand, The Romantic Manifesto (New York: World Publishing Company, 1969), p. 63.

24. Thorstein Veblen, The Theory of the Leisure Class (New York: Mentor Books, 1953), p. 30.

25. R. A. J. Walling (ed.), The Diaries of John Bright (New York: William Morrow and Company, 1931), p. 41.

26. Chester McArthur Destler, American Radicalism 1965-1901 (New York: Octagon Books, 1945), pp. 215, 14, 19, 86, 165.

27. Goldman, Rendezvous, pp. 79-80, 177, 276, 80, vii, 66-81, 146-161.

28. Jurgen Herbst, The German Historical School in American Scholarship (Cornell University Press, 1965), pp. 1, 8, 16, 130, 146, 148, 54, 55-6, 56-7, 71, 100, 155, 67, 129, 142, 178, 187, 188-9, 201, 196.

29. Wallace K. Ferguson, Geoffrey Bruun, A Survey of European Civilization (Boston: Houghton Mifflin Company, 3d ed., 1962), pp. 766, 767.

30. Joseph A. Schumpeter, Capitalism, Socialism and Democracy (New York: Harper and Brothers Publishers, 2d ed., 1947), pp. 320, 341.

31. Albert Fried and Ronald Sanders (eds.), Socialist Thought (Garden City: Anchor Books, 1964), pp. 238, 317.

32. W. E. Burghardt DuBois, The Souls of Black Folk (Greenwich, Conn.: Fawcett Publications, 1961), p. vii.

33. See the chapter on "The Sins of Legislators" in Herbert Spencer, The Man Versus the State (Baltimore: Penguin Books, 1969), pp. 112-150.

34. Herbert Croly, The Promise of American Life (New York: Macmillan Company, 1914), pp. 415-416, 426. We should notice, though, that Charles Forcey, in The Crossroads of Liberalism (New York: Oxford University Press, 1961), p. 5, disagrees with the view that Croly exercised a substantial influence over Theodore Roosevelt. This, of course, is a factual question, albeit one that may be hard to tie down. It is clear, however, that over a period of several years Croly and Roosevelt had an active and well-disposed acquaintanceship.

35. Dow Votaw, Modern Corporations (Englewood Cliffs, N. J.: Prentice-Hall, Inc., 1965), p. 96.

36. Joseph W. Towle (ed.), Ethics and Standards in American Business (Boston: Houghton Mifflin Company, 1964), pp. 20-29.

37. Forcey, Crossroads, pp. 185, 201.

38. Sinclair Lewis, Babbitt (New York: Harcourt, Brace Co., 1922). The simplistic nature of this stereotype of the businessman is apparent from a

critical reading of Lewis' book itself, but it is
nowhere more evident than in George Bernard Shaw's
characterization in his play Candida of a certain
Mr. Burgess. Witness the following stage description included in the script by Shaw: "The door
opens; and Mr. Burgess enters unannounced. He is
a man of sixty, made coarse and sordid by the com-
pulsory selfishness of petty commerce, and later
on softened into sluggish bumptiousness by over-
feeding and commercial success. A vulgar ignorant
guzzling man, offensive and contemptuous to people
whose labor is cheap, respectful to wealth and
rank, and quite sincere and without rancor or envy
in both attitudes. The world has offered him no
decently paid work except that of a sweater; and he
has become, in consequence, somewhat hoggish.
But he has no suspicion of this himself, and honest-
ly regards his commercial prosperity as the inevitable and socially wholesome triumph of the ability,
industry, shrewdness, and experience in business
of a man who in private is easygoing, affectionate,
and humorously convivial to a fault. Corporeally
he is podgy, with a snoutish nose in the centre of
a flat square face, a dust colored beard with a
patch of grey in the centre under his chin, and
small watery blue eyes with a plaintively sentimental expression, which he transfers easily to his
voice by his habit of pompously intoning his sen-
tences." I might add, although it is beside the
point, that Shaw is perhaps the most asinine of
all the world's well-known intellectuals. See, as
a case in point, his The Intelligent Woman's Guide
to Socialism and Capitalism.

39. Henry May, Discontent, pp. 24, 9, 10, 12,
15-16, 17, 23, 27, 32, 49-50.

40. Charles A. Reich, The Greening of America
(New York: Bantam Books, 1971), pp. 1, 4-7.

41. Robert Theobald, An Alternative Future for
America (Chicago: Swallow Press, 1968), pp. 47-48.

42. Herbert Marcuse, _An Essay on Liberation_ (Boston: Beacon Press, 1969), p. 62.

43. William O. Douglas, "Redress and Revolution," _Evergreen Review_, April 1970, p. 41.

44. Garrett de Bell (ed.), _The Environmental Handbook_ (New York: Ballantine Books, 1970), pp. viii, xiv, 2.

45. Theodore Roszak, _Where the Wasteland Ends_ (Garden City: Doubleday & Company, 1972), pp. 414, 426, 92-99.

11

CAUSES OF THE ALIENATION

The preceding chapter's discussion of the alienation of the intellectual was descriptive in nature. It simply told the story of the alienation. We still need to understand its causes, which is the subject of this chapter. And then in the next chapter I will discuss the major consequences which have come from it.

The alienation can't be explained by a single cause. Any simplistic explanation is inadequate and, as a consequence, unfair. One such partial analysis comes from the alienates themselves: anyone who is immersed in the literature and rhetoric of alienation will naturally be inclined to think of it as the direct result of the defects in our society about which they feel the alienation is a complaint. If we asked Emerson why he was alienated, he would have pointed to the "abuses in which all connive." From this perspective, the alienation would be satisfied and disappear if the defects were cured. But I hope to make it clear in this chapter that this explanation -- which I call the "substantive" explanation -- would be seriously deficient if taken just by itself. The substantive defects do in fact play an important role in creating the alienation; but they are by no means the only cause. I will even express my own conclusion that they are secondary.

Among the opponents of the alienates, on the other hand, there are those who would just as quickly assign an unflattering cause and let it go at that. In this vein, they may speak of the intelligentsia's rivalry, as a social class, for power in a secular, commercial civilization. This makes the alienation an expression of a desire for power and status. Or on the individual level such critics may speak of the envy which each individual alienated intellectual may feel toward the success of the businessman. Here, too, I am struck by how insufficient and unfair such explanations are. I can't see my way clear to write a book which will attribute the alienation exclusively to sociological rivalry or to personal envy. To do so would be to engage in too partisan a failure to see the part of the truth the alienation puts forward. An important byproduct of this injustice would be that we would thereby limit our own understanding. We would fail to come to grips with the full attraction which the alienation has had for so many sincere and capable people.

I have appreciated the open intellectual qualities that were demonstrated by John Stuart Mill in his essay On Bentham and Coleridge. His intellectual breadth permitted him to see that each of these polar opposites of the early nineteenth century -- Bentham and Coleridge -- had hold of a portion of the truth. Mill emphasized that we gain a little and lose a lot when we close our minds to the partial truths contained in opposing points of view. Many views that seem to contradict each other are really focusing on different things. It would be silly to draw from Mill's example the conclusion that we should adopt an unthinking eclecticism. Nor should we ignore real conflicts between points of view. But where a civilization and its problems are highly complex the "truth" -- viewed as a whole -- will almost certainly consist not of a single perception or value, but of a balance of values and a large body of complementary insights. Because of this, I expect that future thinking will look back upon each of our current ideological systems as in various ways correct and in other ways insufficient -- at least as they have been stated.

I will discuss several contributing causes of the alienation. Although each will be separable from the others, they are mutually consistent. Each mirrors a different part of the civilizational context within which the alienation occurs. I

244

will point to six such causes and will evaluate
their relative importance when I have finished.
The six, briefly stated are:

   1. A substantive explanation which will look
to the spiritual and cultural defects of the society at large. This explanation also involves
all economic and political issues. It is from the
alleged defects of capitalistic and bourgeois
society that the alienation says it is in rebellion.

   2. The sociological rivalry between the intellectual subculture and the acting man of business.

   3. The role of envy.

   4. The difference in personality and temperament between the contemplative and the active
man.

   5. The fact that many of the value systems
we have received from the past have looked with
disfavor upon the man of commerce and the type of
culture he creates.

   6. The continuing process by which the
alienation of one generation of intellectuals is
reproduced in the next. This is not an initial
cause, but it is an important secondary one.

The Causes

   The substantive explanation. A highly intelligent but at the same time alienated collection
of essays about American society appeared in the
1920's under the title Civilization in the United
States. In his book about alienation in the
Twenties, Henry May summarized the charges the
essay leveled against our culture: "(1) emotional
barrenness, (2) enforced conformity, (3) excessive
moralism, (4) commercialism, and (5) hypocrisy."[1]

I am not sure such a list gives a sufficently fair picture of the subtlety of the essays, but it does at least present a summary. If we look at the items on the list, we see that its content is similar to the spiritual problems I discussed in Chapter 9 in the context of the split between the radical solitude of each individual and the trivialized outer reality of social contacts. I won't repeat that discussion at this time, but we should note that everything that I discussed there has to be taken into account now in terms of its bearing on the alienation of the intellectual.

The contemplative man is the one who most cultivates his own internal solitude. It is this man, then, who will feel most acutely the impact of a culture which trivializes and blanks out the things he considers most meaningful. There are many passages in which men of learning and sensibility have spoken with great relish about good conversation, and there are just as many in which they have abhorred a lack of conversation where that has existed. But the matter goes much deeper than simply into whether or not there is good conversation. These men will be offended by the entire style of life in a situation in which their companions are by their existential make-up steeped in meaninglessness. Where trivia prevail, sensitive men will form the most far-reaching dissatisfaction with the culture and its works. Its tastes, fashions, economics and politics -- all of these and more will seem to him to be built out of nothing. He will see them as reflections of the false values which he understands to lie at the heart of the culture.

Lostness is one of the consequences of the split between the inner and outer realities. It has been brought up again and again in modern literature. Lostness was the main characteristic of Benjamin in The Graduate. It is basic to much existentialist thought and to the "loss of meaning" which Viktor Frankl has described as the most prevalent spiritual problem in the twentieth century.[2]

The associated tendency toward withdrawal has also been apparent. In the counter-culture of the New Left we saw the classic symptoms of extreme withdrawal.

The "mask of hypocrisy" is another of the problems I mentioned in Chapter 9. It, too, has been commented on many times in modern literature. In fact, the charge of hypocrisy is one of the most frequent complaints the alienation makes against bourgeois culture.

The alienated intellectual has stressed the emptiness of contemporary life in all of its aspects. This isn't to say that the explanations that are given in the literature to explain this emptiness are always the same as I have given. There are many different explanations. There is often a desire to explain the emptiness in economic rather than existential terms, such as in Veblen's The Theory of the Leisure Class. Veblen attributed the false values to the adoption a long time ago of private property and of a "predatory" competitive economic nexus.[3] In so saying, he followed Rousseau. This analysis is different from my own, although in some ways it overlaps with my existential view.

There is another aspect of the substantive cause of the alienation which we still need to consider. The substantive causes are not all matters of culture and lifestyle. We would miss a major aspect if we overlooked the role played by the many difficult social questions that people have had to face during, say, the past three centuries. It could hardly be expected that all reasonable men would share a consensus on these issues. Socialist thought has not consisted exclusively of alienation. It has also been a response to some pressing questions about the role of the industrial "masses" and the means to their well-being in a society which has witnessed the Industrial Revolution and the accompanying "explosion of the multitudes." Since there are several

247

options, it isn't likely that all sensitive men would agree with classical liberals that what has been needed has been more and not less capitalism. There are bound to have been some whose judgment would opt for a socialist solution.

It is diversity rather than consensus that we have inherited from the past. The shattering of the medieval worldview left men unprepared to share a common interpretation.

The capitalism we have known is historically quite new. It has necessarily been less than fully mature. It has not had all of the answers. This would have been true even if the theory of capitalism had been carried out to the letter -- which, of course, it has not. It isn't hard to find much to be alienated against in an immature, imperfect society. Even if classical liberalism had been fully implemented, the cultural existential problems still would have been there to contend with. And classical liberalism would have needed to go much further in developing voluntary solutions to such "social welfare" needs as job security, disability income and old age protection. The difficult issues of the business cycle, of monopoly and of urban development would still cry out for solution. There have been many real, substantive issues. The branches of the Left have proposed a variety of solutions for them. Although I don't think they have offered ultimately constructive solutions, it is obvious that many people will have approached these issues from a socialist perspective.

Herbert Spencer was a thorough-going defender of capitalism, but he was well aware of the imperfections of his age. He readily acknowledged that "it is not to be denied that the evils are great and form a large set-off from the benefits. The system under which we at present live fosters dishonesty and lying. It prompts adulterations of countless kinds; it is answerable for the cheap imitations which eventually in many cases thrust

the genuine articles out of the market; it leads
to the use of short weights and false measures; it
introduces bribery, which vitiates most trading
relations, from those of the manufacturer and
buyer down to those of the shopkeeper and servant."
Spencer joined with the alienate in speaking of
the "depravity of the age." He saw that there
were problems which could elicit the concern of
sensitive men. The reason he was able to retain
his philosophical identification with the culture
was that he realized that "it is not a question of
absolute evils; it is a question of relative
evils." He knew that a depraved humanity had
better not look to socialism for its answers. The
same human qualities which vitiated capitalism
would vitiate socialism, too -- and with much more
dangerous results.[4] But this is the sort of conclusion Spencer and I might reach. Other men who
see the same evils may analyze their causes differently or be more impatient for a remedy.

Emerson wrote along lines that were very
similar to what I have just quoted from Spencer.
We could hardly attempt to explain Emerson's
alienation without addressing ourselves to the
abuses which he himself thought were the source of
it.

The world we live in is exceedingly imperfect.
The imperfection is partly concealed by our affluence, but in many ways it is laid bare. The speed
of change is so great that hardly anything has had
a chance to become settled upon solid foundations.
We haven't had time to develop subtle ways of
dealing with many problems. There are countless
rough edges and there is even a basic inanity.
Needless to say, there are many legitimate substantive issues.

The displacement theory. One of the main
explanations of the alienation of the intellectual
is that the intellectual in modern society has
been displaced from a top-most position in society
and has, as a result, been engaged in an extended

rivalry for prestige and power with the acting man. This "displacement theory" was expressed by Eric Hoffer in The Ordeal of Change in his chapter on "The Intellectual and the Masses." He said that "the rise of the militant intellectual in the Occident was brought about . . . by the introduction of paper and printing . . . The new men of words, like those of the eighth century B. C., were on the whole unattached -- allied with neither Church nor government."[5] The key element is that "they had no clear status, and no self-evident role of social usefulness. In the social orders evolved by the modern Occident, power and influence were, and to a large extent still are, in the hands of industrialists, businessmen, bankers, landowners, and soldiers. The intellectual feels himself on the outside. Even when he is widely acclaimed and highly rewarded he does not feel himself part of the ruling elite . . . Small wonder that he tends to resent those in power as intruders and usurpers."

Hoffer went on to say that "the antagonism between men of words and men of action . . . reappeared in the sixteenth century in the life of the modern Occident and set it apart from all other civilizations." He talked at length about the alliance which the alienated intellectual has so consistently sought with the "masses" -- an alliance which has been essential if the intellectual were to have enough political weight to win in his rivalry with the man of commerce. This alliance is one of the consequences of the alienation which I will discuss in the next chapter. It arises out of the rivalry of the intellectual subculture with the acting man.

Edmund Burke's description of the eighteenth century intellectual sheds some light on the uniqueness of the modern intellectual as a social type. Burke said that "along with the monied interest, a new description of men had grown up with whom that interest soon formed a close and marked union -- I mean the political men of letters. Men of

250

letters, fond of distinguishing themselves, are
rarely averse to innovation. Since the decline
of the life and greatness of Louis the Fourteenth,
they were not so much cultivated either by him or
by the regent or the successors to the crown, nor
were they engaged to the court by favors and emolu-
ments so systematically as during the splendid
period of that ostentatious and not impolitic
reign. What they lost in the old court protection,
they endeavored to make up by joining in a sort of
incorporation of their own." Burke commented on
the negativism which was already apparent: "To
this system of literary monopoly was joined an unremitting industry to blacken and discredit in
every way, and by every means, all those who did
not hold to their faction. To those who have observed the spirit of their conduct it has long been
clear that nothing was wanted but the power of
carrying the intolerance of the tongue and of the
pen into a persecution which would strike at property, liberty, and life."[6]

Marc Raeff describes the development of the
nineteenth century Russian intelligentsia in a way
that corresponds to Burke's observations. Raeff
says that "frustrated and exasperated, the generation of the 1820's turned to the organization of
secret societies and staged the abortive revolt of
December 14, 1825. Their failure, as is well
known, created an irrevocable gulf between the
elite and the state -- the one institution that
through service had been an anchor for the educated class since Peter the Great. The elite had not
yet overcome its isolation from the people, and
now its ties to the state were cut too."[7] This
involved a deep social displacement.

The upshot, according to Raeff, was a sense
of group identity and an emphasis on transforming
society. "Left alone and adrift, its members
turned their energies to find new roots, using the
mental and spiritual traits that had been developed during the eighteenth century. Lacking solid
roots in their family, their region, or their

people, the new generation of the elite sought
meaning for their life in thought and action aimed
at transforming the men and society surrounding
them . . . . The intelligentsia was coming into
being."

A similar development took place in the United
States. Jurgen Herbst's The German Historical
School in American Scholarship tells about the un-
certain status of the American intellectual during
the late nineteenth and early twentieth centuries
and of the intellectual's irritation over his lack
of clear leadership. "In democratic America politics was everybody's business, whereas in Germany
it was the business of experts. When a German-
trained professor returned to his native shores,
eager to contribute his knowledge and skill to the
shaping and guidance of American domestic and
foreign policy, he met with deaf ears on the part
of the statesmen and politicians. Instead of citizens eager for sage counsel and specialized infor-
mation he encountered Americans preoccupied with
their own selfish advancement and cynical toward
scholarly disinterestedness."[8]

In light of the commentaries I have just
cited about the sense of displacement that was felt
by intellectuals in England, Russia and the United
States, Hoffer's explanation makes a great deal of
sense. It seems to me that this is as it should
be. There is no reason to suppose that the intellectual as a human being operates outside the
common tendencies of mankind. A sociological
explanation that is based on the intellectual's
self-interest and his sense of collective identity
is bound to be as true of him as it is of others.
(It is also important, though, to realize that
"economic" or "self-interest" explanations are
rarely the whole truth about anybody. They are
no more likely to be the whole truth about intellectuals than they are about others.) Modern
thought, especially on the Left, has often viewed
the acting man as mainly a creature of his economic
self-interest and his power cravings. A "realistic"

252

portrait of this type amounts to a Machiavellian perception of human motivation. This perception has been a product jointly of the empiricism which has been characteristic in modern thought and of the Left's ideological desire to debunk the motives of its opponents. Because of the latter, the "self-interest" explanation has often been used as a cynical acid. The same acid can just as validly (and invalidly) be used against the intellectual, who is by no means immune to the appeal of self-interest and of drives for power and prestige.

The importance of the displacement theory as an explanation of the alienation is suggested by precisely those many writings in which modern intellectuals have told us that economic and class interest is the main mover of men. When Marx tells us of the all-encompassing importance of class theory, he is by implication telling us that the same applies to himself. When Charles Beard and Thorstein Veblen and Marshall McLuhan describe in subtle detail how human actions are formed out of economic influences, we can hardly think them exempt. Surely such analyses contain a grain of subconscious autobiography.

The role of the intellectual as "intelligentsia," as a distinct social class or subculture engaged in a struggle for power, is evidenced by the frequent elitism of the intellectual and his desire to occupy the topmost place of status and leadership. This elitist striving is apparent in many famous books: the philosopher king was to be on top in Plato's Republic; the intellectual was to constitute a priesthood which would share the topmost spot in Auguste Comte's utopia; in late nineteenth century Germany the "socialist of the professorial chair" valued his role as advisor to the state; in Edward Bellamy's Looking Backward the intellectual was to receive the highest honors.[9] An endless string of authors have wanted to use the modern state for an essentially theocratic purpose -- with the intellectual in the position

of primary influence. Even the socialist movements
which have involved the alliance between the intellectuals and the so-called "masses" and which
have accordingly been most ostensibly democratic
have had this element at their ultimate center,
since it isn't to be supposed that after the
alienated intellectual has succeeeded in his long-
standing rivalry with the man of commerce he will
be satisfied with the quality of those masses.
He will be eager at that time for their reformation
and will dominate them, if he can, for that purpose. If he can't dominate them, he will probably
become their bitter enemy.

The Envy Theory. The displacement and envy
theories are really two sides of the same coin.
The first explains the alienation in terms of
class interest, the other of individual unhappiness.
One is "macro," the other "micro." In the envy
theory we see the psychology of personal resentment.
This individual resentment tends to become an
ideology among those who are equipped to rationalize and articulate it.

A century ago, Sir Henry Maine wrote his famous discussion of the movement of civilization
from status to contract.[10] The individual, Maine
said, is no longer being assigned a place in
society from which he cannot deviate. He is becoming free in modern society to arrange his own
place through voluntary relationships he establish-
es with others. Maine saw this as having been the
tendency within Western society up to the time of
his writing Ancient Law. But during the century
which has followed its publication the tendency has
been very much back the other way. We have continuously added to the status aspects of our society.
This shift back was so evident by the late nineteenth century that Herbert Spencer commented on
it in Man Versus the State.

A comparison has often been made between the
position of an individual within a status society
and his position within a competitive culture. It

254

is argued that the individual in a status society has a basis for being at peace with himself. This was Samuel Johnson's view in the eighteenth century when he argued that "subordination tends greatly to human happiness."[11] The idea is that if a man has inherited, for example, the job of chimney sweep from his father, and his own son will inevitably inherit it from him, he is under no pressure to rise higher. The "system of society" won't let him rise. Accordingly, he feels no nagging frustration over his failure to do so. His status is not a personal reflection on him, since everyone knows it is beyond his control. He has no tendency, then, to form scapegoats to rationalize his lack of success.

I don't agree that this is a totally adequate view of a status society. History shows continuing frustration and alienation within such cultures. The plebeians in the early Roman Republic were not content with their status; they devoted three hundred years to a fight for equal status with the patricians. In the Greek city-states there was a continual "struggle of the orders" between the aristocracy and the have-nots. And in the Middle Ages, the aristocratic hegemony eventually felt the pressure of the tradesman to rise. Contentment is not an accurate portrayal of a status society. Herbert Spencer told how the removal of the restraints of a status society by the old Whigs had been felt as a great positive benefit.

Although this qualification is necessary, a comparison with a status society is still helpful to highlight an aspect of competitive society. In a competitive culture, a person can attend his twentieth year high school reunion and see many who succeeded better than he has. The individual is peculiarly sensitive to his failures. Emulation and "invidious comparison," to use Veblen's phrase, are important to him. But he won't usually accept his inferiority (as he sees himself or as he imagines his friends and especially his wife see him) graciously as the result of a system of

255

natural justice. He will very likely develop defense mechanisms by blaming those who have done
better than he has -- or by blaming "the system."

This rationalization of failure is bound to
be an important psychological mechanism within a
competitive nexus. Richard Weaver said of modern
man that "because he has been assured that he is
'just as good as anybody else,' he is likely to
suspect that he is getting less than his deserts."[12]
Weaver added ominously that "resentment, as Richard Hertz has made plain, may well prove the dy-
namite which will finally wreck Western society."

It's noteworthy that the analyses of Thorstein
Veblen, who was anti-capitalist, and Ludwig von
Mises, who was pro-capitalist, correspond quite
closely on this point. Veblen observed that "as
fast as a person makes new acquisitions, and becomes accustomed to the resulting new standard of
wealth, the new standard forthwith ceases to afford
appreciably greater satisfaction than the earlier
standard did . . . and this in turn gives rise to
a new standard of sufficiency and a new pecuniary
classification of one's self as compared with one's
neighbors." The result bears heavily on the frustration we are discussing: "So long as the comparison is distinctly unfavorable to himself, the
normal, average individual will live in chronic
dissatisfaction with his present lot."

Veblen, of course, arrived at negative value
judgments about the culture he was describing in
these terms. But I commented earlier that John
Bright drew just the opposite conclusion. Bright
thought a "spirit of emulation" was necessary for
human well-being. He took its absence to be an
important cause of the degraded condition of the
average Turk in the nineteenth century.[13] Ludwig
von Mises agreed with Bright when he saw competitiveness and social striving as parts of progressive society and of the freedom of the individual.
This did not blind Mises, though, to the realization that envy is one of the main sources of anti-
capitalist feeling.

Mises said something very close to the passage I have just quoted from Veblen when he commented in The Anti-Capitalist Mentality that "television sets and refrigerators do not make a man happy. In the instant in which he acquires them, he may feel happier than he did before. But as soon as some of his wishes are satisfied, new wishes spring up." He differed from Veblen, though, when he added a favorable value judgment: "This lust (for goods) is precisely the impulse which leads man on the way toward economic betterment."[14]

He distinguished between the situations under status and contract. "In a society based on caste and status, the individual can ascribe adverse fate to conditions beyond his own control." But "it is quite another thing under capitalism . . . Everybody whose ambitions have not been fully gratified knows very well that he has missed chances." He agreed with Veblen when he said that "whatever a man may have gained for himself, it is mostly a mere fraction of what his ambition has impelled him to win . . . Everybody is aware of his own defeat and insufficiency."

The result is an anti-capitalistic philosophy -- a philosophy of alienation. "In order to console himself and to restore his self-assertion, such a man is in search of a scapegoat . . . (He will say that) he was too decent to resort to the base tricks to which his successful rivals owe their ascendancy . . . The more sophisticated do not indulge in personal calumny. They sublimate their hatred into a philosophy, the philosophy of anti-capitalism." Mises said the intellectuals "loathe capitalism because it has assigned to this other man the position they themselves would like to have." He also pointed out how wealthy Americans have made this reaction worse by not including intellectuals in "society," as is done in Europe.

This resentment -- commented upon by both a friend and an enemy of an individualistic society

257

-- is an important cause of the alienation. And
yet, I have already expressed my opinion that it
would be unfair to make it the only explanation.

There are, in fact, good reasons for resentment in human life. This is as true within individualistic society as it is elsewhere. Emerson
said that a young man, on entering commerce, must
forget the prayers of his childhood and take on
the yoke of routine and obsequiousness. Is the
resentment felt by such a man as Emerson something
which we can understand as pure envy? Is there
nothing more to it than a petty man's response to
the achievements of those who work harder and
think better than he does? To think so would be
to entertain far too narrow a perspective. Mises
had one of the finest minds and some of the most
decent instincts in modern thought, but he missed
the complexity of the matter when he wrote that
under capitalism there is "the sway of the principle, to each according to his accomplishments,"
and concluded that the resentment is almost totally a rationalization for inadequacy. No doubt
such rationalizations occur. But so will the quite
distinguishable anger of the sensitive, decent man
against those features of human relationships which
Herbert Spencer referred to as "the depravity of the
age." The resentment can be toward the actual defects in human relations and not just toward personal failure.

At the same time, it is important that the
alienated intellectual come to see that his alienation has some roots which are not as noble as
he has thought them to be. What is needed is that
all parties to the modern controversy take a
broader and fairer look at the polarization.

Before I conclude my discussion of the envy
theory, I should mention that a related part of
its dynamic lies in the psychology of spoiledness,
which I discussed in detail in Chapter 8. Anyone
who takes gratifications for granted as a matter
of entitlement is predisposed to feel resentment.
Since such a person will resent any obstacle or

frustration, resentment is a normal part of his frame of mind. This is itself a source of alienation. It can also be played upon by opportunists and demogogues, both literary and political. Such demagoguery, unfortunately, is a significant part of the Left's program and rhetoric.

A number of years ago, Herbert Spencer remarked sagely that "the more things improve the louder become the exclamations about their badness." He observed that "there has been . . . a conspicuous progress in the condition of the people. And this progress has been still more marked within our own time." But nevertheless there has been perpetual discontent. This is sometimes spoken of as "the revolution of rising expectations." If we analyze it, we see that it is a complicated matter: In part the unhappiness reflects a legitimate sensibility on the part of those who have known that the average man has been held in bondage in the past and have tried to eradicate any vestige of that bondage; in part, though, it reflects the spoiled child mentality; and in part it reflects the manipulation of the "masses" (in a new form of bondage?) by politicians and intellectuals who have used the "masses" as pawns in the strategic game of politics and ideology.

I am especially struck by the trait of spoiledness which is shown by an intellectual who chooses to devote his life to books and self-cultivating things, and then envies the attainments of the man who has been out sweating and grunting. It is an example of "wanting to have your cake and eat it, too." The facticity of life means that years of preoccupation in one direction necessarily carries with it the cost of not having been able to spend years becoming successful in another. To resent that something has not come to him when he has not worked for it is simply to reveal a spoiled state of mind.

Temperament. Despite all of these considerations, I can't be altogether sure just what it is that makes one man live life as it has been presented to him and another stand back and pick it

to pieces through an extraneous sensibility. I
am not sure I understand the root difference, for
example, between Benjamin Franklin and Henry David
Thoreau. Part of the difference was existential:
Franklin enjoyed intellectual communion with
others in the library society that he formed with
some friends, while Thoreau felt deeply isolated
by the poverty of soul he sensed around him. It
may be that there was an increase of an academic
type of intellectuality between their respective
periods, so that the displacement theory plays a
part; but there was an apparent difference in
temperament. These causes were undoubtedly played
upon by the rising Romantic movement in Europe,
which repudiated the Enlightenment and voiced an
intense alienation against bourgeois values.

I have felt the difference in temperament
within myself. It comes up readily even in so
simple a thing as a game of volleyball. A few
years ago, the law firm I was in put on an annual
summer picnic, and part of the afternoon was spent
playing volleyball. I noticed that my own attitude as I played the game differed substantially
from that of most of the other players (who as
lawyers epitomized the aggressiveness of the acting man). My expectation was that I had a certain zone and that if the ball came to me there I
would be entitled to hit it back, but that if it
seemed clearly to be going into someone else's
zone I had a reciprocal obligation to let him get
it. But the result was that I rarely got to hit
the ball at all, even when it came straight toward
me. There were invariably one or two players
muscling in to get in over me, rudely but oblivious-
ly making a spectacular play.

These other players didn't preoccupy themselves with punctilio about how the game was to
be played. They just played it, and they did so
with all the gusto they could muster. They were,
as a result, better players, at least in this in-
formal game where discipline was not a major factor. The main thing was to see that the ball was
returned. These other players were very much in

the game, absorbed in its give-and-take. My own
sensitivity and sense of the decencies withdrew
me into a spectator role, even while the game
raged around me.

This was a difference of personality. It was
too small a matter to reflect a "sociological
rivalry." It was a contrast between contemplation,
introspection and sensitivity, on the one hand,
and a thorough-going absorption in the active
processes of energetic life on the other.

Once this difference is apparent, we can
easily see its ramifications. The intellectual
playing volleyball will resent the other players'
lack of consideration. He will feel himself
absolutely right in saying that "that player does
so well only because he doesn't care anything
about the decencies of the game." And he will
be right. But at the same time, the volleyball
situation is good to show that there is another
side to the story. There is something to be said
for the active man who is able to go ahead effec-
tively without a Hamlet-like introspection. The
case isn't clearly for either type of man.

This difference in temperament deeply separates the two types. They are bound to see most
of life differently. They will espouse contrasting
values, live different lifestyles -- and be antagonistic in many ways. The divisions between them
which relate to the other causes of the alienation
will probably relate in some way to this difference
even though this difference in personality isn't
the sum total of the split between them. The other
causes continue to play their separable but complementary roles.

In a newspaper column, Jeffrey Hart commented
on this aspect of temperament as it relates to
those who select an academic career. "I think that
one main factor can be singled out," he wrote.
"It has to do with the nature of the decision to
enter upon an academic career. I have worked
closely with undergraduates who were considering
a teaching career and with graduate students who

261

were preparing themselves for such an occupation
. . . Quite characteristically, the decision (to
enter academic life) is . . . powerfully negative
-- not, very definitely not, to become a doctor
or an engineer or an admiral or an executive, not
to participate in quite that direct a way in the
ordinary life of the society" (Emphasis added).
He went on to say that "this negative decision,
the decision against the ordinary life of society,
may flow from any number of sources --temperamental,
ideological, neurotic, and so on. It may even be
only half-conscious and unavowed. But it is a
reality in a great many instances." He said that
"the intensity of the No said to society varies
in a fairly predictable way from department to department. Those that tend to be involved with
the life of the outer society . . . attract a personality type likely to be on much more genial
terms with society than do, say, religion, philosophy, and higher mathematics." He concluded
that "in my opinion this is the main factor in
faculty leftwardness."[15]

Anti-bourgeois intellectual traditions. The
problem of understanding the alienation isn't
entirely one of explaining its immediate causes.
In part, at least, it is a matter of seeing
that the alienation against commercial culture has
always been a strong factor in European thought
and that the modern alienation is a continuation
of it. The alienation wasn't made up out of
wholecloth at some point in the eighteenth or
nineteenth centuries. The more I have studied the
history of ideas in Europe, the more weight I have
been convinced to give to the aspect of continuity.
The alienation was fed by powerful streams that
flowed into the modern era.

There was, of course, a torrent of aristocratic thought that never admitted the case for
modernity. Among other things, it looked on the
tradesman and the average man as vulgarians. If
we consider even the milder expressions of such
views as they were voiced in England, major

262

literary names stand out: Samuel Johnson, Edmund Burke, Thomas Carlyle, Samuel Coleridge, John Ruskin, Matthew Arnold and Robert Southey. By the time socialism began to rise in England in the middle of the nineteenth century, the alienation was already at a high pitch. And the situation in England paled by comparison to the continent, where the anti-rationalist, anti-bourgeois backlash following the French Revolution carried a great many intellectuals to mystical and totalitarian extremes.

Another stream was the socialist theory that had been extant throughout history. It can be seen in the writings of Campanella and Sir Thomas More. It offered the foundation for a collectivist critique of society.

There were also some important strands of Christian thought which lent themselves to an opposition to a competitive, secular, individualistic social order. Christian thought has had so many different sides to it that it is misleading to generalize about it as a whole. There is much in it that would support capitalism and the middle class, and there is at the same time much that would provide a strong basis for opposition. We should recall that when Bernard Mandeville wrote The Fable of the Bees he had to speak of individual self-interest as though it were a vice -- and then to argue a paradox, that it is precisely men's "vices" that are a source of human betterment. The British Fabian socialist R.H. Tawney was able to relish a good many medieval values that contrasted with later capitalist values.

Reproduction of the alienation. Once the alienation existed, it reproduced itself from generation to generation, passing from aristocrat to socialist. The ideas have been passed on by an immense and continuing literature. If a present-day college student, for example, has the slightest tendency to feel hostility toward the society in which he lives, he will find instant reinforce-

263

ment in countless books and movies. These will provide him with an extensive and sophisticated rationale for his alienation.

In Chapter 16 I will talk about the youth movement in Germany both before and after World War I. The movement involved a passionate dislike for bourgeois society. This movement led directly to the totalitarian ideologies and reflected them as they existed at that time. Both Marxism and National Socialism were nourished by the youth movement's alienation. But it is worth noticing that the movement was just picking up the alienation which already existed in the preceding generation of intellectuals. Despite the movement's emphasis on youth and novelty, its members embraced the many forms of alienation that came down to them through the Romantics and Hegel and the Volkish thinkers and the Historical School and the Marxists, to mention just a few of the many sources. It was a movement that in many ways is analogous to the New Left of the 1960's. In neither movement did the young originate their own ideas, despite a lot of talk about a "generation gap"; they wrapped themselves, instead, in the ideas of the rebels of the preceding generation. They were in rebellion against their middle class parents, but this was not the same thing as a repudiation of the already-existing intellectual subculture. Such New Left authors as Marcuse, Brown and Alinsky, who were themselves not young, embodied the earlier influence of Fourier, Marx and Rousseau. The slogans of the Russian Revolution were popular, although they weren't recognized by an historically illiterate American public.

The alienation has not existed just in such visible outpourings, however, as the German youth movement or the later New Left. The alienation has colored the Left in general and was profoundly important in National Socialism in Germany. It has also been one of the main roots of modern liberalism in America.

Alternative explanations. The six explanations I have given are the ones that seem to me to be the strongest, but our society is sufficiently complicated that a good many other factors can be pointed to in an even more extensive list.

Jeffrey Hart surmised that still another cause may exist in the rationalism of the modern intellectual, since this questioning frame of mind may lead to dissatisfaction with an unplanned society. It is satisfying, for example, to be able to spell out the optimum operation of the Mexican economy in a set of equations on a blackboard. The intellectual as a model-builder and specialist may prefer a nice predictability which isn't to be found in a voluntaristic society.

Hart also suggested that the alienation may stem in part from personal problems in people's lives. Some problem may cause a verbalized response if the person doesn't feel he can come to grips with it.

At the end of his anthology on alienation in the 1920's, Henry May included a brief chapter on the causes. Although he didn't personally endorse each of the explanations he listed, they include:

• The view that the intellectuals of the period were "deluded . . . immature and ignorant" and took a superficial view of the society they criticized. According to May, this was the view taken by V. L. Parrington in 1929 and Bernard DeVoto in 1942. May acknowledged that some of the alienates of the 1920's may have been superficial, but he didn't think that this was sufficient to explain the alienation as a whole. For my part, I agree with May. The alienation often involves, either as cause or effect, a loss of balance of values; but it just isn't sensible to try to dispose of the serious issues that are raised by the alienation by attacking the thinkers themselves as ignorant. The alienation is too deeply rooted in a number of significant aspects of modern life.

• The possibility that they were correct in their criticisms. This is the same thing as the "substantive explanation" that I have talked about already.

• The idea that World War I brought on the alienation. May says that the alienation preceded the war, so that the war can't be the main explanation. This becomes especially apparent when we consider that the alienation existed for a century before World War I. But this doesn't mean that a war is totally irrelevant. As with the Vietnam War, a conflict can serve as a catalyst to bring the alienation into the open and to attract additional people. In some cases, as with Tsarist Russia, war can play a major role in weakening the existing regime and can set the stage for effective political action by those who are alienated.

• The Marxist interpretation that capitalism was in decline and that it was predictable that the intellectual would become alienated at some point in the dialectical movement toward revolution. May correctly says that this point depends upon the validity of the Marxist interpretation of history. Since I consider "dialectical materialism" an unscientific pretension, I don't give this explanation any weight.

• The possibility that the middle class was in decline. I agree that a growing void or insufficiency in classical liberal thought was both a cause and a consequence of the alienation. I have chosen to discuss it among the consequences of the alienation when we review them in the next chapter.

• The related view that there has been a "loss of faith." This attributes the alienation to the loss of consensus that occurred as Europe emerged from the age of faith. This point is similar to what I said in my chapters on Greece, Rome and the Middle Ages when I argued that modern society has received a rich variety of suggestions from the past, but no paradigms. Rationalism and secularism have left the world open for debate, just as the Romans were left without a consensus by the disintegration of the mos maiorum. No thorough-going consensus has come in to take the place of the shattered hegemony of traditionalism and faith. I might add that a Burkean conservative would argue that modern man has lost sight of the reality of God, and that this would inevitably lead to quarrels among the many competing gnostic creeds.

• A suggestion that the Puritan heritage left an intensity of emotion and even fanaticism which carried over to the modern intellectual. Both in the United States and Russia the clergy was an important source for the alienated intelligentsia, and in each case the clergy had a tradition of intense emotion and "righteousness." The history of nineteenth century American radicalism shows clearly that the New England clergy was an important factor.

• The thought that democracy lends itself to conflict of opinion, even though it also involves aspects of conformity. This point undoubtedly has some profound implications, but even superficially we can see that a free society permits the expression of alienation. This contrasts sharply with a totalitarian state such as the Soviet Union, where a great deal of alienation is simply not allowed to become an overt movement.

These many suggested causes show that the subject is by no means closed. There are as many assignable causes as there are facets of the civilization.

My Evaluation of the Causes

So far, I have discussed a number of contributing causes, but without trying to weigh their relative importance. It seems to me, though, that some are clearly more important than others.

At first, I was inclined to give the substantive explanation the highest priority. I was sensitive myself to the cultural and intellectual deficiencies to which the alienated intellectual pointed. And it is far more charitable to give the intellectuals credit for responding mainly to defects than it is to emphasize other causes for their dissatisfaction.

I have reluctantly changed my mind from this more charitable view to conclude that the envy-displacement-temperament causes have been the most important. The reason for my change of mind is that the response which the alienated intellectual has made to his alienation has been inconsistent with the type of response that could be expected if the substantive problems were his main grievance. It is a response which only makes sense in the context of the intellectuals' tactical position in modern society and their alliance with the have-nots.

One part of the substantive causes have to do with the existential problems of the middle class: the trivialization, the suffocation of higher values, the isolation of the radical solitude, the heightening of hypocrisy, the "political" nature of human relationships and the loss of connection with other human beings. If these defects had been the main cause of the alienation from bourgeois culture, what would have been the intellectuals' most effective and natural reaction? In answering, we must keep in mind that the bourgeois society has been a free society and that, in addition, it has made abundant means available to its intellectuals as a part of its general affluence. In such a setting, the intellectuals could have immersed themselves in their own serious work, flooding their own academic communities and a good deal of the remainder of the society with excellent art, music, literature, research and thought.

They could have affirmed in countless ways a creed that would <u>not</u> be trivial and would <u>not</u> involve hypocrisy or a suffocation of higher meaning. They could have announced a creed of elevation and ennoblement.

Tens of thousands of intellectuals creating an ennobled, elevated, humanistic literature, art and music could do everything that would be necessary to give the culture in which they live the elements they have felt it to lack. Even our tenth-rate universities bring together more people with doctorates than Athens was ever able to aggregate in credentialed intellectuality in any one generation. Just from the universities themselves the culture could be flooded with great art and sculpture. The intellectuals themselves and those they could inspire among their millions of students could constitute a readership for a literature which could be the finest the world has ever seen. There would be enough such people to create a market for worthwhile things. When we would turn on our car radios we would be able to find perhaps one or two or even three stations playing beautiful music. A profound cultural renaissance would emanate from the university campuses. If there were people in the broader community who were somehow able to go untouched by its influence, their presence would be of little matter to the intellectuals themselves. The creative man would have his own rewarding life within a milieu which in countless ways would offer him a sense of community with others.

But it is necessary instead to compare this natural response with the actual response most modern intellectuals have made. Instead of throwing themselves into creative effort for an easy transcending of the mediocrity they have seen around them, they have been willing -- even anxious -- to become chronic complainers. They have been pleased to create a literature, art, and music of complaint and dissonance. They have elevated the anti-hero and, consistently with the

269

alliance with the have-nots and their rivalry with the acting man, they have launched a relativistic attack on standards and values.

The dissonance does nothing to ennoble or to give meaning. It doesn't make sense if we think that the intellectuals' main concern has been to overcome triviality and lack of meaning. But it becomes quite understandable when we think of attack and complaint as weapons. They have been weapons against the acting man of bourgeois culture.

Likewise, the anti-hero is hard to fathom if we think the intellectual has mainly resented the emptiness of bourgeois life. But the anti-hero is an appropriate vehicle in the context of the alliance with the have-nots and of the opposition to so-called "middle class values." The have-not has had real needs during the past two centuries, but one thing is, in general, clear about him: he is not a hero himself. Those who pander to him can't do so by elevating the hero. They have to put themselves on the level of the have-not and speak to him on his own terms. He will often be receptive to an attack on the "middle class virtues" of hard work, prudence, thrift, responsibility and self-reliance. By opposing such bourgeois aspirations, the alienated intellectual can attack the society he dislikes and at the same time cultivate his political, ideological alliance with the have-nots.

Much of the specific ideology of the Left follows from this: the relativism which denies the possibility of values, the "environmentalist assumption" which takes all responsibility off the individual and places it on "society," the view of the state as the protector of enfeebled men, the theory that capitalistic society is overwhelmingly exploitive.

William Barrett praised "modern art" in Irrational Man because of its "confession of spiritual poverty." He said this has been its "greatness and its triumph."[16] Such praise, for such a reason, will seem incredible to anyone who is not deeply affected by the spiritual neuroses of the Left. "Realism" has appeal as an expression of truth, but this is a far cry from dwelling for decade after decade on the depravity of man. Such a dwelling is by no means a realistic view of man. Our age has mastered technique, but I have no doubt that the future will look back on much of our art as an aberration. It will probably see the finest work of our time in the paintings, instead, of such men as Andrew Wyeth and Norman Rockwell.

Tennessee Williams contributed an introduction to Carson McCullers' Reflections in a Golden Eye. The back cover describes the book as "an artistic vision of a human hell." The cover goes on to say that "this particular hell is an army post in the South. Its inhabitants: a sexually disturbed officer; his sensual animal of a wife; his fellow-officer and wife's lover; a delicate, sensitive woman who must live with her husband's infidelity; and the driven young Private who brings the searing drama to a head. From these elements, one of America's superlative writers has produced a vision of existence as terrible as it is real." In his introduction, Tennessee Williams wrote that "Reflections in a Golden Eye is one of the purest and most powerful of those works which are conceived in that Sense of the Awful which is the desperate black root of nearly all significant modern art, from the Guernica of Picasso to the cartoons of Charles Addams."[17] (Emphasis added)

The relationship of this literature and art to the Left was apparent in the "revolutionary theater" of the late 1960's. Screams and writhing bodies and dissonant rhetoric constituted the dramatic medium. The Sense of the Awful was a direct anti-bourgeois tool.

Joseph Schumpeter reached the same conclusion I am expressing that the social rivalry of the

271

intellectual has been a more important determinant
of the intellectual's ideology and behavior than
has his concern over defects in bourgeois lifestyle. In Capitalism, Socialism and Democracy,
Schumpeter spoke of "a group interest shaping a
group attitude that will much more realistically
account for the hostility to the capitalist order
than could the theory -- itself a rationalization
in the psychological sense -- according to which
the intellectual's righteous indignation about the
wrongs of capitalism simply represents the logical
inference from outrageous facts."[18] He also spoke
of the effect on the intellectual of the political
necessity of appealing to the have-not: "Having
no genuine authority and feeling always in danger
of being unceremoniously told to mind his own
business, he must flatter, promise and incite,
nurse left wings and scowling minorities, sponsor
doubtful or submarginal cases, appeal to fringe
ends, profess himself ready to obey -- in short,
behave toward the masses as his predecessors be-
haved first toward their ecclesiastical superiors,
later toward princes and other individual patrons,
still later toward the collective master of bourgeois complexion."

    Nietzsche made a similar point when he said
that "decadence is only a means for the type of
man who demands power in Judaism and Christianity,
the priestly type."[19] We can see this in practice
when the modern intellectual dwells on "the
poverty of the soul." He has a definite interest
in making mankind sick.

    I have commented at length on the existential
emptiness within our society, but one thing must
be said: that our society has nevertheless made
vast resources available to its intellectuals.
They enjoy magnificent university facilities, great
libraries, excellent concert halls and galleries,
and a leisured campus life. This suggests that it
is most appropriate to blame the emptiness, when
it continues, not so much on the acting man as on
the intellectual. It has been by becoming a

chronic complainer and a spokesman for the anti-
hero that the intellectual has made George Babbitt
a continuing reality.

There is still another aspect of the substantive cause for the alienation to consider,
though. Matters of aesthetics and lifestyle
have not been the only basis for the intellectual's
complaints. As I commented earlier, the substantive issues also include all of the economic and
political arguments against capitalism.

But even here, there are good reasons to
assign the substantive cause a secondary place.
One is that, on balance, the economic and political criticisms of capitalism do not have nearly
enough merit to account for their influence. Since
this is a major subject in itself, I will have to
leave the various economic and political issues
for discussion in my books that survey the competing ideological systems. All I can do at this
point is to express my conclusion.

But there is a more definitive point, too.
It is that the chronology of the nineteenth century
shows that the alienation preceded, did not follow,
the period of classical liberal ascendancy.
Capitalism wasn't tried and seen to fail before
the intelligentsia developed its hatred for it.
The hatred came first. In the United States, the
alienation began in the generation of Emerson and
Thoreau. This was still during the pre-Civil War
age of local, small-shop capitalism, well before
the smokey industrialism and tendency toward concentration that are usually pointed to when we
receive our impression of why intellectuals abhorred capitalism. In England, the landed aristocracy -- not the middle class -- controlled both
the politics and the economy until after the passage of the Reform Act of 1832. Even then it
took Richard Cobden years of struggle to gain even
a partial adoption of the Free Trade position.
When Chartism showed its hostility, the bourgeoisie and capitalism had hardly been given a chance.

273

In Germany, there was little capitalism until late
in the century. But this didn't deter Karl Marx
from devoting his life (mostly in England) to
excoriating it. His theories, and those of Lassalle and others, were not precipitated by terrible experience. They were a priori, the product
of agitated minds, not of history itself. In
Russia, socialist radicalism began before mid-
century. There was almost no capitalism at that
time.

It is noteworthy that socialist thinkers have
often assigned the vices of landed aristocracy
to the incipient capitalism, as though classical
liberalism and the landed aristocracy were a single
continuous phenomenon and had not been bitter
enemies. In England, the achievements of the factory system in raising the length of life and the
standard of living were overlooked. The over-
crowding and misery captured all the attention --
and it made no difference that these were in large
measure caused by the landowners' tariff on grain,
the Enclosure Acts by which aristocrats had long
forced people off the land and into the towns, and
the immigration from poverty-stricken Ireland.
There is an apparent overeagerness to dress capitalism with a crown of thorns when socialists blame
it for these things.

The answer can be, of course, that thinkers
don't have to wait to see how something will turn
out before they can conscientiously oppose it.
And that will be true. But it is an argument by
way of "confession and avoidance." It confesses
or bypasses the aspect of whether or not the
socialist authors were justified in their condemnation of capitalism by the facts as they then
existed. It then leaves the question of whether
an a priori condemnation was called for. In order
to answer this, we need to think back to what the
situation was. Europe was just emerging from the
age of kings and aristocracy. Omnipresent feudal
remnants were just being brushed away. The liberty of the individual was being championed. Was it

274

a time for optimism, for hope, for an enthusiastic
exploration of what a society of free men could
do? Classical liberalism certainly thought so.
But not the socialist critics. To them, it was
already self-evident that a market economy would
breed entrapment and exploitation rather than
meaningful freedom. And why did they opt for that
conclusion? I believe it was not because the conclusion was irresistible, but because they already
felt a profound alienation from other causes. If
I am correct, the other causes of the alienation
have to be given greater weight than the substantive complaints.

NOTES

1. Henry May (ed.), The Discontent of the Intellectuals: A Problem of the Twenties (Chicago:
Rand McNally, 1963), pp. 31, 56-59.

2. Viktor E. Frankl, Man's Search for Meaning
(New York: Clarion Books, 1962), p. 108.

3. Thorstein Veblen, The Theory of the Leisure
Class (New York: Mentor Books, 1953), pp. 30,
38-39.

4. Herbert Spencer, The Man Versus the State
(Baltimore: Penguin Books, 1969), pp. 315-316,
63-77, 70, 312, 313.

5. Eric Hoffer, The Ordeal of Change (New York:
Perennial Library, 1963), pp. 38-39.

6. Edmund Burke, Reflections on the Revolution in
France (New York: Liberal Arts Press, 1955),
pp. 126-128.

7. Marc Raeff, Origins of the Russian Intelligentsia (New York: Harcourt, Brace & World, Inc.,
1966), p. 170.

8. Jurgen Herbst, The German Historical School in American Scholarship (Cornell University Press, 1965), p. 173.

9. Edward Bellamy, Looking Backward (New York: Modern Library, 1942), p. 132.

10. Sir Henry Sumner Maine, Ancient Law (New York: Charles Scribner, 1964), p. 163.

11. James Boswell, The Life of Samuel Johnson (New York: Modern Library, 1952), p. 121.

12. Richard M. Weaver, Ideas Have Consequences (Chicago: University of Chicago Press, 1948), p. 43.

13. R. A. J. Walling (ed.), The Diaries of John Bright (New York: William Morrow and Company, 1931), p. 41.

14. Ludwig von Mises, The Anti-Capitalist Mentality (Princeton: D. Van Nostrand Company, Inc., 1956), pp. 4, 11-13, 14-16, 19, 12.

15. Jeffrey Hart, newspaper column entitled "What Makes a Ph.D. Run?"

16. William Barrett, Irrational Man (Garden City: Doubleday & Company, Inc., 1958), p. 40.

17. Carson McCullers, Reflections in a Golden Eye (New York: Bantam Books, 1941), p. xiv.

18. Joseph Schumpeter, Capitalism, Socialism and Democracy (New York: Harper and Brothers, 1947), pp. 153, 154.

19. Friedrich Nietzsche, The Portable Nietzsche, trans. Walter Kaufmann (New York: Viking Press, 1968), pp. 593-594.

12

CONSEQUENCES OF THE ALIENATION

Modern life has its own dynamic, with major forces pulling and tugging within it. I hope I have said enough to show that the alienation of the intellectual is one of the more important factors in the dynamic. The history especially of the past century has been significantly different than it would have been if the alienation hadn't been present. In the absence of the alienation, modern society would have had a far more "normal" development. With it, though, the European and American cultures -- and through them all other peoples, too -- have grown in an atmosphere tainted by bitter tension. The hegemony of the Middle Ages has given way to major conflicting value systems. The tension has given rise to mass ideologies and secular religions. At the same time, other needed developments have atrophied.

Nothing was so important to the rise of European socialism as alienation. It was a major contributor to the cultural and intellectual chaos that led to Hitler in Germany and consequently to World War II. It incubated Marxism and Leninism. The consequences of this have been evident in the Soviet Union, China, Eastern Europe, and in such places as Korea, Vietnam, Cambodia, Cuba and Chile. They have appeared in the "protracted conflict" of the Cold War which has made (and which, despite "detente," continues to make) the intellectuals' alienation a discoloring element in the future direction of the so-called Third World. The alienation has deflected the spiritual and intellectual essence of American life; it has led to modern American liberalism and most recently to the New Left, while the classical liberalism which has supported the great middle class and individual liberty has suffered from severe undernourishment.

277

The alienation has had these effects within the context of the "explosion of the multitudes" and of expanding technology, secularism and science. It has by no means been the only force at work. But without the alienation, who can say what modern history might have been or the present map of the world would show?

The remaining chapters of this book will each deal with one aspect or another of the alienation's consequences. The purpose of the present chapter, though, is more general; it is to discuss the many consequences in their overall sweep. I'll be doing this under three large headings. The first will deal with the immensely significant rise of the Left during the modern period. The second will relate the alienation to the otherwise inexplicable hierarchy of values within the psychology of the alienated intellectual. And the third will discuss the effect of the alienation on the development of capitalism and of classical liberal thought.

The Rise of the Left

I will attribute the rise of socialism very largely to the alienation, but I am afraid that this may create a false impression. It would be a mistake to think that the alienation created socialist thought per se. Socialist models were full-blown at least as long ago as the ancient Greeks. One of Aristophanes' comedies explored the scheme of a fully egalitarian community, having a hilarious time with the fact that it included equality among even the beautiful and the ugly in sexual relations.[1] When we consider the entire history of humanity, it is collectivism rather than individualism that has been most typical of the human experience.

However, if we ask why there has been a vast socialist movement during our particular period of history -- an angry movement which has chal-

lenged capitalism, the middle class and individual
liberty despite the visibility of their achievements --, we find a number of contributing factors;
but the towering hatred the modern intellectual
has felt against the culture in which he has lived
stands out as the foremost among them. This hatred
has given continuous impetus and articulation to
the socialist movement for two and a half centuries
since Rousseau, elaborating it, picking it up if
ever it has flagged, kindling it into a major intellectual and spiritual force. It has stood out
in the literature of our time and has been the
powerful dynamic factor within the emergence of
socialism.

A subculture. The dissatisfaction felt by
the modern intellectual has been the link which
has brought together the diverse factions in
modern social thought. It's symbolically significant, for example, that Werner Sombart was able
to move from a prominent place in the German Historical School into Marxism and then into National
Socialism. This was an extensive intellectual
migration which involved moving from one faction
to another and then to another, despite all the
vituperation which each faction voiced against the
others. But each of the movements embodied an
extreme anti-bourgeois alienation. What was constant was that throughout his migration Sombart
was able to maintain this alienation.[2] When I say
that modern intellectuality has constituted a subculture, I shouldn't be taken to mean that all
alienated intellectuals have shared the same views.
In fact, there has been an amazing diversity. The
lack of homogeneity is just as evident within
socialist thought as it is elsewhere. And yet
overwhelmingly the intellectuals have been set off
against the rest of the culture. They have differed internecinely about the particular model of
society they would substitute for bourgeois culture and about the best way to effect change, but
they have been almost unanimous in their antipathy
toward the predominant culture. They have formed,
as Burke said, a "corporation" of their own.

The existence of a subculture of the intelligentsia is what gives modern social thought the
"herd quality" that is so often evident. Conservatives in the United States have often referred
to "knee-jerk liberals." This refers to the
kind of person who responds predictably, both
intellectually and emotionally, in line with the
current fashion of the intellectual mass.

This involves considerable faddishness. The
subculture is swept by fashions of opinion and
emotion, sometimes of lifestyle. While this is
true with regard to political and social issues,
it is also true within academic subject-matter.
Intellectuals yearn to be "in the swim." Anyone
who isn't is made aware of his anti-social mal-
evolence. The subculture, having a virtual monopoly on the articulation of ideas, constitutes a
modern Orthodoxy. But no orthodoxy perceives itself as such. The modern Left is convinced that
the ideas it espouses aren't ideas at all: that
they are realities. In academic life the truisms
of the subculture take their place as the criteria
for scholarly performance; they permeate the
journals and the research; they become the basis
for doctoral dissertations and even of entire dis-
ciplines. And by occupying all spaces, they
smother alternatives. The orthodoxy has intricate-
ly institutionalized itself. In turn, the institutions drive off those who by temperament or intellectual inclination would prefer a different approach. For example, a student who isn't disposed
toward highly mathematical and narrowly empirical
studies in a modern liberal environment finds himself profoundly at odds with higher education in
the United States today.

The alliance with the "have-nots." The subculture is politically impotent just by itself.
It lacks the power it wants in modern society.
The result is, as Eric Hoffer has said, that the
modern intellectual "has consistently sought a
link with the underprivileged. So far, his most
potent alliance has been with the masses."[3]

The intellectual has sought this alliance far more avidly than have the masses themselves. Very often the masses have been totally lethargic toward it. It has required a prodigious effort on the part of the intellectual.

The alliance is what most typifies the modern left, however. What we call the Left is a coalition between the alienated intellectual and the have-nots against the main society. The alliance is a unique feature. Because of it, the Left includes an ingredient that makes it distinct from generic socialist thought as that thought existed among the ancient Greeks and will probably exist in future ages. The alliance means, too, that the Left is as much a matter of tactics and of sheer political expedience as it is of pure thought. And it embodies its own "internal contradiction" (to use a Marxist phrase) born out of the difference between its elitist and vulgarian elements.

Marxism is a good example of the alliance. Marx wrote an elaborate theory of class struggle that described the struggle of the proletariat against the bourgeoisie. But who was Marx himself other than an intellectual who was proselytizing in favor of alienation, socialism and revolution? He worked to create the very "class consciousness" he predicted.

One of the leading New Left philosophers, Herbert Marcuse, did the same. He began by acknowledging that the coalition foreseen by Marx had not actually produced a revolution. Instead of the rich getting richer and the poor poorer, the worker had become better off. In light of these things, we could expect that if it weren't for the alienation everyone, including Marcuse, would rejoice at capitalism's accomplishment. But Marcuse merely shifted his sights. He looked for a new ally for his alienation. If there were still to be a revolution, he said, it would have to come from the oppressed minorities and the disaffected young.[4] We see again the formula of in-

281

tellectual seeking an alliance with the have-not.

In the United States, modern liberalism has involved the alliance. American political writing often refers to "the Roosevelt coalition." Franklin Delano Roosevelt was able to bring together the intellectual, organized labor, the racial and religious minorities, and (by historical accident) the Solid South. This meant that the intellectual was again aligned with the have-nots. In recent years, the Roosevelt coalition has tended to break up, and this has led to considerable consternation inside the liberal movement. There has been much talk of a "New Coalition" which will continue to link the intellectual with the unassimilated elements of society. The McGovern campaign in 1972 sought it unsuccessfully. President Carter was able to put the pieces together in 1976, at least enough for a narrow victory, even though he wasn't identified with the intellectual subculture.

Both in European socialism and in American liberalism, the alliance has resulted in an egalitarian movement with an elitist underlay. Friedrich Hayek was right when he said that "socialism has never and nowhere been at first a working-class movement." He pointed out that "it required long efforts by the intellectuals before the working classes could be persuaded to adopt it as their program."[5]

A tactically warped worldview. Both the alienation and the alliance's incongruous mixture of forces mold the specific content of the Left's ideology. The result is a gigantic warping. The effects are felt in the Left itself and in the larger society. In what follows, I will want to examine some of these effects.

(1) If it weren't for the alienation, modern literature would be very different from what it has been. The alienation is necessarily a major part of the Left's own literature and rhetoric.

This has meant that for well over a century our literary emphasis has been on opposition and social criticism. It is probably safe to say that modern literature has been more incessantly negative than any other literature in history.

(2) Many of the Left's intellectual movements and many aspects of modern thought in general have involved "relativism." The relativism has resulted from two very different sources: empirical science, and the alienated intellectual's tactical need to debunk bourgeois life. Several prominent movements (such as pragmatism, positivism, situation ethics, historicism and cultural relativism) have involved this dual aspect. They have been in tune with a non-provincial empiricism; but they have also served as "debunking" mechanisms.

It's easy to understand how the scientific mind becomes aligned with relativism. An anthropologist, for example, who studies several cultures becomes aware that the customs and beliefs within a given society are just one cultural alternative among many. His breadth of intellectual exposure works against a narrow provincialism. He sees that things are relative to their circumstances and history. I might add that I myself endorse this form of relativism, since it is a valid mode of perception.

On the other hand, there is nothing in relativism which should allow it, by itself, to debunk any culture. It isn't intellectually sound to tell someone to "forget your beliefs and principles and acculturations; everything is relative and there are no truths." The Left does this constantly with bourgeois culture. But it is one thing to strip a people of their provincialisms by showing them that there are alternative approaches; it is quite another thing to be able to show that their beliefs, social structurings, institutions, etc., are wrong on the merits. When relativism is used as a debunking tool, it never takes the argument as far as it has to to be valid. If the

283

argument doesn't actually get into the merits and show that human values aren't well served by the society's existing customs and beliefs, it has no basis for debunking that society. Since Rousseau, relativism has been used as a corrosive acid to undercut bourgeois acculturations and beliefs. But it is doubtful whether the relativistic critics could win the argument on its merits. Even with all its faults, bourgeois society has many features that sustain and advance civilization.

This abused relativism has been the Left's most frequent weapon. Situation ethics was most important for its negative feature -- its opposition to codes of socially enforced moral conduct. Eric Goldman was candid enough to point out that pragmatism has been a "method of doing without the conservative philosophy."[6] Historical relativism has sanctioned a refurbishing of the Middle Ages (a reinterpretation which has been intellectually important to the Left).

There is an example in American Constitutional Law which will help us understand why there has been so much enthusiasm for relativistic approaches. To someone reading twentieth century legal writing for the first time, it seems odd that there has been so much praise for Oliver Wendell Holmes, Jr.'s, statement that "the life of the law has been experience, not logic." By itself, it seems prosaic. We understand the enthusiasm only when we realize that Holmes' statement summed up an important line of attack against the Rule of Law. The Rule of Law is an ideal which seeks stable, known law, applied through general norms which are to be administered even-handedly through a logical process. It is a part of the classical liberal model because it serves two important purposes for an individualistic society: it frees the acting man by giving him dependable guideposts; and it chains down governments by making them govern by known law rather than by short-term command. The refutation of the Rule of Law was vitally necessary for modern liberalism, since the refutation was needed in order to overcome the Constitutional restraints which were holding back the Welfare State and the growth of the federal government. There was an easy link between Holmes' "the life of the law has been experience, not logic" and Charles Evans Hughes' "the Constitution is what the judges say it is." As soon as the latter view was accepted, the door was open for the immense Constitutional changes which have occurred since the late 1930's.

Before leaving this point, it is worth noticing that the opposition to middle class values even goes beyond a relativistic attack. It also distorts the values which the members of the Left would otherwise hold. I doubt whether the "anti-hero" would be a major theme in modern literature if it weren't for the alienation against the so-called middle class ethic and for the alliance with the non-achievers. Nor, in the absence of alienation, would the "Sense of the Awful" which runs through so much modern writing, art, music and poetry be prevalent. When a critic argued that the merit of modern art lies in its portrayal of the "poverty of the soul," he praised a type of art which appeals to the intellectual precisely because of its denial of middle class values. By contrast, bourgeois art doesn't dwell on anguish and poverty of spirit; it deals with the themes of ordinary life.

(3) The reader will recall that we are discussing the ways in which the alienation and the alliance have warped the Left's worldview. One area where the effect has been profound has been the area of social and economic theory. I will want to mention briefly several of the ways this theory has been affected.

Perhaps most importantly, the Left has developed theories of exploitation which interpret life in ways which, if true, make a classical liberal society unthinkable.

Alienation has strongly colored the Left's in-

285

terpretation of the economic history of the Industrial Revolution. It is an interpretation which magnifies the bad and virtually ignores the good.

The Left's opposition to private property is, in one sense, a purely intellectual preference; but in another light it can be seen as a severe weapon against the acting man of commerce.

The alliance with the have-nots has led to significant differences between the ways a classical liberal and a member of the Left perceive the role of the environment in relation to the individual. The Left places little emphasis on the self-starting capabilities of the individual himself; it opposes any deliberate creation of a "moral environment" which will inculcate self-reliant values; and it stresses the pressing, entrapping, monolithic nature of the environment. The Left arrives at this set of prejudices because of its opposition to middle class ethical values and because of its alliance with the have-nots. These two factors are at work in the Left's usual way of seeing welfare recipients: the Left isn't about to advise them about, or judge them by, their responsibilities; and it will almost always accept the recipient's own view that his problems are mainly the fault of "society."

(4) In my book on socialism, I will discuss the "layered" quality of the Left. The Left's outer mask is often majority rule. But egalitarianism is a more basic value, and will be pursued independently of the majority if the majority isn't disposed to support it. Deeper still, underneath the egalitarianism, there is the elitism of the intelligentsia. To this elitism, equality is not ultimately a goal; it is only a crucially important tactical device as a way of cutting down the acting man and of gaining political support from the have-nots. The Left can only be understood by reference to this hierarchy of elements.

By leading to the rise of the Left, the

alienation has profoundly affected the world at
large. We often hear that the entire globe has
been Westernized during the past century. But
the Westernization has been accomplished in two
ways, and this dualism has carried into the other
areas of the world the divisions which have
characterized modern Western civilization. First,
the world has been Westernized by the spread of
Western technology and cultural influences. This
would have happened even if the alienation had
been absent. But second, the West's intellectual
influences have infected Asia, Africa and Latin
America with the same neurotic relationship between the intellectual and the culture as has
been so typical of Europe and America. This means
that the world has fallen heir to a civilization
which has long suffered an existential crisis.
This makes even more problematic the future of
the non-European world which is filling up and
becoming more participative. As the whole world
"comes into its own," it does so with considerable
cosmic immaturity and without really constructive
leadership -- especially in the intellectual and
spiritual areas -- from the catalytic civilization
of the West.

The Alienated Intellectuals' Hierarchy of Values

        The intellectual's alienation against the
predominant culture necessarily affects his perception of values relating to that culture. Instead of the "balance of values" that a person
who is more attuned to the culture would seek,
he will tend to place a high value on the reformist
measures that he thinks are desirable and to deni-
grate all else. Precisely because of his alienation, these other values will be given little or
no weight, or will be rejected totally. The result
will be an orientation which people who identify
with the culture will view as extreme. The
extent of the extremity will depend largely on the
extent of the alienation.

This difference in value-orientation is illustrated if we compare the positions of the Abolitionists and the Jacksonians before the Civil
War. In his Farewell Address in 1837, Andrew
Jackson spoke of the Union with reverence. He
said that "at every hazard and by every sacrifice
this Union must be preserved." He pointed out
that Washington had considered the Constitution
an experiment, but he added: "The trial has been
made. It has succeeded beyond the proudest hopes
of those who framed it. Every quarter of this
widely extended nation has felt its blessings
and shared in the general prosperity produced by
its adoption."[7] Jackson valued American society
and its institutions. And because he did, it wasn't
surprising that he went on in his speech to warn
against anything that would tend to shatter the
union. He spoke first against movements of
nullification and secession. Then he spoke against
the anti-slavery agitation, warning that it could
break the bonds that had been formed by the
Constitution. He used fairly strong language:
"Rest assured that the men found busy in this work
of discord are not worthy of your confidence, and
deserve your strongest reprobation." Martin Van
Buren expressed similar views in his Autobiography
when he said that the original union of the thirteen former colonies had necessarily subsumed that
the slavery which existed in the Southern states
didn't befoul them. Van Buren felt that it
wouldn't be honorable both to declare their institutions intolerable and to insist that the political union with them be continued. "If our
participation in the protection which the Federal
Constitution extends to the institution of slavery
had become intolerable to us, and we had satisfied
ourselves that the interests of humanity would
gain more by our release from that obligation
than they would lose by a dissolution of the
Union, there was one way in which we could obtain
an honorable discharge and that was by tendering
to our brethren of the slave holding states a
peaceable and voluntary dissolution."[8] During the
years that preceded the Civil War, the Jacksonian

288

presidents continued to say that the problem of slavery was subordinate in importance to the value of preserving Constitutional order.

The values held by the alienated intellectuals, however, stood in sharp contrast to these views. In Walden and the Essay on Civil Disobedience, Henry David Thoreau voiced strong alienation against American culture -- and also against its politics and institutions. On the slavery issue, he said he would be disgraced to be associated with the American government. "I cannot for an instant recognize that political organization as my government which is the slave's government also."9 In an extremely illuminated passage, he said that "seen from a lower point of view, the Constitution, with all its faults, is very good; the law and the courts are very respectable; even this State and this American government are, in many respects, very admirable and rare things, to be thankful for, such as a great many have described them; but seen from a point of view a little higher, they are what I have described them; seen from a higher still, and the highest, who shall say what they are, or that they are worth looking at or thinking of at all?" In saying this, he was expressing a hierarchy of values which was diametrically opposed to the balance of values held by the Jacksonians. The difference between them is explained by Thoreau's alienation, which raised his reformist objectives in his mind and devalued everything else.

We know what followed in American history: the Civil War, the freeing of the slaves, the Reconstruction, and much else. Slavery was abolished and the Union was kept together. Many people conclude, then, that the abolitionist was right. But the success of northern arms obscures the nature of the choice men had to make in the 1830's, 1840's and 1850's. Thoreau's choice ran a terrible risk. The American union could have been destroyed. The likelihood was that the South would secede without the North being able to force it back. In

289

that case, slavery would not have been abolished. The two countries would almost certainly have continued to fight wars over the extension westward. It was this that was most likely. Thoreau was willing to risk it because he hardly valued the things that would have been destroyed.

The circumstances and issues of Russian history were different, but the behavior of the Russian intelligentsia during the nineteenth and early twentieth centuries shows the same relationship between alienation and a value-orientation which denies a balance of values. The nihilist Nechayev proclaimed that "we live in the world to destroy it."[10] The Tsar Alexander II was known as "The Great Reforming Tsar," but the nihilists rejected his work and eventually, after many tries, succeeded in assassinating him. In the next generation, their counterparts rejected the constitutional system established after the revolution of 1905. Twelve years later, they overthrew the Kerensky regime, which was ineffectual but democratic. In their hierarchy of values, few if any values existed which counted other than the revolutionary values they held so high.

The same is evident in revolutionary Marxism. No matter what the accomplishments of the contemporary world may be, they are to be smashed and ruled over by a dictatorship so that a utopian ideal may (hopefully) be achieved. From the point of view of anyone who does not share in the intense alienation and who therefore sees modern life as a gigantic human enterprise that involves countless competing values and interests which must be harmonized into a free and civilized order, Marx's prescription is insane. If that person is to understand Marx, he must understand the alienation's effects on value structures.

The same was true of the revolutionary portion of the New Left in the United States in the late 1960's and early 1970's. We have seen that Herbert Marcuse expressed a total alienation from American culture. Because of this, he was able to formulate a type of Marxism which interpreted American freedom and well-being as mere soporifics that were intended to put a sheep-like population to sleep. Even though he acknowledged the improvement of the condition of the average person during the past century, he still craved revolution -- and again in the name of a utopian vision. His alienation made a balance of values impossible.

A "balance of values" shouldn't be used to defend all existing social orders regardless of their content. But in each of the instances I have cited, and in many others besides, the singleness of purpose has sacrificed other important values. The alienation is caused by some legitimate complaints and other not-so-legitimate reasons, but in either case it has created a value-distortion which has led away from rather than toward a free society.

The value-orientation of the alienated intellectual has a potential affinity for fanaticism. Fanaticism involves an inability to see any but a narrow range of values. When the alienated intellectual is willing to raise certain values high while he denigrates others, he is only slightly separated from fanaticism. This is something we need to understand if we hope to comprehend modern extremism.

I would now like to move to another aspect of the alienated intellectual's psychological make-up: his elitist moral perception. Even though he has consistently sought an alliance with the have-nots and this has resulted in an emphasis on "democracy," the alienated intellectual has felt strongly the exclusive rightness of his perceptions. He has had little doubt but that the drum to which he has marched has been the right one and that those to which the rest of the world has marched have been false. This necessarily makes him an elitist. I point this out without denying that some elitism is valid; I would have to hold to a radical rela-

tivism to deny that some men and ideas are superior
to others. But the elitism of the alienated intellectual is noteworthy because it contradicts the
outer garment of democracy and egalitarianism which
the alienated ideologies have often assumed. It
is also doubtful whether the intellectual has a
sound basis for his elitism, since the reality he
perceives is by no means as assuredly correct as
he thinks it is.

The elitism is inferentially present in the
psychology of alienation, but it is also directly
evident in many statements that have been written
during moments of candor. In my review of the
alienation in Chapter 10, I referred to Ezra Pound's
comment about a "half-educated, Zoroastrian rabble
of 'respectable' people more stupid and sodden than
is to be found even in America." He followed up
this comment by saying that "the Lord of the universe sends into this world in each generation a
few intelligent spirits, and these ultimately
manage the rest."[11] We should also recall Burnette Haskell's observation that "we found that
the masses of working men were densely ignorant,
cowardly and selfish" -- to which he added that
"any pretext will do . . . that will rouse the
people."[12] Henry May observed generally about the
collection of essays edited by Harold Stearns in
1922 that "many of the articles hinted . . . that
the real enemy was none other than democracy itself, with its deification of the average man and
its hatred of superiority."[13] Alienated literature contains many disparaging references to the
public as being, for example, "the herd."

The unique psychology of the alienated intellectual is also reflected in his desire to use the
State or a Revolution or a Collective as an essentially <u>theocratic</u> instrument. His ideology is a
social <u>religion</u> and the state or collective is,
in effect, a Church. Because he feels himself to
be right, to be superior, and because he despises
so much of what he sees around him, he has taken
for granted the moral validity of a coercive,

intolerant reformation of mankind. The question of means, involving the different poles of rapid-versus-gradual, violent-versus-peaceful change, has always tortured the Left, dividing it into many factions. But the alienated intellectuals have been virtually unanimous in their willingness to use statist or collectivist power as a means. They have politicized most human values. Even though modern society is secular, the modern world has seen no real separation of church and state. Those who have proclaimed the cultural Truths of secular religion have sought as fervently as the advocates of any prior religion to impress that Truth onto the rest of humanity through the power of the state. If we were to deny it, tens of millions of ghosts from the twentieth century would rise up to reassert it.

A classical liberal conception of a free society denies the legitimacy of any such use of state power. It doesn't deny that powerful cultural, spiritual, ethical and legal bonds are needed to maintain even a free society, but the bonds are necessary to establish and maintain a framework for voluntarism. The classical liberal considers it a terrible distortion of the proper role of the state to assign it the job of reconstituting mankind. Because of this, classical liberal theory will consider it just as necessary to insist on a separation of the state from secular religion as on the more traditional separation of the state from theistic religion. It is inconsistent with individual liberty to politicize cultural transformation.

There has been some ambivalence about the direction toward which the intellectual should reform mankind. The intellectual has often wanted to remake mankind in his own image. This has been apparent in the utopias of Theobald and Bellamy and perhaps also of Reich. At other times, though, the intellectual has just settled for a hierarchical order in which he would be on top -- as in the visions of Plato and Comte.

293

The Effect on Classical Liberalism

The "alienation of the intellectual" is important in its own right. We have been studying it for its visible consequences. But if we look beyond these, we see that there has been a negative, a void, created by the presence of the alienation that has also been of great significance. Certain needed features of our civilization have been absent because of the alienation. By itself, this is worth noting. What is missing from a period of history is often as important as what is present.

As Western civilization emerged from superstition into reason and science, and from hierarchical political and cultural domination into a "rising of the multitudes," it urgently needed a philosophy appropriate to the new setting. Classical liberalism took great strides toward becoming such a philosophy. It attacked the Mercantilist worldview that equated liberty with chaos, and instead presented a rationale for an economy in which a harmonious division of labor could lead to increasing productivity and well-being through a nexus of contractual exchange. The early emphasis was on economics and politics -- so much so that classical liberalism and classical economics were largely the same. Beyond this, it adopted at first the outlook of the Enlightenment and shared in the rationalistic perspective of the eighteenth century. As intellectual modes changed, it changed too; the natural rights emphasis gave way to the utilitarian emphasis, with Bentham and James Mill leading the way; and when later in the century the prevailing fascination was with evolutionary conceptions, Herbert Spencer translated classical liberal values into that idiom.

It would have been extremely beneficial if this philosophy of freedom had continued to be the direction of modern thought. Much that is constructive could have been accomplished by a philosophical consensus which would have been consistent with the values of the broad new "bourgeoisie" and

at the same time sensitive to the spiritual needs
of the time. But instead, the actual developments
have been disappointing. In America there was no
suitable mind to replace Jefferson after he was
gone. Emerson might have done it, but his mind
was already reacting to the incipient alienation
and to influences that were incompatible with
classical liberalism. In England, the mantle fell
to John Stuart Mill. He might have accomplished
the needed integration if his mind had been a shade
tougher, his powers a bit greater and his scope a
few degrees broader. He had an open, receptive
mind that was able to reach out to see the partial
truths that were contained in competing philosophies, so he was the one who came closest to
adapting the central lessons of classical liberalism, conservatism and socialism. But the ultimate
product of his thought on social philosophy didn't
succeed in making these elements a cohesive, far-
reaching affirmation of a free society. Neither
Utilitarianism nor On Liberty accomplishes this.
More toughness would have brought him deeper into
his own classical liberal origins and might have
led him to affirm them more forcefully, so that he
would have been shielded from his eventual flirta-
tion with socialism. Somewhat greater powers
might have made it possible for him to state in
more satisfactory terms the principles of a free
society and, also, of utilitarianism. A broader
scope (which I would like him to have had despite
his already open-ranging mind) might have suggested
to him the need for a more complete discussion of
the spiritual, intellectual and cultural requirements of the new "mass man" whom he already knew
to be present.

But it is probable that even if Emerson and
John Stuart Mill had been thoroughly suited to the
demands of a fully adequate classical liberalism
their voices would have been drowned out by the
surge of the intellectual community to the Left.
It would be superficial to believe that the direction of modern thought lay so fatefully in just
two men. If the main body of intellectuals had not

295

gone to the left, the fuller, more comprehensive classical liberalism would have come about in any case.

But since the shift was to the left, a more adequate formulation of classical liberalism would probably have been ignored. And the determinants of whether such a shift was to occur were only partly intellectual.

Whatever the responsibility of individual thinkers, the drain of resources to the left had the effect of weakening the intellectual supports of capitalism and classical liberalism. There was a drain of intellectual talent that has weakened the formulation and articulation of classical liberal thought. The import of this is that modern Western civilization has been left without an appropriate head and heart. It has had to get by without an intellectuality appropriate to itself. The absence of this intellectuality has deeply affected the development of the institutions of modern society. It has also had an impact on the cultural and spiritual questions which have remained so pressingly open, and on the theory of classical liberalism itself. And finally, it has reacted back on the Left, reinforcing its alienation.

There are a number of areas in which classical liberalism has been left immature by the drain of intellectual resources. One of them has to do with monetary theory and the trade cycle. This is a crucial issue both for economics as a science and for capitalism as a working system. Classical liberal theory is split between the advocates of the gold standard, as perhaps supplemented by a system of "free banking," and the advocates of central monetary management guided by a "Rule of Law" standard. Ludwig von Mises ranks as a leading proponent of the first, Milton Friedman of the second. Because of the statement of these widely varying positions, it would be possible to say that the theoretical aspects have been covered;

but that would obscure the total lack of follow-up
discussion which should have occurred relative to
each theory. Instead of there being a vigorous
intellectual community developing each, working
out its nuances and comparing it with the other,
the theories have existed virtually still-born.
In the meantime, the practical direction of American economic institutions has for many years been
led off at angles which haven't been conceived or
rationalized in terms of classical liberal values
and priorities. The disturbing thing about this
divergence between sound theory and practice is
that there is now almost a total lack of theory
giving a classical liberal critique of the practice. As it has become more evident that the
Keynesianism of recent years hasn't been able to
limit inflation and at the same time keep unemployment in check, serious writing has emerged from
a socialist point of view suggesting that the
federal government be made an "employer of last
resort" to hire anybody who hasn't gotten a job in
the private sector. There has been very little
offsetting literature, though, analyzing the problem from a classical liberal perspective.[14] Many
difficult issues, both in the popular arena and
in the quieter domain of scholarly reflection, are
going by default at this point in the twentieth
century. Although not always to the same extent,
the lack of intellectual resources has been
present in Europe for perhaps a century and in the
United States for a century and a half. Classical
liberal thought receded before it had reached a
full flowering.

The same is true when we consider the question
of economic concentration and the associated issue
of anti-trust. Classical liberalism is again
split: some feel that concentration is no real
problem in a free market, that it is due mainly if
not exclusively to collusion with government and
that it can best be met by a simple laissez-faire
policy which will remove all government intervention; others, though, feel that concentration is
a genuine problem both theoretically and practical-

ly in a free society, that it is a threat to some
important classical liberal values and (even
though they dislike the ambiguity and capricious-
ness of anti-trust law as we know it) that it
should be restrained by law. Again, this is a
disagreement which under certain circumstances
could reflect intellectual vitality. But in fact
the two schools aren't locked in vigorous discussion. Even though the difference is unresolved,
the debate is dormant.

Monetary policy and anti-trust are just two
examples. There are a great many public issues
which would benefit from a larger and more active
classical liberal intellectuality, especially if
that intellectuality enjoyed the means that are
available through the institutions of higher
learning. Things would be very different if there
were professors and graduate assistants in significant numbers reviewing from a classical liberal
point of view the "energy crisis," consumer protection, ecology, the operation of the courts,
urban renewal, the welfare program, city planning
and all of the countless other processes and
issues of contemporary life. It is here that the
intellectual vacuum is most telling. The cumula-
tive loss is immense.

Another aspect that suffers has to do with
the fundamental theoretical questions that underlie
classical liberalism itself. If we survey the
metaphysical foundations for the various forms of
classical liberal theory and the types of ethical
methodology they use, we see that these aren't
satisfactorily settled. It is true, of course, that
these aren't well settled in any philosophy, but
the failure just illustrates the cosmic immaturity
of the human race in our century. I would hope
that a deeper form of classical liberalism would
resolve these questions despite their evident difficulty. In my article in Religion and Society in
February, 1970, I urged classical liberals to adopt
a secular concern for the basic spiritual and
metaphysical questions. Classical liberalism has

barely touched these matters in any depth. They
can be an extremely fruitful source of future study.

This is linked with an associated problem.
Until now, classical liberalism has largely been
oblivious to the great cultural, spiritual,
existential questions that are inherent in modern,
secular life. Every other philosophy has had much
to say on these matters of lifestyle and meaning
(usually to castigate the middle class and commercial civilization). If a free society is to meet
these issues appropriately, it needs an intellectuality which will both remain loyal to its values
and be sensitive to its failures. The cultural
issue has in my opinion been of greater importance
than the economic and political issues, which have
been more symptomatic. If the intellectual void
in American culture is to be overcome, what is
needed is a classical liberal intellectuality that
understands Rousseau and Veblen and Charles Reich
-- and will address itself to that part of their
perspective that has raised genuine questions about
the meaningfulness of everyday life. Commercial
society does in fact have its spiritual defects.
The defenders of that society, not its enemies,
should have the most to say about them.

Many fine intellectuals have contributed to
classical liberalism -- but far fewer than
have contributed to the Left or than have been
needed.

Because of the loss of nourishment and renewal, classical liberalism has often been fragmented,
dormant and atrophied, defensive and dogmatically
apologetic. It has been a philosophy in extremis.
The current preoccupation of many of its devotees
with anarcho-capitalism is symptomatic. It reflects the loss of touch with social reality and
responsibility which occurs when a cause is assumed
by its supporters to be hopeless and only self-
justification is left. In much of classical liberalism's writing during the past century there
has been a defensiveness which has been narrow and

doctrinaire; this has affected both its soundness and its effectiveness. The fragmentation is evident in the unwillingness of the various factions to entertain the ideas of the others; it is as though each were hermetically sealed in its rightness. Accordingly, even though there is still much that is valuable in its writing, the movement is in far from a healthy, vital condition.

The problem is in its center, at its intellectual heart. It is true that it needs more of a popularizing literature and more political action, just as it needs more of everything; but the fundamental need is for a resurgence of serious intellectual work of the finest sort. Whether it obtains this work and the many other supports it needs will depend upon whether the civilization within which we live will be able to witness a cultural integration of its intellectuality. The split between the intellectual and the bourgeoisie will have to be overcome. Whether this occurs will depend only in part upon the efforts of intellectuals who see the need for it; it will depend even more on the future direction of unconscious, unplanned determinants which will either augment or reverse the causes of the alienation.

NOTES

1. See Joseph B. Gittler, Social Thought Among the Early Greeks (Athens, Ga.: University of Georgia Press, 1941), pp. 150-157.

2. Ludwig von Mises, The Historical Setting of the Austrian School of Economics (New Rochelle: Arlington House, 1969), pp. 33-34.

3. Eric Hoffer, The Ordeal of Change (New York: Perennial Library, 1963), p. 39.

4. Herbert Marcuse, One-Dimensional Man (Boston: Beacon Press, 1964), pp. 256-257; also, An Essay

on *Liberation* (Boston: Beacon Press, 1969), pp. 56, 58.

5. F. A. Hayek, *The Intellectuals and Socialism* (Menlo Park: Institute for Humane Studies, Inc., 1949), p. 5.

6. Eric Goldman, *Rendezvous With Destiny* (New York: Vintage Books, no date), p. 123.

7. James D. Richardson (ed.), *A Compilation of the Messages and Papers of the Presidents* (Washington: Government Printing Office, 1896), Vol. III, pp. 294-295.

8. Martin Van Buren, *Autobiography* (Washington: Government Printing Office, 1920), p. 137.

9. Henry David Thoreau, *Walden-Essay on Civil Disobedience* (New York: Airmont Publishing Company, Inc., 1965), pp. 237, 251.

10. Robert Payne, *The Terrorists* (New York: Funk & Wagnalls Company, 1957), pp. 21-27.

11. Henry May, *The Discontent of the Intellectuals: A Problem of the Twenties* (Chicago: Rand McNally, 1963), pp. 11, 12, 31, 17, 27, 41.

12. Chester McArthur Destler, *American Radicalism 1865-1901* (New York: Octagon Books, 1946), p. 86.

13. May, *Discontent*, p. 31.

14. Gottfried Haberler's *Economic Growth and Stability* (Los Angeles: Nash Publishing Co., 1974) may be such a book.

301

PART III:

REFLECTIONS OF THE CRISIS

THE FRENCH REVOLUTION

In the preceding chapter, I discussed several of the consequences that have emerged from the alienation. Both the alienation and its consequences are of major importance if we are to understand the "modern predicament." I wouldn't have us lose sight, though, of the other interrelated aspects of the picture I've painted: the half-maturity of mankind at its present state of development, the lack of paradigms from the past, the rise of the average person to predominance in society, and the spiritual vacuity that trivializes our way of life. These have all played a part in creating our unique situation.

The essential point is that the ground under our feet is not entirely solid, and that much of what we do can best be understood as an adjustment to that fact.

One of the most pervasive results of this continuing adjustment has been the rise of the major ideologies. They have provided us "systems of interpretation." We see ourselves and others through -- and consequently base our actions on -- these organized systems of perception. They are fundamental to our ontology, defining the reality in which we live. These social philosophies are so influential and are so affected by the factors we are discussing in this book, that I will devote additional books to discussing them.

The remainder fo the present book will have to have a more limited purpose. It will be to show the problematical nature of our civilization by reference to some of the main historical events of the past two hundred years. The present chapter will discuss the first of those -- the French Revolution.

305

My discussion of the French Revolution will
be limited to showing how it illustrates the
continuity of three features of immaturity: the
abuse of power, the questionable capacity for
self-government, and the lack of a sufficient
spiritual basis.

The first of these -- statism -- was present
under the autocracy of the Old Regime. It wasn't
abolished, though, by the Revolution, which continued the abuse of power through its many Fears
and Terrors and through the way many of its leaders viewed the role of the state. Later, it reached a high-point in the dictatorship of Napoleon;
and it has continued as one of the most important
facts of the twentieth century.

The second feature -- the problematical
capacity of the average person to maintain a high
civilization and a free society -- was also present before, during and after the Revolution. One
way of understanding the social structurings of
the medieval system as they existed under the Old
Regime in France is as an adaptation to the fact
of human weakness. In its own way, the Revolution
revealed this weakness through the savagery and
fickleness of the Parisian mobs. And notwithstanding the improvement that has occurred in the condition and education of the average person during
the two centuries that have followed, it is still
very much an open question just how sufficient a
human base we have for advanced civilization.

The third aspect is one that I won't do much
more with than just mention. It has to do with
the lack of a proper religious foundation for
human life. Robespierre attempted a short-lived
Cult of the Supreme Being, which symbolizes the
yearning men still feel even after we have left the
Age of Religion and have become increasingly secular.

Statism. The famine during the winter of
1788-89 was one of the factors that led to the

Revolution. It's significant that Leo Gershoy
tied the famine to the statism of the Old Regime.
"Lack of resources and primitive methods of agriculture alone do not explain the recurrent food
shortages and famines that France suffered in the
Old Regime. Internal trade, if it had functioned
smoothly, could have brought the surplus from one
district to other districts where a shortage
existed. But innumerable restrictions hampered
internal trade. Customs barriers, transit fees,
market and fair dues, and varying weights and
measures made transportation expensive."[1]

A long history of abuses under the Old Regime
preceded the violence that was so spectacular a
part of the Revolution. Alexis de Tocqueville
said that "I have no hesitation in affirming,
after a careful study of the facts on the record,
that a great many of the practices we associate
with the Revolution had had precedents in the
treatment of the people by the government during
the last two centuries of the monarchy. The old
regime provided the Revolution with many of its
methods: all the Revolution added to these was
a savagery peculiar to itself."[2]

As we assess the horrors of the Revolution,
we need to appreciate that French society was in
extremis. France as a cauldron contained all
factions and ideologies. The Revolution had the
enormous task of overcoming the accumulated feudal
institutions, and it had to do this in a contested
situation. The devotees of the old system were
not about to acquiesce in it, and France was surrounded by monarchies that were anxious to restore
the Old Regime. The circumstances were such that
France could hardly have enjoyed America's sort of
moderate revolution. The enormities were born out
of suspicion, tension, fear, recrimination and
hatred.

Just the same, the enormities make the Revolution, with its guillotine, the appropriate symbol
for the statism that has plagued all ages. This

307

is especially so since they are personified so well
by a number of peculiarly bloody individuals who
stand out with romantic ghastliness from the history of those years. Marat was such a figure.
His vague and contradictory theories justified an
"eternal call to massacre." "On the day of the
fall of the Bastille," Beraud says, "he asked for
five hundred heads. A year later, he demanded
five or six hundred more, not for vengeance, but
for national security. As time went on, he showed
more avidity. In August, 1791, he wanted eight
hundred gibbits; towards the end of 1791, he
insisted upon five thousand, six thousand, twenty
thousand. 'And,' he said, 'let us not hesitate
for an instant.' With the new year, his demands
grew; he asked for seventy thousand!"[3] It isn't
surprising that in the dialectic of violence
Marat would himself be assassinated -- as he was
in his bathtub by Charlotte Corday.

The Revolution was bourgeois and moderate in
its early stages. The Declaration of Rights was
founded on classical liberal ideals of personal
liberty. If the Revolution could have been
stabilized at that point, the later horrors would
have been avoided. But, of course, it wasn't.
Things went from bad to worse: The King escaped,
was recaptured and was eventually executed; the
Terror began in September, 1793; in October, the
revolutionary tribunal guillotined Marie Antoinette
and then the Girondins, so that in all twenty
thousand people were killed at that time; the
Hebertists were executed in March, 1794, and Danton
and his supporters in April. The "Great Terror"
guillotined thirteen hundred during June and July.
At that point, Robespierre himself was overthrown
and guillotined. The next year, when the Jacobins
tried a coup that failed, the "White Terror" re-
taliated against them. The time was ripe for Napoleon to seize power. At first there was a glow
of hope that he would reaffirm the aspirations of
the Revolution; but this faded as he made himself
more and more kingly and as his militarism bathed
Europe repeatedly in carnage.

A few years later, the French economist Frederic Bastiat blamed statist philosophies for much of the revolutionary abuse. In The Law, he wrote that "like Rousseau," the radical Jacobin leaders "desire to force mankind docilely to bear this yoke of the public welfare that they have dreamed up in their own imaginations."[4] He quoted Saint-Just: "The legislator commands the future. It is for him to will the good of mankind. It is for him to make men what he wills them to be." Robespierre, Le Pelletier and Billaud-Varennes expressed similar views. Bastiat ascribed this in part to classical studies. "These centuries were nourished on the study of antiquity. And antiquity presents everywhere . . . the spectacle of a few men molding mankind according to their whims, thanks to the prestige of force and fraud." This points to the continuity I have been stressing, since statist influences from the past, even from the ancient Greeks and Romans, have served as the backdrop for modern society.

Human weakness. A system of "estates" within the Old Regime separated the common people into a class of their own. It is entirely possible that under the circumstances of earlier centuries this subordination served a needed purpose; it may have been an essential expedient to fill the void left by humanity's weakness. It may have been needed, as Edmund Burke said of Christianity, to "cover our nakedness."

If we reverse the assumption, it becomes clear that the hierarchical social system was a void-filling makeshift: Would truly competent people have allowed themselves to be held in subordination? A system like that is per se a symptom of an underlying deficiency.

One aspect of the social hierarchy was that the average person was "below the threshold" of the empathy of those on top. Tocqueville spoke of this psychological division when he said that "we are reminded of the conduct of Mme. Duchatelet, as reported by Voltaire's secretary; this good lady, it seems, had no scruples about undressing in the presence of her manservants, being unable to convince herself that these lackeys were real flesh-and-blood men!"

But even the makeshift had eventually weakened. Commentators disagree about the viability of the aristocracy before the Revolution. Burke thought the aristocracy in France was sound, but Tocqueville wrote that "while ceasing to be a ruling class, they had remained a privileged, closed group, less and less an aristocracy and more and more a caste."

Needless to say, the Revolution radically changed the outer structures of society. But it could not remove the problem of human weakness. The will of the multitudes to stand as free individuals has been an open question ever since. John Bright's democratic optimism has been severely tested. You'll recall my earlier observation that modern society has not been in a position where it could receive a clear reading of this propensity. The alienation of the intellectual will have to be overcome before we can judge the tendencies of the so-called "masses" themselves. Up to this point, the move toward socialism and totalitarianism hasn't come even primarily from the average person; the influence of the intellectual, especially through Leftist ideology which panders so much to the worst instincts of the have-nots, has been enormous.

The picture the Revolution gives us of the multitudes isn't a favorable one. It's a picture of savage fury reduced to pitiful dimensions by fickleness and vacuity. The "masses" were inconstant and intemperate, literally cheering every excess. It's amazing that on his way to the guillotine Camille Desmoulins received no support from the mob when he called out: "People! Your friends are being killed! Who called you to the Bastille? Who gave you your cockades? I am

310

Camille Desmoulins." It's not surprising, in light of this, that the same people were able to become the cannon fodder for Napoleon.

The population grew rapidly during the final years of the Old Regime, especially in the cities. Crane Brinton says that "literacy now began to extend to a considerable part of the population in the West. The masses did not yet read, though by the end of the century the skilled workers in the more advanced countries could and did read."[6] But, of course, this advancement was hardly enough to prevent superstition. Gershoy points out that "the Age of Enlightenment was also an age of superstition, particularly in Paris, where spiritualists and charlatans like Mesmer and Cagliostro had a tremendous following. Along with the works of the philosophes there was a tremendous vogue for books on magic, sorcery and alchemy." It's true that the Revolution was sponsored by the rising commercial class; but it was "carried out by (the nation's) least educated and most unruly elements."

At the same time, the French were passing through a "revolution of rising expectations." Stanton Coblentz observed that the French Revolution occurred despite the fact that "the French masses, even if one takes the darkest possible view of their situation, were less oppressed than other Europeans who did not rise in revolt."[7]

Demagogic manipulation of the "masses" wasn't absent. It's noteworthy that even the nobility had pandered to their inertia and discontent. Tocqueville said that "the very men who had most to fear from the anger of the masses had no qualms about publicly condemning the gross injustice with which they had always been treated. They drew attention to the monstrous vices of the institutions which pressed most heavily on the common people and indulged in highly colored descriptions of the living conditions of the working class and the starvation wages it received." A continuous thread runs from this to Emile Zola's

311

novel _Germinal_ and to President John F. Kennedy's well-known appeal on behalf of "seventeen million Americans who go to bed hungry every night."

The rise of the multitudes has been full of democratic promise -- but it has left Western civilization with a strangely problematical aspect. Coblentz quoted the concern that was voiced by Albert Guerrard in _The_ _Life_ _and_ _Death_ _of_ _an_ _Ideal_: "If we compare France in the middle of the nineteenth century with France in the middle of the eighteenth, we cannot suppress a feeling of loss. It ought not to be so: material progress is undeniable; knowledge as well as comfort were more widely diffused; poetic sources long sealed had been opened, science assuming profounder meaning. Yet, with it all, we are conscious of a vulgarization, a rebarbarization." This sensibility has been widely discussed in the literature of the nineteenth and twentieth centuries; it is itself part of the alienation many sensitive people, including the alienated intellectual we have examined, have felt toward modern culture.

Intellectual weakness. Edmund Burke and Samuel Johnson in England articulated superbly the intellectual position that underlay the Old Regime. I am not one who believes, though, that that worldview was a satisfactory paradigm for humanity. It rationalized a closed system, accepted many enormities which people cannot be expected to accept once they can do otherwise, and idealized certain things which the photographic eye of modern realism knows to have been less than actual. The medieval worldview has bequeathed us some partial truths, but it is essentially false. The fact that it is false means that to that degree men were left mentally and spiritually "to their own devices" as they entered the modern period. The earlier age didn't provide a solid set of answers. The modern age, as symbolized for us in this chapter by the Revolution, has experienced a loss of consensus; but in my opinion the existential indecision which appears in the modern period

312

is a significant improvement over the medieval consensus. The Middle Ages seemed to offer solutions
because it possessed an agreement on a makeshift.
But agreement of this sort is itself a type of
transciency. The indecision of our own time may
not affirm Truth, but at least it is not a stasis
of error.

However, although this is true of the Old
Regime's mindscape, it is also true that the fool-
ish and simplistic philosophies of the Revolution
pointed ahead to the severe intellectual weakness
of the modern period. A few years ago I heard a
respected scholar praise Rousseau's thought as
genius par excellence (even though he disagreed
with Rousseau's position); but his praise of
Rousseau ran counter to my own impressions. We
would be hard pressed to name a writer who has
been more influential than Rousseau during the
past three centuries. Sophisticated reiterations
of his worldview have been published tens of
thousands of times. They have included the writings of Thorstein Veblen, for example, and more
recently of Charles Reich, Theodore Roszak and
Herbert Marcuse. But notwithstanding Rousseau's
continuing influence as a father of the Left's
cultural relativism, his writings should, in all
honesty, be recognized as simplistic makeshifts.
When I first read his Discourse on the Origin of
Inequality Among Men, I was amazed that it could
be taken seriously; and I was puzzled about the
mentality of Rousseau's contemporaries who awarded
it a prize. It has no substance whatsoever outside of a single observation about human society
which is the theme of the essay and which is utterly trivial. His point was that so long as men
simply existed as animals, living and dying with
neither foresight nor memory and merely responding
in a stimulus-response way to their environment
as do other animals, they lived with the content
simplicity that is typical of animals. He said
that all of the other qualities of human life,
both good and bad, including political inequality,
have come about because men left that isolation

313

and shortsightedness and came into society.

When confronted with this point, we have to ask "So what?" Even Rousseau didn't want mankind to revert to that animal condition. If not, then why should that condition be used as the standard by which civilization is judged? Rousseau fashioned a simplistic and useless tool by which he and his alienated followers could undercut, by a perpetual cultural relativism, any existing society. He stood outside the culture and refused to accept any of its values. The desire by so much modern intellectual culture to undercut the predominant culture has been complex and has even contained some important truths. But Rousseau's own formulation was pure artifice.

A similar criticism applies to his Social Contract. Rousseau argued that men should follow the General Will. He wasn't able to indicate how this mystical General Will is to be known, though, since he said that it can't be ascertained by taking a vote. The result is that there is a fundamental ambiguity in his central concept. Accordingly, his idea of the General Will has been used equally well to justify democracy or despotism. Anyone can claim an insider's intuition about what it is.

Although Rousseau's thought wasn't the only intellectual precursor of the Revolution, its influence was immense, especially with Robespierre and the other Jacobins. This indicates to me that there was intellectual weakness on the part of those who held him in such esteem. Their mental "void" played a significant role in the Revolution -- and a similar void has continued throughout the modern era. It has been apparent in the Jacobins, in the nihilists of nineteenth century Russia, in the more extreme Abolitionists before the Civil War in the United States, in the anti-bourgeois fanatics of the German Youth Movement both before and after World War I, and in the counter-cultural alienates of the American New Left. Each included

314

a type of intellectual who mixed idealism with fanaticism, energy with uncivilized impatience, virtue with cruelty, and high purpose with vulgar demagoguery. Such a mixture carried the French Revolution to the bloody heights of Robespierre's "Republic of Virtue."

I have already mentioned Marat's call for ever more heads. Saint-Just dreamed of utopian socialism and spoke to his troops in a style that foreshadowed Napoleon. He personified sincerity and virtue; and yet in the name of virtue and for supposed reasons of state he was able to call first for the head of Louis XVI and then to agitate to bring about the execution of the Girondins. He later arranged the execution of the Hebertists and the Dantonists.

The Revolution does more than illustrate this type of immature intelligentsia. In a broader sense, it shows the "loss of consensus" which has existed in modern society. Innumerable factions followed each other in power in rapid succession. The struggle against monarchy and feudalism pitted the emerging democratic forces against the nobility and king; but even on the democratic side we see the beginning of the crisis over what direction the new society should take. Instead of representing of newly-found consensus, Robespierre's Cult of the Supreme Being and Republic of Virtue were ludicrously short-lived. Eventually, as a result of the excesses of the Revolution and of Napoleon, there was an intense reaction against rationalism itself. The anti-rationalistic Romantic movement of the early nineteenth century was part of this overall failure of consensus.

Jose Ortega y Gasset's theory of history emphasizes the alternation of consensus with "crisis." In the eighteenth century, he said, Europe had been held together by the belief that "kings rule 'by the grace of God.'" This was the unifying conception even though it was false. As such a unifying conception is lost, as it was

315

during the Revolution, "the social domain falls prey to passions. The ensuing vacuum is filled by the gas of emotion. Everyone proclaims what best suits his interest, his whims, his intellectual manias."[8]

While all of this was happening, the still inchoate alienation of the intellectual was beginning to take form. Certainly the devotees of the Old Regime have never stopped despising modern culture. And among the revolutionaries such men as Rousseau, Babeuf, Robespierre, Saint-Just and others began the cultural critique that eventually led to the alliance of the intellectuals with the have-nots and to the rise of socialism. Burke had some pertinent observations about the intellectuals of his own day: "To this system of literary monopoly was joined an unremitting industry to blacken and discredit in every way, and by every means, all those who did not hold to their faction." He continued: "To those who have observed the spirit of their conduct it has long been clear that nothing was wanted but the power of carrying the intolerance of the tongue and of the pen into a persecution which would strike at property, liberty and life." This description seems contemporary today; it is very descriptive of the process that has occurred during the two centuries since Burke wrote.

Unresolved spiritual questions. There are those, such as Eric Voegelin and Richard Weaver, who consider Christian theology to encapsulate the true reality of man's existence. For my part, though, I consider that theology to have been non-reality bound; by this I mean that the questions it asked were unanswerable by normal human means. In the secular age which has characterized the modern period, we have tended (however imperfectly) to move away from questions which can never lead beyond unresolved speculation.

This does not mean, however, that we do not face profound spiritual questions with regard to the meaning and nature of our lives. Many people

316

assume that spiritual issues disappear in the absence of a theistic faith; Mario Pei recently wrote, for example, that without God man would find it all right "to behave like an animal."[9] But this is far too doctrinaire and simplistic. A serious secularist would hardly join him in asserting it. There are a great many indications that in our secular age many people still feel deeply that they need answers to the ultimate questions.

Robespierre sought a solution in his rationalistic state religion. Its failure left an open question which we still face. The psychotherapist Viktor Frankl has written that a "loss of meaning" is the central neurosis people experience in the twentieth century. The point I would make, which relates to the theme of the early chapters of this book, is this: that modern man is existentially still wandering; that he has received no final paradigms, religiously or otherwise, from the past.

We feel a morbid fascination toward the French Revolution. It is much the same as the feeling we have toward the Nazi period. Each, in its own way, was a brutal caricature of humanity. Each makes essential the theory of man's continuing immaturity. And each was a modern event.

NOTES

1. Leo Gershoy, The French Revolution and Napoleon (New York: Appleton-Century-Crofts, Inc., 1953), pp. 47, 77.

2. Alexis de Tocqueville, The Old Regime and the French Revolution (Garden City: Anchor Books, 1955), pp. 192, 183, 204, 207, 180.

3. Henri Beraud, Twelve Portraits of the French Revolution (London: Cayme Press Ltd., 1929), pp. 122, 154.

4. Frederic Bastiat, The Law (Irvington-on-Hudson, N.Y.: Foundation for Economic Education, Inc., 1964), pp. 52, 50.

5. Edmund Burke, Reflections on the Revolution in France (New York: Liberal Arts Press, 1955), pp. 103-4, 126-7.

6. Crane Brinton, The Shaping of the Modern Mind (New York: Mentor Books, 1957), p. 117.

7. Stanton A. Coblentz, Ten Crises in Civilization (London: Frederick Muller, 1967), pp. 111, 133.

8. Jose Ortega y Gasset, Concord and Liberty (New York: W. W. Norton & Company, Inc.), p. 20.

9. Mario Pei, The America We Lost (New York: Signet Books, 1968), p. 87.

14

THE RUSSIAN NIHILIST

The history of Russia during the nineteenth and early twentieth centuries is both fascinating and instructive. In part, the fascination comes from the colorful texture of that distinctively Russian culture, which was to us half familiar in its European flavor and yet half remote and exotic. But, too, the fascination is the product of our hindsight. There is an element of foreboding. We know that Old Russia was a society pregnant with the monstrous fetus of Soviet totalitarianism -- which was born eventually out of the society's chaos and weakness.

The instruction consists, at least for my purposes in light of the themes I have been stressing, of two major points. First, those years demonstrate -- perhaps better than any other example we might give -- the impact and destructiveness of the alienated European intellectuality when it was exported from Europe to the other peoples of the world. And second, they illustrate the dependency and weakness of the emerging peoples of the non-Western world. When Europe ceased to lead constructively, Russia offered no visible alternative of its own. Instead, it allowed itself to be seduced and eventually overwhelmed by the most brutal illusions emanating from the alienation.

So that we can see these things in the context of the specific history, I will want to review the events after 1800. It is a history which is only vaguely known to most Americans.

The reign of Tsar Alexander I began in 1800 and ended in 1825. Although as a young man he was tutored in the liberal ideas of the Enlightenment by La Harpe, his liberalism later became mixed with the mysticism that was so prominent a part of the Romantic reaction that followed the Napoleonic wars. Accordingly, it was mysticism rather than liberalism that dominated his later years. He delegated much of his power to an autocrat, Arakcheyev, whose approach was just the opposite of

La Harpe's. As late as 1812 Alexander had appeared as the enlightened savior of Europe. He had seemed a man of advanced ideas who represented positive forces after the Napoleonic bloodbath. But he soon gave the liberals within the Russian nobility and army reason to become disillusioned with him and with the principle of Tsarist autocracy. The liberals began to form secret societies; Murayov drafted a constitution that was based on the Constitution of the United States; Pestel began to urge revolution and wanted a dictatorship that would clear the way for an egalitarian republic. They planned a revolt for the spring of 1826.

As luck would have it, though, Alexander's death in December, 1825, trigered the revolt prematurely. The "Decembrist" uprising proved ineffectual -- and resulted in the execution or exile of its leaders. The Tsarist regime continued, with Nicholas I taking Alexander's place.

For his part, Nicholas was firmly committed to autocracy. During his reign, which continued until 1855, he used his powers to restrict the nobility and repress education and innovation. But this wasn't enough to stem the intellectual ferment that was occurring underneath the surface of Russian life and that was producing an "intelligentsia" which was no longer drawn just from the army and the gentry. This intelligentsia became, eventually, the most important fact in Russian history. Its members listened thirstily to the revolutionary ideas that were emanating from Europe, ideas which were by this time not simply anti-monarchical and anti-feudal, but which were profoundly alienated from the bourgeoisie and from liberalism itself. Herzen yearned for socialism through peasant communes; Belinsky was a Christian socialist; Petrashevsky wanted a Fourier-type socialism. It's interesting that the magnificent literary figure Dostoyevsky began as a member of the Petrashevsky circle, even though he later turned to other ideas that were Christian but not socialist.

Alexander II -- the next Tsar -- is described as having been of mixed character; he was at once gentle, indulgent, humane, sentimental, peevish, indolent and lacking in conviction.[1] His initial impulse was toward a liberal program sponsored by the monarchy, an impulse he probably received from the humanitarian education given him by Zhukovsky. He rejected the idea of a national representative assembly, at least partly because he feared it would be controlled by landowners; but in several areas he took major liberalizing steps. Perhaps most importantly, he declared the emancipation of the serfs in 1861. His judicial reforms in 1864 sought to establish the "rule of law." In 1863, his university reforms permitted universitites to elect their own councils, rectors and deans (although the Minister of Education retained a veto). In the armed services, he replaced the barbarous twenty-five-year recruitment of peasants with universal conscription; and he began efforts to educate the soldiers. And in 1864 he establish-ed local representative government through elective bodies known as the zemstva.

These were major steps forward, at least from the point of view of anyone who was receptive to a peaceable reform of Russian autocracy. Needless to say, the reforms didn't carry Russia fully into participative democracy; but they were significant beginnings. The Emancipation, for example, had imperfections; but it would have been enormously meaningful even if it had been no more than a for-mal change in the serfs' legal status.

The important point, however, is that the alienated intelligentsia were intractable. The reforms weren't well received; the intelligentsia viewed gradual improvement with contempt. Alexan-der's reward was intense criticism -- and assasina-tion. He was killed by a bomb in 1881 after several unsuccessful attempts. His last words were: "They hunt me like a mad dog."

This reaction struck a severe blow at the

process of gradual reform. After his initial
"Epoch of Great Reforms," Alexander himself drift-
ed from the process, probably in large measure
because of the response he received. He was,
however, planning further reforms during the year
before his death. The next Tsar, Alexander III,
was unsympathetic to reform, and earned himself
the reputation of "the last true autocrat of the
Romanov dynasty."[2]

It is often overlooked by those who seek at
least some extenuation of the later Soviet tyranny
on the grounds that Tsarist Russia had been so
intolerable, that a constitutional monarchy did in
fact come into being as a result of the revolution
of 1905. But, again, although this reform satisfied most liberals, the intelligentsia remained
adamantly committed both to socialism and to terrorism. They continued their efforts and in 1917
waged what was from the first an essentially leftist revolution. The moderate socialist Kerensky
held power for a few months, but even he was un-
acceptable; he was overthrown by Lenin.

I would suppose it's not unworthy as a paren-
thesis at the end of this history to add that the
Socialist Revolutionaries and even most of the
original Bolsheviks were put to death within a few
years by the totalitarian state they helped create.

The liberals' limitations. Probably the
greatest significance of the liberal movement, as
distinguished from the socialist, during those
twelve decades is to be found in its limitations.
The Decembrists had themselves been ideologically
split. After the liberals were defeated in that
uprising, they did not become a major element in
the intelligentsia as it emerged. The intelligentsia was increasingly radical. Liberals were found
mainly in the nobility, the zemstva and in a small
circle of writers and newspaper editors. Their
position was in the middle, melioristic and benevolent, seeking the improvement of existing institutions. Primarily, they were anxious to support the

Tsar in reforms whenever he would take the lead.
Their goal was the gradual development of a constitutional legal order -- and, if possible, they
hoped this would incorporate certain peculiarly
Russian elements. In the 1860's they wanted a
central representative assembly that would be based
on the zemskii sobor of the sixteenth and seventeenth centuries rather than on the model of a
Western-style parliament. In common with a great
many liberals on the continent of Europe, they
associated reform with an enlightened monarchy.
But in the context of the leftward tendency of
most intellectuals and of the absence of a viable
middle class, the liberals weren't able to give
the predominant leadership. Russian history accordingly offers an excellent example of the "brain
drain" toward alienation that was depriving classical liberalism of its dynamic thrust at the very
time it needed it most.

The intelligentsia. The subculture which we
know as the "intelligentsia" began to form at
Moscow University during the 1830's. As the preceding history has made clear, its creed was not
liberalism, but alienation and utopian socialism.
The socialisms of Fourier and Saint-Simon, the
ideals of the French Revolution and the philosophies of Hegel and Feuerbach -- all of these and
more, imported from Europe, received lively interest.

Alexander Herzen was the leading intellectual
of that early period. As time went on, the subculture became increasingly removed from the liberals of the Decembrist period. In Sons Against
Fathers, Lampert makes the point that "the intelligentsia was no longer what it had been in 1825
or 1835. It differed in mood, in conviction, in
social status and composition. It still included
a few army officers and a few members of the gentry, but they had been largely displaced or absorbed by the raznochintsy, the declasses of Russian
society." They were "most of all teachers, students, and scribblers of every sort," according to

a secret report at the time. As of a still later time, Hugh Seton-Watson has given some interesting statistics about the make-up of the intelligentsia. He says that "of all (the revolutionaries) condemned to prison or administratively exiled between 1873 and 1877, 279 were children of noble parents, 117 of non-noble officials, 197 of priests, 33 of merchants, 68 of Jews, 92 of meshchane, and 138 of peasants. The last two categories refer to the legal status rather than the actual occupation, and it may be assumed that these were in fact children of city workers. The large number of children of priests is particularly striking."3

By mid-century, there was considerable intellectual ferment in Russia. We know, of course, that the "Golden Age" of their literature -- consisting of the writings of such men as Tolstoy, Dostoyevsky, Pushkin, Chekov and Turgenev -- continued into the 1870's.

The first small groups of revolutionaries began to form in the early 1860's. This was the decade of the "nihilists" -- as they were called by Turgenev. Since the label is somewhat deceptive, it is worth noting Robert Payne's description of them in The Terrorists: "They possessed no philosophy except their simple faith in science and their repudiation of existing conventions, and while attempting to create a morality of their own, they were trapped into an extreme form of asceticism which could have no popular appeal. Turgenev gave them the name 'nihilists,' but he did not mean that they believed in nothing; he meant that they believed in the destruction of the existing state."4 Historians frequently comment on their similarity to the Puritans, at least in single-mindedness and moral fervor. They were also in the tradition of Savonarola; more than austere virtue was involved -- there was also extreme militancy. They had that icy moral fury which has sometimes typified the more saintly intellectuals in Western civilization, personifying a fanaticism imbued with piety which has subordinated all other values to its own point of concentrated focus. Such a temperament has occurred several times historically and has to be understood if certain periods in the history of Western society are to be understood.

Despite the fact that many of them were atheists, the movement had a good deal in common with the religious mysticism that was widespread in Russia. At mid-century, there were as many as ten million "religious dissenters" in Russia. "Some of them," Lampert says, "were attracted by visions of a better and freer life or by the teachings of messianic prophets, or by the wild emotional indulgences of the khlysty (flaggelants) and the manichaean skoptsy (castrates); others were sober evangelicals." It isn't surprising, therefore, that the nihilists drew heavily from the children of priests. Even though the child was outwardly very different from the parent, the inner spiritual base was similar. The child had lost his specific religious base, but had gained a secular one; his fervor continued. Two of the leading nihilists, Chernyshevsky and Dobrolyubov, were the children of Orthodox priests.

Socialism was yet another ingredient, combining with the atheism and the opposition to prevailing values. Chernyshevsky was a socialist before he was a revolutionary. Dobrolyubov held to an uncompromising socialist ideology even though he repudiated all fixed moral law; and although he died quite young -- at age twenty-five -- he is thought to have been the person who inspired Turgenev to use the label "nihilist." Tkachyov sought "a new socialist order." And although Nechayev possessed only a hazy vision of the type of society he wanted, he essentially shared the anarchism and socialism of his mentor Bakunin. He was the author of The Revolutionary Catechism, in which he proclaimed that "the revolutionary lives in this world only because he has faith in its speedy and total destruction."5

325

There was a period during which the intelligentsia sought wide support from the peasants. "Populism" held center stage in the 1870's, and consisted of a program for agrarian socialism. We can imagine the scene in 1874 as described by Richard Freeborn: "Dressed in peasant clothes and carrying socialist tracts, about 3,000 young members of the intelligentsia, mostly students, left the universities and urban centers in order to live and work among the peasants." The upshot, however, was that the peasants proved quite conservative, contrary to Bakunin's expectations. They were not the "dry tinder of revolution," Freeborn says, that the intelligentsia hoped they would be. In effect, this was a lesson that a Marx, but not a Mao, could understand: that the revolution could not rely on the peasants.

The violent revolutionary activity suffered a lull because of police activity after the attempted assassination of Alexander II in 1866, but it gradually revived. The Socialist Revolutionary Party mixed Populist Agrarian socialism with terrorism. A group called "The People's Will" concentrated on killing the Tsar. It succeeded in 1881 after several attempts.

By the end of the nineteenth century, Marx began to dominate socialist ideology in Europe. His influence began to be felt in Russia (and here again we see the exportation of ideas from Europe) in the 1880's. This led to theoretical arguments among the various types of socialists; the Populists wanted to rely on peasant communes as the basis for socialism, while the Marxists argued that the "dialectic of history" required that Russia could not attain socialism until it had first passed through the capitalist phase. Plekhanov, the leading Marxist, learned the new creed while he was in exile. Maxim Gorky was among the many later Marxists. He supported the Bolsheviks and created the literary form known as Socialist Realism.

There were four main political movements in

326

Russia during the decade that preceded the revolution of 1905: liberalism; a revived Populism; nationalism for the non-Russian peoples; and Marxism, which by this time had become a separate movement. The Left was torn by serious factional disputes based on the intricacies of Marxist theory; e.g., in 1905 the Mensheviks supported the more orthodox Marxist view that a bourgeois, liberal revolution should occur first, to be followed later by a proletarian revolution that would bypass the bourgeois phase.

The revolution of 1905 did in fact create a constitutional, liberal regime; and although the Tsar was not deposed, a national parliament, the Duma, was established. But it's noteworthy that this moderate solution suffered much the same fate that the early phase of the French Revolution had suffered: the Duma became increasingly dominated by the radicals, and there was an escalation of revolutionary activity. By now, the universities had been granted autonomy -- and they became centers for revolution. The Socialist Revolutionaries began a series of executions through their "combat organization." The Left, with its hierarchy of values that placed great weight on its utopian goals and thoroughly devalued everything else in the society, was plainly unwilling to accept a liberalized Russia.

Social changes. Important social changes were taking place during the nineteenth and early twentieth centuries. Not counting Finland, the population of the Russian Empire rose from 74 million in 1860 to 133 million in 1900 (although a small part of the increase was due to some minor annexations). This enormous burgeoning of population means, in effect, that the "revolt of the masses," in the sense that Jose Ortega y Gasset later wrote of it, was occurring in Russia just as it was in Europe and America.

Russia was still an exceedingly backward country. Freeborn says that "except for a small

327

proportion of kulaks and bigger, more progressive,
landowners, the average peasant farmer was abys-
mally ignorant and inefficient." Agriculture, he
says, was done almost entirely with manual labor.
In 1913 there were only 166 tractors in all of
Russia, despite its huge land mass. Nevertheless,
the beginnings of industrialization doubled the
Russian output between 1893 and 1900; the urban
population doubled during the second half of the
nineteenth century. One consequence of even this
rudimentary movement toward an urban, industrial
society was, according to Freeborn, that an urban
proletariat began to emerge that was much more
revolutionary than the peasantry.

Some Significant Voids

The events that actually occur in a society
and that catch the eye of historians are only part
of the story. Sometimes the events themselves
are void-filling make-shifts. If we seek an interpretive understanding, we need to appreciate
the factors that were missing from the society --
the voids. As we look back on Russian history
with the hind-sight that we now enjoy, we can see
that the positive factors were weak and the negative ones strong.

The intellectual void. The "Golden Age of
Russian Literature" produced some of the world's
enduring writing, but even within it we can see
the existence of a profound intellectual void.
Tolstoy was the giant -- but do we have grounds
for thinking that his writings included clear and
civilizationally satisfactory concepts about political philosophy, economics and jurisprudence?
He was essentially a lost soul even though his
magnificent fatalism and spiritual yearning provoked the most creative genius. His lostness was
especially apparent during the last years of his
life when he renounced literature and turned to
mysticism. It stands out, too, in his most monumental works, War and Peace and Anna Karenina.

328

But if we were to find balanced reason anywhere
among the Russian authors it would mainly have to
have been with Tolstoy. We could hardly expect
clear leadership to have come from the delightfully
warped Dostoyevsky, whose novels were works of art
giving flesh to the Russian torment of spirit and
intellect.

There is no difficulty in seeing how the
tormented, mystical mentality could relate to
utopianism. A mystic may easily forsake the day-
to-day tedium of ordinary life for a distant panacea. This in itself will reinforce a tendency
which I have already commented upon about the
alienation of the intellectual: the propensity to
place an extremely high value on a utopian goal
and to devalue everything else. Visionaries rarely appreciate that a civilization requires a
balance of values. Their distortion of values
comes at terrible expense.

Such a mentality arrogates all claims to piety,
morality, compassion and Godliness. It deserves
credit for its sincerity, but we should fault it
for usurping man's common morality by its incom-
parable presumptuousness. The success of this
moral stake-out is in part due to the failure of
sounder, more balanced, men to express an ethic
which can serve as an alternative to such claims.
The effectivenss of the militant intellectual as
an agitator is enhanced by the acting man's passive
acceptance of the moral code offered by that intellectual. One of the major insights Ayn Rand has
stressed has been that productive men often fail
to proclaim an ethical philosophy which is consistent with their own values. By this default they
leave themselves open to be victimized by the in-
sistent claims of the alienates who champion the
worldview of the have-nots.

Reflection of the European void. Because of
the Russians' absorption of European intellectual
modes, Russian thought in the nineteenth century
embraced as its own the void that existed in

329

Europe and America. Most of the ideas adopted by
the intelligentsia were from alienated European
thought; some were from America. To an American,
it is surprising to notice how little influence the
American example had; the liberal Murayov drafted
his constitution based on the United States', but
America's influence was minor compared with Europe's.
The ideas of most of the intelligentsia after mid-
century were socialist. And European thought gave
the Russian intellectual a complete mental inven-
tory: socialism was combined with positivism,
relativism, utopianism and alienation in the nihilist mind.

But European socialism didn't provide a constructive philosophy. The bleak horrors of the
Soviet Union are not surprising; they stem from a
philosophy and a system which makes coercion an
instrument of social religion. The Russian nihilist imbibed the worst features of Western civilization's existential crisis.

Russia's own intellectual void. The blame,
though, isn't all Europe's. Russia obviously suffered from its own intellectual void. If there
had been a consensus truly fitted to Russia the
Russian intellectuals would not have run so naive-
ly to Europe for their ideas.

The lack of a democratic tradition deprived
all Russians, including the intellectuals, of a
chance to gain experience in real life. Without
his "feet on the ground," a person who cares deeply about humanity will tend to become a dreamer.
This immaturity is at least part of what we mean
when we say that a people is not prepared to govern
itself.

One important effect is that the society loses
the benefits that could come from on-going intellectual participation. Such a drain of intellect
occurred in America, and in Russia it was a contributing factor in the decadence of the Tsarist
regime.

330

This is not to suggest that other aspects of Russian life did not also contribute to the internal weakness. Each of three wars had a telling effect: the Crimean, the Russo-Japanese and World War I. It is no coincidence that the revolutions of 1905 and 1917 each came in the wake of military disaster.

Lack of a viable middle class. There was no large human base, such as a middle class, which would support a free society on the American model. The peasantry's "conservatism" amounted almost entirely of their not being revolutionary. As people who had just recently emerged from serfdom, they weren't a sufficient base if freedom and democracy were to be achieved. In another connection, Wilhelm Röpke has written about how essential it is that there be a "middle class properly so called, that is, an independent class possessed of small or moderate property and income, a sense of responsibility, and those civic virtues without which a free and well-ordered society cannot, in the long run, survive."[6]

The Russian example suggests a strong analogy to the more recent situation of the so-called "Third World" countries. In the absence of a sound intellectuality and a broad middle class, there is no viable "middle." The wealthy and the privileged stand on one side and multitudes of people who are not yet ready for self-government stand on the other. In most such situations, a movement toward a free society has to come from the top. But this can prove chimerical if there isn't a sufficient human base -- and if an alienated intellectuality won't permit it. Yet at the same time, the rapid change and rising expectations taking place within all societies during the past century have made a slow preparation seem intolerable.

Human weakness. The combination of factors I have just mentioned -- an immature, alienated intelligentsia, growing multitudes of ill-prepared

331

people (or in advanced societies a spoiled, shallow and rootless public) -- means, in effect, a rise of internal barbarism. In such a context, civilized values become problematical. In light of the history we have just reviewed, Russia stands as an apt symbol for the crisis within Western civilization and, because of an unfortunate causal connection, within the rest of the world.

NOTES

1. E. Lampert, Sons Against Fathers (London: Oxford at the Clarendon Press, 1965), pp. 2, 85, 70.

2. Richard Freeborn, A Short History of Modern Russia (New York: William Morrow & Company, Inc., 1966), pp. 123, 112, 130, 160, 130, 133.

3. Hugh Seton-Watson, The Russian Empire, 1801-1917 (London: Oxford at the Clarendon Press, 1967), p. 423.

4. Robert Payne, The Terrorists (New York: Funk & Wagnalls Company, 1957), p. XV.

5. Nechayev is described in Payne's The Terrorists, pp. 3-130. His "The Revolutionary Catechism" is published in full there at pp. 21-27.

6. Wilhelm Röpke, A Humane Economy (Chicago: Henry Regnery Company, 1960), p. 32.

15

COBDEN, BRIGHT, PALMERSTON AND WORLD WAR I

As we look back on World War I after these many years, we lose track of the enthusiasms and animosities that made our grandparents think it so worthy a cause, and we can hardly avoid thinking of the war as having been one of the more senseless agonies mankind has ever visited upon itself. It was a ghastly war; and it's amazing that it was fought without even a major principle or a genuine conflict of interests being involved. It was, instead, the product of a massive neurosis.

The present chapter, as the reader knows, is one of a series in which I am discussing some of the more obvious reflections of the modern crisis. World War I could hardly be omitted from such a series. It was a symptom of the cosmic immaturity that resides within even the civilized man; and it tells us a lot about our intellectual failures. But before I discuss the war from this perspective, I will want to take time to review its specific origins and to summarize briefly the debate that has raged among historians over the question of fault. These will then serve as a concrete backdrop for my more general discussion.

The event that sparked the war occurred at Sarajevo on June 28, 1914, when a Serbian conspirator from the Pan-Slavic "Black Hand Society" shot and killed the heir-apparent to the throne of Austria-Hungary's Dual Monarchy, the Archduke Francis Ferdinand, and his wife (while, trivially but interestingly, they were on their way to celebrate their fourteenth wedding anniversary).

The Black Hand Society is known to have acted in complicity with various Serbian officials, and the conspiracy may even have extended to some members of the Russian government. The Society's existence was part of the Greater Serbian agitation which at least in part had originated in the ethnic nationalism that swept across Europe during and after the Napoleonic era. The agitation had been a long-standing problem for Austria-Hungary, a country which under Metternich had been a major European power but which had been seriously weakened by exclusion from Germany as a result of the Austro-Prussian War in 1866. The exclusion had made Austria-Hungary prey to the struggle of nationalities that eventually led to the Sarajevo assassinations and which in turn motivated the Dual Monarchy's severe reaction.

The historians of the period disagree over a great deal of what led up to the assassinations and over what happened after them. Some argue that Germany and Austria-Hungary used the Archduke's murder as a pretext to launch a general European war which those countries had hoped for for other reasons. Other historians say these countries only wanted strong diplomatic steps and a limited war with Serbia which would stop the agitation. At Versailles after World War I, the victors imposed the first of these views as the official theory of the war.

The events show that Germany gave her ally pretty much a blank-check during the first few days after the assassinations, but later tried to keep Austria-Hungary from going too far. One of the points of argument among the historians is whether the eventual restraint was either timely or genuine; but in any case the Dual Monarchy didn't heed the restraint. It went ahead with its declaration of war and mobilization against Serbia.

Even at this juncture, the conflict might have remained restricted if Russia hadn't mobilized to support Serbia. It's significant that many Europeans considered a general mobilization equivalent to a declaration of war. Again, historians disagree -- first over Russia's justification for mobilizing and then over the importance other

334

countries should have assigned to it. Some historians assert, in fact, that the mobilization carried out a scheme by pro-war factions in Russia and France in favor of a general war which would hopefully gain the Dardanelles for Russia and Alsace-Lorraine for the French. Others see the mobilization as a justified intervention on behalf of Serbia in keeping with Russia's "traditional role" as protector of the slavs.

Germany's Kaiser Wilhelm held back long enough to send the Tsar an ultimatum demanding that the mobilization be abandoned. When Russia continued, Germany went to war. And the way it did so is itself the subject of one of the main points of contention; Germany followed a strategy that had been worked out for it years earlier by Chief of Staff Alfred von Schlieffen which was designed to eliminate Germany's geographical problem of a two-front war. The plan called for an immediate attack through Belgium and northern France to defeat the French before the Russians (who were allied with France) could have time to enter the war from the east. This violation of Belgian neutrality gave rise to world-wide revulsion against Germany, and provided at least a pretext for England's intervention. Historians disagree over whether the English government under Asquith and Grey was responding genuinely to the attack on Belgium; some think it used the attack to justify England's entering the war pursuant to secret commitments to France and Russia.

From this point, the war was underway. Millions died; countless others were gassed and maimed; and the setting was established for World War II. But even now there is a general inability by intelligent world opinion to say why it all happened. As we have seen, almost every nuance of the circumstances that led up to the war is subject to conflicting interpretation. These nuances are combined together into three basic theories: the theory, adopted at Versailles, that Germany plotted the war; the view that France and

335

Russia plotted it; and what we might call the "tinderbox" theory.[1]

At Versailles, the Allies' "Commission on the Responsibility of the Authors of the War" declared that "the responsibility for it lies wholly with the Powers which declared war in pursuance of a policy of aggression, the concealment of which gives to the origin of this war the character of a dark conspiracy against the peace of Europe." This is a view that Camille Bloch has endorsed in The Causes of the World War: "William II and the German General Staff, although they had maintained a pacific attitude during the recent Balkan wars . . . ., were fully aware of the unpreparedness of France, Russia, and England; they believed that the moment for agression had come, and determined to seize the first favorable opportunity to adopt a policy of force."[2]

The exactly opposite conclusion -- that France and Russia had plotted the war -- was argued by Harry Elmer Barnes in The Genesis of the World War. He said that "for several years previous to the outbreak of the World War, Izvolski (the Russian ambassador to France) had become convinced that the most important point in Russian foreign policy was the securing of the Straits, and that they could only be obtained by a European war." He continued that "Sazonov was converted to this view by December, 1913, and he expressed himself as be-lieving that with British help, France and Russia could easily dispose of Germany and put an end to her existence as a first-class power . . . To pre-pare for such an incident, the Russians had en-couraged Serbian plots against Austria, supplied the Serbians with arms, and twice promised them Russian aid against Austria. Russian army, and possibly diplomatic, circles knew of the Sarajevo plot in advance and gave it their approval."[3] Barnes also tied in France through its Premier and later President, Raymond Poincare; he said that in 1912 Izvolski "was joined in his program by . . . Poincare (whose dominating ambition was

336

the restoration of Alsace-Lorraine," which had been lost to Germany in the Franco-Prussian War in 1870.

Another historian of this same school of thought is Erich Brandenburg, one of Germany's leading historians. In From Bismarck to the World War, Brandenburg said that "so far as guilt can be brought home to individual personalities in the world war, these two men (Izvolski and Poincare) stand convicted . . . It was they, not Germany, who wished for conquests at the expense of others."[4]

I have called the third interpretation of the war the "tinderbox" theory. It says that Europe stumbled into the war after years of arms-race and mutual suspicion without anyone's premeditation. A group of French and German historians has concluded that "the documents do not permit attributing a premeditated desire for a European war on the part of any government or people in 1914. Distrust was at a peak and ruling circles were dominated by the idea that war was inevitable. Each one accused the other of aggressive intentions; each accepted the risk of war and saw its only hope for security in the alliance system and the development of armament."[5] Consistently with this, Raymond Aron says in The Century of Total War that "search was made . . . for the men who had knowingly embarked on aggression. They were not discovered or, in any case, they were not discovered in the simple guise of storybook villains."[6]

I have made a list of some of the main open questions left by the welter of conflicting interpretations. When we see that they often involve subtle questions of judgment, we can understand why it is that historians will never evaluate them all the same way:

• Whether Izvolski and Poincare intended a general war.
• Whether Germany plotted war.
• The extent of Serbian and even Russian complicity in the Sarajevo killings.

337

• Whether (as Sir Edward Grey in England so strongly asserted) Germany was actually more nationalist, imperialist and militarist than the other major powers in Europe.

• Whether Russian mobilization was justified on behalf of Serbia.

• Whether Kaiser Wilhelm's pre-war role was militaristic and bombastic -- or was instead that of a peace-maker.

• How closely England was allied before the war with France and through France with Russia.

• Which nation or bloc was responsible for the arms race that preceded the war -- or whether exclusive blame can be assessed at all.

• Whether it was reasonable to understand Russian mobilization as equivalent to a declaration of war.

• Whether Germany's invasion of Belgium caused England to enter the war or whether the invasion was just used as a pretext by Asquith and Grey.

• Whether it was reasonable for Austria-Hungary to think that a war with Serbia could be localized.

• Whether Germany was wrong in giving Austria-Hungary a free diplomatic hand, and whether Germany's eventual restraint was timely and genuine.

• The justification, if any, for the Pan-Slavic agitation.

• Whether Austria-Hungary was justified in desiring war with Serbia after the assassinations.

To list these issues is to suggest that the causes of the war pose a very difficult intellectual question. It is remarkable that in England and the United States public opinion was able to reach so overwhelming a consensus that Germany was the villain. In his memoirs, Sir Edward Grey said that Germany had possessed a criminal nature that had been a threat to European civilization.7 Woodrow Wilson saw World War I as a war "to make the world safe for democracy." But these conclusions were by no means clearly supportable; and since they weren't they seem to reflect hysteria and the effects of massive propaganda. As we place the

338

war in perspective, it will be worthwhile to note precisely the closed-mindedness of millions of people, their dogmatic certainty about something that will always be inextricably complicated to historians, and their enthusiastic willingness to die without any real attempt at understanding. The elements of human nature that were involved seem timeless. I am reminded of the people who rejected Balavignus' suggestions about the plague in the fourteenth century, since they too died in large numbers while wilfully distorting reality.

Intellectual Precursors

The war wasn't an unrelated event; it occurred in a civilization in which the preconditions for it had been established well in advance. These preconditions included a savage strain of intellectuality which had raised the tensions within Europe to a frantic pitch. Countless viewpoints screamed in Jacobinical excess. Many glorified war and "direct action."

Julien Benda's famous The Betrayal of the Intellectuals described this intellectual milieu in detail. He saw intense political passions that were clothed with all the drapings of ideology and which spoke with the authority of science, claiming that their actions were not only supremely valuable but were also propelled by historical necessity. These passions had all become self-conscious and were now fine-honed with the traits of universality, coherence, homogeneity, precision and continuity, so that they outshown all other emotions. All of this was carried to a perfection never before seen in Western civilization. With considerable anguish, Benda cried that "today there is scarcely a mind in Europe which is not affected -- or thinks itself affected -- by racial or class or national passion, and most often by all three." (Emphasis added) He said that "in the last half

century France has possessed a fanatically nationalist literature." And he saw that "the cult
of success, I mean the teaching which says that
when a will is successful that fact alone gives it
a moral value, whereas the will which fails is for
that reason alone deserving of contempt . . . is
professed by many a modern teacher in political
life (it may be said, by all in Germany since Hegel,
and by a large number in France since de Maistre)."
He wrote of the "denunciation of liberalism . . .
by the vast majority of contemporary men of letters."

This milieu raised the State high and looked
upon war as a spiritual elevation. "The modern
realists," Benda said, "are the moralists of
realism. For them, the act which makes the State
strong is invested with a moral character . . . ,
and this whatever the act may be. The evil which
serves politics ceases to be evil and becomes good."
He added that "our moralists who sneer at pacific
civilization and extol a warlike life, do so
because the former seems a dull sort of a life
to them and the latter an opportunity for sensa-
tions." He wrote between the world wars, and he
concluded that "this humanity is heading for the
greatest and most perfect war of classes." In the
intellectuality Benda described, we can spot,
among other things, the origins of Hitler's contempt for "the peaceful contest of nations" and
for bourgeois life. This was a contempt which
caused Hitler to cry out "why couldn't I have been
born a hundred years earlier? Say at the time of
the Wars of Liberation when a man, even without a
'business,' was really worth something?"

Benda made it clear that such ideas weren't
simply German. Nevertheless, the observations by
Reinhold Aris in his History of Political Thought
in Germany are illuminating. "One of the favorite
heroes of the Storm and Stress poets was the noble
criminal who struggled against the law as the
incarnation of a narrow-minded rationalism."[9] He
says that "in Schleiermacher's thought the organic

340

concept allied itself with the national idea and thus all the strength which could be derived from the concept of an organic state was transferred to the national movement." He writes of "Hegel's glorification of the Prussian military state as the embodiment of the world spirit." Muller, in turn, "uses his philosophical principle of antagonism for the justification of war . . . In his opinion a state can only thrive if it is continuously challenged by other states and it is itself only the product of war." Nietzsche expressed the same thought in Twilight of the Idols. "Out of life's school of war: What does not destroy me, makes me stronger."10 "One has renounced the great life when one renounces war" (his emphasis). In 1880, Nietzsche described the situation in Europe: "All states are now ranged against each other: they presuppose their neighbor's bad disposition and their own good disposition." To which he added two years later that "I welcome all signs that a more manly, a warlike, age is about to begin, an age which, above all, will give honor to valor once again. For this age shall prepare the way for one yet higher . . . For, believe me, the secret of the greatest fruitfulness and the greatest enjoyment of existence is: to live dangerously!" (his emphasis). Benda later noted Nietzsche as among those who came to equate justice with power.

Cobden, Bright and Palmerston

If a student of the causes of World War I becomes enmeshed in the detail of events after the turn of the century, he loses the perspective which he could have if he were to look at the war in light of the attitudes and events of fifty or sixty years earlier. If we read the biographies of Richard Cobden and John Bright -- the two leading members of the Manchester School in England whose political activity spanned the middle forty years of the nineteenth century --, we will notice a striking similarity between the international

341

issues of their time and those which later culminated in World War I. We will also find that their peace-oriented and yet thoroughly practical philosophy is an excellent touchstone by which to measure the voids that led to war.

The emphasis in Bright's political life was on democracy. In keeping with this, he associated peace with the extension of the franchise. George Trevelyan says that "he regarded our warlike foreign policy as the result of our aristocratic system of Government."[11] In the second half of Bright's life (following his fight alongside Cobden for the abolition of the tariff on grains), he devoted himself to extending the franchise.

Richard Cobden had a somewhat different emphasis during the second half of his political life. Cobden avidly sought a policy of free trade, which he saw as integral to a world-wide order in which peaceable commerce rather than warlike suspicion would be the nexus among nations. He referred to "the question of Free Trade as the means -- and, I believe the only human means -- of effecting universal and permanent peace."[12] John MacCunn has painted a broad picture of Cobden's vision: "It was not an insular or one-sided Free Trade that could content him -- though he never hesitated to prefer that to Protection. His expectations went out to nothing less than a complete international division of labor, under which the production of the whole world would be maximized, and the wants of each several country supplied on a basis of a free international exchange of commodities . . . Above all, it was to be not only the harbinger but the cause of Peace, and the breaking down of hostile barriers between nation and nation. 'Free Trade!' he cries in one of his most vehement passages, 'What is it?' Why, breaking down the barriers that separate nations; these barriers behind which nestle the feelings of pride, revenge, hatred, and jealousy, which every now and then burst their bounds and deluge whole countries with blood!"[13]

342

Cobden's philosophy included several implications. He favored the international arbitration of disputes. He considered colonies "the costly appendage of an aristocratic government." And he argued that the concept of "the balance of power" was a "chimera."[14] Cobden observed about the "balance of power" (which was a concept that bred distrust and caused the system of alliances) that "it is not a fallacy, a mistake, an imposture, it is an undescribed, indescribable, incomprehensible nothing; mere words, conveying to the mind not ideas, but sounds." Further, he opposed the idea that England should police the world. He stood against the existence of a large standing army, opposed the colonization of India, sought to abolish the need for passports, worked for the reduction of armaments, was a vigorous critic of England's involvement in the Crimean War, and served successfully as England's representative in negotiating a commercial treaty with France based on free trade principles.

To Cobden during those years, Prime Minister Palmerston was an apt symbol of the whole warlike syndrome. R. A. J. Walling gives William Gladstone, Richard Cobden and John Bright credit for having done "more than anything else to check the mad jingo dance in which Palmerston beckoned on a panic-stricken country to war with France."[15] Trevelyan gives us an illustration: "The first two years of the new Whig cabinet (June 1859-1861) saw a terrible danger draw near and recede. The panic-mongers, headed by Palmerston himself, long held the country on the verge of war with France, for no reason except the utterly false belief that Napoleon intended to attack us." Cobden argued that England was itself a source of the distrust: "I sometimes hear it very complacently said, 'everybody knows that England is only armed in self-defense, and in the interests of peace.' But when France looks at our 500 ships of war, our 180 war steamers, and hears of our great preparations at Alderney, Jersey, and other points close to her shores, she has very different suspicions."

343

He wrote an essay on the subject, which he summarized by saying that "it has been demonstrated in the preceding pages, by evidence drawn from our own official statements, totally irrespective of the French accounts, that, as a nation, we have borne false witness against out neighbors; that, without a shadow of proof or justification, we have accused them, repeatedly, during a long series of years, of meditating an unprovoked attack on our shores, in violation of every principle of international law, and in contempt of all the obligations of morality and honour." He pointed out that "for a century and a half we have been fighting, with occasional intermissions, for the Balance of Power, but I do not remember that it has ever been made the subject of peaceful diplomacy, with a view to the organisation of the whole of Europe." Speaking of the Crimean War, he added that "in the present case, our Government has entered into war on the assumption that the European balance has been, and still is, endangered by the ambition of Russia." According to Trevelyan, Cobden and Bright "worked together between 1846 and 1854 (for) resistance to military expenditure and to Palmerston's interference in European affairs which caused it."

From all of this, we see that the syndrome that carried Europe into World War I had existed for a good many years, despite the presence of men such as Cobden and Bright who offered a change of philosophy which might have put an end to the madness. The causes of the war are to be found most immediately in the events at and after Sarajevo, but the real underlying factors existed in the intellectual and spiritual void which had caused Europe to turn a deaf ear to constructive alternatives.

Some Additional Observations

An awareness of the factors that led to World War I is important if we are to understand certain attitudes which have existed during the Cold War

since 1945. Classical liberals and Burkean traditionalists hold philosophies that would incline
them toward a deep revulsion against Marxism-
Leninism. They accordingly have seen the overriding international issue since 1945 as having been
the expansionist nature of Communist totalitarianism.
Such thinkers see world events since 1945 as similar to the situation during the 1930's when Hitler's
expansionist Nazism was the central problem. From
this point of view, the problem is not so much one
of "distrust" and "misunderstanding" as it is one
of a world divided by ideology in which all of the
factors we have considered about bourgeois culture
and about the intellectuals' alienation from it
are pertinent. Although the pre-World War I problems of distrustful nations still exist, they are
present as an underlay. Over and above them, we
find the struggle between the factions within a
profoundly divided civilization.

On the other hand, the very nature of the
Left's orientation has caused it (including most
modern American liberals) to minimize the threat
posed by Communism, often to the point of denying
it as a problem altogether. When detente was en-
gineered with Peking and Moscow by Richard Nixon
in the early 1970's, liberal voices were raised
which argued that the entire Cold War had been due
far less to a genuine threat from Communist expansion than to a jingoistic perception arising in
America.

When this perspective abstracts Communism
virtually out of the picture, it comes to see the
world's problems in a way that is identical to the
way Cobden saw those which existed in the nineteenth
century: a balance of power, a lack of mutual
understanding, a destructive national pride, pro-
fiteering in armaments, and the like. Anyone who
sees the world in this way will tend to call for
an American foreign policy of conciliation and
detente. Such measures as cultural exchanges are
calculated to reduce provincialisms. The Communist
"wars of national liberation" around the world are

looked upon as simply local civil wars, albeit wearing a superficial mask of ideology -- and it is suggested that American policy should be one of non-intervention.

It is worth noticing this vast difference in perception. A conservative has a difficult time understanding why a liberal sees things as he does; and it is just as hard for a liberal to understand the conservative's system of interpretation. Each starts with different premises about the world, and those premises are related to his overall ideology.

I am myself a classical liberal and I accordingly hold Richard Cobden in considerable esteem. I agree with his understanding of nineteenth century international affairs. And yet, I also agree with the anti-Communist perception of the world following the Second World War. A world that is threatened by expansionist totalitarian ideology is, in my opinion, substantially different from one that is threatened only by the vagaries of the anarchy of nations. At the same time, I would stress that anti-Communists should keep in mind that the pre-World War I neuroses still exist as an underlay. Whenever we can do so consistently with our adversary role in the conflict with Communism, we should try to edge the world a bit closer to Cobden's vision. It will be a tragedy if the energies of the twentieth century are totally absorbed by the need to fight totalitarian forces, with the effect that when those forces no longer occupy the stage we will have made no progress toward solving the syndrome which was so evident before World War I. A program for doing what we can toward "improved understanding," free trade, the international arbitration of disputes, etc., should ideally be developed concomitantly with an anti-Communist policy to the extent that we can do so without giving up our necessary sense of moral outrage over the totalitarian nature of that system.

346

The difficulty is that our own weakness and division make this impossible. If we enjoyed a deep consensus within our own intellectual culture about the evils of Communism and about the benefits of a classically liberal free society, we would be armed with a spiritual force of our own to meet that of our totalitarian opponents. This would mean that we would be much stronger than we now are. From such a position of strength we could afford some conciliatory measures which might help solve the pre-World War I syndrome. But our actual weakness of mind and of spirit produces a different effect; it means that very little goes truly well for us under any policy, whether militant or conciliatory; and it means that conciliatory measures tend to vitiate such moral force as we are able to muster.

It is doubtful whether Richard Nixon made the characteristic mistake of a "liberal" view of the world. He knew the nature of Communism too well for this. He sought conciliation out of what he considered shrewdness and strength. It wasn't Communism that he misunderstood, but ourselves. His policy overestimated the moral, spiritual condition of the West. We act from division and apathy mixed with some surges of will, and this is hardly a sufficient basis for the dual policy I have mentioned.

There is something else to consider, too. Although we should work toward a Cobden-like resolution of international anarchy, I have no conviction that the world, in its immaturity, is ready for a definitive solution. The civilized base isn't sufficiently present. It would help immensely, of course, if the divisions within modern Western civilization were cured; but even then we couldn't anticipate that humanity, including the people of the United States and Europe, would give up its "direct action" tendencies and its varied attitudes sufficiently to agree upon Cobden's suggestions. The internal barbarization occurring within the West and the civilizational weakness of

347

Asia, Africa and Latin America will hardly dissolve in the foreseeable future. This means that the world will retain a substantial amount of turmoil in any case. If Communism were to disappear but the alienation of the intellectual were to remain, countless people would simply throw themselves into new totalitarian movements; and if even so profound a change were to occur as the evaporation of the alienation, the world would still be inhabited by an immature humanity.

Nor can the world be made peaceable by an international "rule of law." There is nothing to make us suppose that today's boundaries reflect a final equilibrium. Tremendous demographic changes are taking place, and submerged peoples are rising. There is nothing about the status quo that suggests that it corresponds with the realities that will exist even so soon as fifty or a hundred years in the future. If a full Kellogg-Briand Pact type of peace is to exist under such circumstances, it will have to be the result of nuclear terror; it certainly won't occur naturally. A system of international law would have no way to adjust demographic pressures. Either it would serve as an instrument of the status quo and find itself perpetually challenged; or it would serve as the cutting edge of change, in which case it would have to perform the impossible task of developing a consensus on the principles which would guide the process of change.

There is no basis, certainly, for world government. The voids within modern civilization are simply too great for us to anticipate that a world government would serve the interests of a classical liberal type of freedom for the individual. Such a government would itself tend to become an instrument of "direct action" for whatever peoples or interests predominated within it. Or if it were to fall under the rein of the idealist, it would tend to become the theocratic instrument of the intelligentsia. For better or for worse, we are left with the traditional system of nation-states.

NOTES

1. These views are well represented in an excellent introductory book: Dwight E. Lee (ed.), The Outbreak of the First World War, Who Was Responsible? (Boston: D. C. Heath and Company, 1958).

2. Camille Bloch, The Causes of the World War (London: G. Allen & Unwin, Ltd., 1935), pp. 183-191.

3. Harry Elmer Barnes, The Genesis of the World War (New York: Alfred A. Knopf, 1929), pp. 372-373, 147.

4. Erich Brandenburg, From Bismarck to the World War (London: Oxford University Press, 1929). pp. 518-523.

5. From James A. Corbett, "France and Germany Agree -- on the Past," Historical Bulletin, XXVIII (March, 1955), 158-162.

6. Raymond Aron, The Century of Total War (New York: Doubleday & Company, Inc., 1954), quoted in Lee, Outbreak, p. 69.

7. Sir Edward Grey, Twenty-Five Years (New York: Frederick A. Stokes Company, 1925).

8. Julien Benda, The Betrayal of the Intellectuals (Boston: The Beacon Press, 1930), pp. 22, 1, 43, 116, 81, 85, 140, 145.

9. Reinhold Aris, History of Political Thought in Germany (London: George Allen and Unwin Ltd., 1936), pp. 193, 294, 302, 312.

10. Friedrich Nietzsche, The Portable Nietzsche (New York: Viking Press, 1968), pp. 467, 489, 72, 97.

11. George Macaulay Trevelyan, The Life of John

Bright (Boston: Houghton Mifflin Company, 1913),
pp. 273, 283, 178.

12. John Morley, The Life of Richard Cobden (London: Chapman and Hall, 1881), Vol. I, p. 230.

13. John MacCunn, Six Radical Thinkers (New York: Russell & Russell, 1964), p. 103.

14. Richard Cobden, The Political Writings of Richard Cobden (London: The Cassell & Company, Ltd., 1886), pp. 150, 197, 198, 346, 696-697, 533.

15. R. A. J. Walling (ed.), The Diaries of John Bright (New York: William Morrow and Company, 1931), p. 243.

16

GERMAN YOUTH, VOLKISH IDEOLOGY

AND THE NAZI PHENOMENON

Anyone who has seen Hitler's propaganda film "The Triumph of the Will" and who remembers the scene in which flagbearers at the 1934 Nazi Party Rally in Nuremberg lowered their flags to the ground one by one as the names of the battlefields of World War I were read off will appreciate how much World War II was a continuation of the First World War. The anger, the nationalism, the militancy all carried over through the short span of intervening years.

Again, millions were to die. And again it's hard to understand, in light of the size of the calamity, that we can have so poor an understanding of the causes of the tragedy. We often think of World War II as having sprung from a unique aberration. A recent movie was typical of this when it pictured Hitler as a psychotic.

So far as an historically adequate perspective of the causes of the war is concerned, it is really beside the point whether Hitler was psychotic -- although I am inclined to think that he was not, at least until he drove his health to extremes under the pressures of war and of his eccentric living habits. It is a mistake to focus on Hitler at all. A twentieth century Tolstoy could easily write another War and Peace that would show how particular individuals -- even dominating individuals such as Hitler -- were swept along on a tide which they hardly controlled. The forces which produced Nazi totalitarianism and led to war were rooted in the intellectual and spiritual condition of Europe in general and of Germany in particular. Seen in this context, Hitler wasn't an aberration who just happened by an unfortunate series of cir-

351

cumstances to become the head of the German state.
What is important to understand is that he represented certain major tendencies which were already
well under way before he was born.

I will want to place the Nazi phenomenon in
this larger context, and this involves reviewing
five main antecedents, which will be:

- The psychology of the "mass-man" as described by José Ortega y Gasset. This will take
  us back into some of the things I discussed
  in Chapter 8.

- The role played by modern man's yearning for
  a secular religion.

- The intellectual preconditions.

- The cultural preconditions.

- And the specific factual circumstances which
  led to Hitler.

The psychology of the "mass-man." In Chapter
8 I stressed that our age has been highly problematical not just because of the rapid development
of science and technology, but because of the average man's rise to predominance for the first time
in history. In that chapter, I referred at length
to Ortega. It is worth noting, though, that many
thoughtful men have commented on the dangers that
are inherent in the shallowness, rootlessness and
spoiledness of the type of man who is born into an
advanced civilization but who takes it for granted
without moving himself from his self-assurance
enough to understand and appreciate its wonder and
delicacy.

The state of mind has definite repercussions
in the political life of modern society. During
the past century, great masses of people have
come into being who have been willing to use brutal "direct action" methods without regard to

352

their effect on humane institutions. Young Germans cried in 1932 that they were tired of endless talk, and wanted "only to act."[1] Although each varies in degree, there is a fundamental similarity between Sorel's syndicalist "general strike" technique in France, the sit-ins and mass marches that occurred in the United States in the 1960's, the truckers' mass closing of the highways at the time of the fuel crisis in the United States in 1973, the garbagemen's strike in New York City a few years before, the actions of the New Left in Chicago in 1968, Hitler's relish in breaking up bourgeois meetings, and the like. Hitler expressed a point of view which was in tune with all of these "direct action" movements when he gloated "How many a time the eyes of my lads glittered when I explained to them the necessity of their mission and assured them over and over again that all the wisdom of this earth remains without success if force does not enter into its service . . . ."[2] When means such as these are widely used in a society, it isn't surprising that that society's politics will exhibit the same traits. In fact, as Ortega pointed out, the totalitarian state is the ultimate embodiment of this "direct action" psychology and method. The civilizing principle that force should be the last resort is reversed. Instead, force is made the first or even the only resort.[3]

If we see Hitler in this context, we see that his rise was consistent with the mentality of countless people other than himself. I can't speak for the reader's experience, but my own convinces me that the character traits that Ortega described are prevalent. Far from being the exclusive possession of a few anti-social eccentrics, they reflect a major human failure in modern Western life. (It is always worth while to mitigate Ortega's observations, though, by realizing that this modern failure isn't a fall from an earlier perfection. In the beginning chapters of this book I sought to create a long-term perspective which would permit us to see that our own voids are part

353

of the cosmic condition of mankind as we find ourselves at this point in our development.)

The yearning for a secular religion. Religiously centered philosophers such as Richard
Weaver have argued that because of its preoccupation with secular values the modern age has sunk
into decadence, lacking a God-centered perception
and wandering emptily without spiritual focus.
The psychiatrist Viktor Frankl has observed that
"the loss of meaning" is today's most common spiritual affliction. And even the atheist Jean Paul
Sartre has said that "by forlornness we mean the
absence of God." Lostness is a recurrent theme in
modern literature, philosophy, art and motion
pictures.

The spiritual question isn't wholly absent
from the life even of the commonplace man who seems
to accept a life of averageness without question. Of course, it is possible to say that its
mere absence as a positive factor in his life will
affect his values and behavior. Such a man's spiritual mediocrity is an important datum for himself and for those who live with him even
though it is often unrecognized. But beyond this,
it is often true that, despite appearances, the
spiritual question is felt by him. Since circumstances don't always set the stage for a comfortable acceptance by him of a superficial reality,
they can force him to question the meaning of life.

The great mass movements have, in part, served as substitute religions to satisfy this spiritual emptiness. The religious aspect of National
Socialism can easily be imagined if we compare the
humdrum quality of the daily life of a German factory worker who may have worked all day, stopped
at a beer garden on his way home, spent the evening with his family, and repeated the same round
the next day, with the excitement and transcendent
feeling he probably felt as he heard of German
armies on the march and attended massive rallies
with half-a-million other people. He could easily

354

have been carried away by the large brilliantly
colored flags, the bands playing stirring music and
the collective shouts of "sieg heil" as Hitler
pranced exultantly about. All of this offered
something larger, more meaningful, than the worker
saw in his own small, ordinary existence. The
Nazi Party rallies were secular religious experiences. "Religion? Of course," Howard Becker
says. "Any value-system for the sake of which its
devotees sacrificially live and gladly die is a
religion, regardless of whether or not it has a
god in the traditional sense."[4]

In Mein Kampf, Hitler told of his despair
over having been born "in an age of shopkeepers."
He wished he had been born a century or so before,
in time to take part in the Wars of Liberation
against Napoleon. In the preceding chapter, I
quoted authors who in the nineteenth century
praised war for its spiritual excitement. War,
with its heavy baggage of carnage and destruction,
appears sick and existentially hollow when thought
through, but it has fascinated those who either
have not identified with peaceable society or have
lacked sufficient personal resources to find meaning elsewhere. Walter Laqueur reports that young
people in Germany greeted World War I enthusias-
tically. Ina Seidel was a young German poet who
wrote "O holy fortune, to be young today!" The
war, she said, gave German youth a reason for
existence for the first time; until then, youth
had seemed "a burden and a curse."

The intellectual preconditions. The many
modern thinkers who -- in their disaffection from
mass, industrial, bourgeois culture -- have preached "blood and thunder" philosophies were as much
precursors of World War II and of National Socialism as of World War I. The same intellectual
milieu contributed to each.

But the alienated intellectual temper did
more than extoll violence and the state; it undercut constructive attachment to the more civilized,

humane aspirations of the new age. This intellectuality has not identified with liberal values.
Laqueur says that German young people considered
liberalism the greatest "abomination," and that
they felt "nausea and especial contempt" toward
it. The alienation has fed resentment and a carping, neurotic rejection of society. The result has
been that the main movements of the twentieth century have not been in harmony with the finest potential of the time, but with discordances and
tensions. It's no surprise that after many years
of an intellectual milieu in Germany which included the Storm and Stress movement, the Romantic rejection of the Enlightenment, the Historical School
with its debunking relativism and its anti-bourgeois attitudes, the Lassallean socialists and the
Marxists, the cultural tendencies that led to Hitler were present. Those tendencies reflected the
alienation and shattering of consensus.

It's a mistake to lose sight of the broad intellectual context, but the intellectual movement
that was most directly related to the rise of
National Socialist ideology was the Volkish movement which followed on the heels of Romanticism.
George Mosse has traced the origins of Volkish
thought in The Crisis of German Ideology. He says
that "'Volk' is one of those perplexing German
terms which connotes far more than its special
meaning. 'Volk' is a much more comprehensive term
than 'people,' for to German thinkers ever since
the birth of German romanticism in the late
eighteenth century 'Volk' signified the union of
a group of people with a transcendental 'essence'
. . . The essential element here is the linking of
the human soul with its natural surroundings, with
the 'essence' of nature . . . According to many
Volkish theorists, the nature of the soul of a
Volk is determined by the native landscape. Thus
the Jews, being a desert people, are viewed as
shallow, arid, 'dry' people."[5] He says that "men
like Father Jahn, Arndt, and Fichte began to con-
ceive of the Volk in heroic terms during the wars
of liberation against Napoleon." The Volkish

356

worldview was elaborated later in the nineteenth
century by such authors as Heinrich von Sybel,
Theodor Fontane, Wilhelm Heinrich Riehl, Berthold
Auerbach -- and many others. As it went on, Volkish thought escalated toward the eventual National
Socialist ideology: "In Der Wehrwolf (1910),
the most famous German peasant novel," Mosse says,
"Hermann Lons eventually carried the glorification
of brute force to its heights." In the meantime,
"popular literature, mainly novels (which sold in
the millions), portrayed the alien Jew in growing-
ly distasteful stereotypes."

There were two authors, though, whose names
especially stand out in connection with Volkish
thought. Mosse says that "the ideology was elevated into a Germanic faith, an achievement for
which two men bear a large share of the responsibility: Paul de Lagarde and Julius Langbehn."
"Any humaneness Lagarde possibly possessed was
eventually obscurbed by his call for the extermina-
tion of the Jews like bacillae. This outburst
clearly paralleled his advocacy of physical force
and violence to crush the recalcitrant contemporary
state 'like an eggshell.'" Just the same, "ideas
of race played a greater role in Langbehn's theology than in Lagarde's. Race and vitality of
nature were viewed as equivalent forces." I could
go on quoting Mosse, especially about the extension of an ever more virulent Volkish ideology into the twentieth century, but what I have already
cited is enough to show the extent to which National Socialist ideology found origins in the
earlier Volkish worldview, which in turn had
sprung quite readily from the mystical, nationalis-
tic, anti-Enlightenment attitudes of the Romantic
movement. The latter, of course, had been an important part of the existential struggle which
many thinkers had waged against the advance of
modern and liberal values. We see the connection
between Romanticism, Volkish ideology and National
Socialism in the statement by the Nazi philosopher
Alfred Baeumler that "Romanticism saw man again in
the light of his natural and historical ties.

Romanticism opened our eyes to the night, the past, our ancestors, to the mythos and the Volk."[6]

The cultural preconditions: the German Youth Movement. The German Youth Movement began in about 1896 and continued until it was absorbed into the Hitler Youth in the 1930's. It was a movement which ranks with the Jacobins, the Russian nihilists and the American New Left as a symptom of extreme social and ideological disintegration. A study of it lends a great deal to our perspective of the rise of Hitler, since the movement reveals patterns that are helpful in explaining Hitler's role as a charismatic leader of his peers.

Howard Becker's German Youth: Bond or Free and Walter Laqueur's Young Germany tell about the movement from a scholarly point of view. But because unimpassioned scholarship doesn't adequately convey the appropriate sensibilities of civilized men as they see, with considerable abhorrence, such things as the German Youth Movement or the American New Left, I think it is best to begin with the description given by Ludwig von Mises in Bureaucracy in 1944. Mises is less "objective" and for some reason, perhaps out of sarcasm, falls into a quaintness of style which is not typical of his writing, but the following passage tells us more than an impartial description can:

"In the decade preceding the First World War Germany, the country most advanced on the path toward bureaucratic regimentation, witnessed the appearance of a phenomenon hitherto unheard of: the youth movement. Turbulent gangs of untidy boys and girls roamed the country, making much noise and shirking their school lessons. In bombastic words they announced the gospel of a golden age. All preceding generations, they emphasized, were simply idiotic; their incapacity has converted the earth into a hell. But the rising generation is no longer willing to endure gerontocracy, the supremacy of impotent and imbecile senility. Henceforth the brilliant youths will rule. They

358

will destroy everything that is old and useless,
they will reject all that was dear to their
parents, they will substitute new real and substantial values and ideologies for the antiquated
and false ones of capitalist and bourgeois civilization, and they will build a new society of
giants and supermen.

"The inflated verbiage of these adolescents
was only a poor disguise for their lack of any
ideas and of any definite program. They had nothing to say but this: We are young and therefore
chosen; we are ingenious because we are young, we
are the carriers of the future; we are the deadly
foes of the rotten bourgeois and Philistines.
And if somebody was not afraid to ask them what
their plans were, they knew only one answer: Our
leaders will solve all problems.

"It has always been the task of the new generation to provoke changes. But the characteristic
feature of the youth movement was that they had
neither new ideas nor plans. They called their
action the youth movement precisely because they
lacked any program which they could use to give a
name to their endeavors. In fact, they espoused
entirely the program of their parents. They did
not oppose the trend toward government omnipotence
and bureaucratization. Their revolutionary radicalism was nothing but the impudence of the years
between boyhood and manhood; it was a phenomenon
of a protracted puberty. It was void of any
ideological content.

"The chiefs of the youth movement were mentally unbalanced neurotics. Many of them were
affected by a morbid sexuality, they were either
profligate or homosexual. None of them excelled
in any field of activity or contributed anything
to human progress. Their names are long since
forgotten; the only trace they left were some
books and poems preaching sexual perversity
. . . ."7

359

I believe that Mises missed placing the
Youth Movement in its proper intellectual context
when he spoke of its "lack of any ideas" and said
that it was "void of ideological content." As
other fragments of the above passage indicate, the
Youth Movement did have ideas -- and these were
the ideas that stemmed from a century of intellectual alienation that repudiated the Enlightenment
and the bourgeoisie. It's true that the alienation
that existed throughout the German Youth Movement
did not produce a consensus and that different
factions grasped at a variety of specific ideologies; but the young people who participated clearly inherited the patterns of alienation from the
intellectual subculture of Europe. A similar inheritance took place in the United States as a
pre-condition to the later rise of the New Left.
Such youth movements should not be considered
separately from the context of an alienated intellectual subculture. It's no coincidence that
both the German Youth Movement and the American
New Left followed years of intense intellectual
alienation.

Laqueur and Becker give considerable detail
about the Youth Movement. The Movement's first
phase was that of the Wandervogel between 1896
and 1919. The second was the Bund (or Bünde)
phase which continued from 1919 until the Movement
was absorbed into the Hitler Youth in 1933. The
Movement had no input from the German working
class; it was composed entirely of middle class
young people, who nevertheless were in revolt
against "bourgeois respectability." In his introduction to Laqueur's book, R. H. S. Crossman
writes of the Wandervogel young people as "long-
haired untidy bacchants and super-bacchants." He
says they despised liberalism (by which he almost
certainly means pro-bourgeois classical liberalism,
as the word is used in Europe) and were suspicious
of intellectual analysis.[8]

Alienation from the bourgeoisie was the consistent thread. Laqueur says that the Wandervogel's

360

romanticism expressed social protest. The romanticism harked back to nature, and sought to forsake materialism; it emphasized the value of a "simple life"; and it revived earlier folksongs and folklore, including the use of names and customs from the Middle Ages. He refers to such eccentric lifestyles as residing in a cave or "walking about in bearskins." One group moved nomadically from town to town, sharing a "primitive communism" and advocating the redemption of humanity through "semi-religious, semi-sexual ecstatic surrender to folk dancing and singing." Laqueur says that it was the anti-capitalist point of view of the Wandervogel that pleased Scheler. He adds that the mentality "was not something that could be explained to Philistines in rational terms," and that anyone who was puzzled by the lifestyle's combination of elements would be answered that no one who lacked the unique feeling shared within the movement would ever understand it. Laqueur explains that there was an implicit premise that collective life, involving "intimate association," was much to be preferred to "interest-motivated, atomistic, impersonal society." This desire for a "more immediate and organic way of living together" was shared by the members both of the Wandervogel and the Bünde. Becker emphasizes the alienation when he says that "the older generation had lived through the triumphs of the 'sixties and the 'seventies, the upward zoom of Germany as a first-rate as well as military power in the 'eighties, and the plush-upholstered comfort and respectability of the 'nineties. Were the youngsters grateful for the warmth of Germany's place in the sun? To put it mildly, they thought that the brave new world was brassy and that the brass was badly tarnished, that the warmth was not the warmth of the sunshine but the enervating stuffiness of overheated, tawdrily furnished apartments filled with the reek of stale beer and the acrid fumes of cigar stubs. Specifically, they thought that parental religion was largely sham, politics boastful and trivial, economics unscrupulous and deceitful, education sterotyped and lifeless, art trashy and sentimental, literature spurious and

361

commercialized, the drama tawdry and mechanical,
dance cheaply titillating or excessively formal,
family repressive and insincere, and the relations
of the sexes, in marriage or out, shot through with
hypocrisy." The result, Becker says, was that
"German youth of Karl Fischer's day loathed and
hated the world of their elders." (I would, of
course, have us ask how it happened that so many
young people were suddenly independent philosophers
having so great a sensibility to higher and finer
values. Instead of reaching this subtle and extensive analysis themselves, they were no doubt
picking up the entire body of values and social
critique from the alienated intellectual generation that preceded them. In what I have covered
in earlier chapters, we have seen how often the
alienated intellectual has repeated the bill of
particulars against bourgeois society, as restated
by Becker in the passage above, during the past
two hundred years.)

At the large meeting of the Wandervogel in
1913 at the Hohe Meissner, "practically every
phase of contemporary adult respectability was
assailed and the demands of youth for its own sake
vigorously asserted."

In its first phase, the movement was slovenly
and nondescript; in its second, it became militar-
istically oriented. But at all times a wide
variety of alienated viewpoints existed within it.
The alienation becomes apparent when Laqueur says
the movement's members "were frequently corrupted
in the twenties by the politics of moral nihilism:
It was neither a Hitlerite nor a Communist who
declared that 'even the most heinous means is con-
secrated if used in the struggle for national liberation,' and that 'we must say "no" to humanism,
we must use even the most barbaric means, if it is
necessary to further the national resurrection' --
it was Ernst Niekisch, who enjoyed great authority
in the youth movement."

And the variety appeared in the many ideologi-

cal groups that participated. Laqueur says that
during its publication in 1912 Wiltfeber was gospel
for the "right-wing Wandervogel." Far from being
a narrow "party manifesto," it articulated the
"unformulated discontents of a young German patriot."
Wyneken, who was one of the Movement's most influential leaders between 1913 and 1920, held strongly
to the idea of "jugenkultur" (youth culture). The
Movement's left wing advocated "premarital sexual
freedom" and there was considerable homosexuality.
Anti-semitism was also a significant factor, with
religious anti-semitism giving way to the racial
form. (There had been a "great anti-semitic wave"
in the 1880's and 1890's.) Laqueur says that anti-
semitism underlay the beliefs of many participants
in the youth movement. The circle around Graff
developed the concept of "Aryan racist superiority."
He explains that they were not bothered by objections that they could not explain or define the
"mission" of this superior race or that there had
never been such a thing, especially in Germany, as
a pure Aryan race; they simply answered that "they
would create such a race in the future."

The Movement had its left wing, where, according to Laqueur, probably a majority agreed with
Karl Korsch in thinking that capitalism was near-
ing its end and that "scientific socialism had become a practical necessity." Alexander Rustow
spoke of capitalism as the principal adversary of
the youth movement, and Karl August Wittfogel predicted that the proletariat would emerge victorious.
Wittfogel urged that it was incumbent upon the
better young people within the bourgeoisie to pass
"the cultural treasures of the past to the class
which was destined to establish the classless
society." Laqueur says that Paul Tillich wanted
to meld Christianity and socialism in a "new world
order."

Laqueur reports that on the Movement's right
wing the behavior by Tusk "surpassed the worst
excesses of the White Knight era; emotionalism and
moral relativism ran wild." He says that every

young male in the local branches of the Jungen-
schaft became a "budding warrior" in a situation in
which soldiers were glorified, military values ex-
tolled and even a "death wish" honored. Tusk considered even the Prussian tradition "too mild" and
in a book called The Heroes' Bible praised the
Japanese Samurai. He wrote an article favoring
harikari in which he said that "the most important
virtue was 'demonic, knightly masculinity.'"

From all of this, it's easy to see that Adolf
Hitler and National Socialism were not strange
intruders into a hostile milieu. Almost everything
involved in National Socialism was a pick-up on
already existing factors. Referring to the "Fuhr-
erprinzip, the leadership principle," Becker tells
us that "the general acceptance of this principle
among Germans, of the younger generation in particular, has often been pointed to as the real secret of the strength of the Nazis. And now note
this: The principle goes back at least as far as
1896, when Karl Fischer introduced it among the
Roamers, whose unquestioned leader he was. The
leader was not the elected or delegated representative of the group; on the contrary, a man who
felt himself 'called' simply proclaimed himself
leader."

Becker goes on to inform us that even "the
great ritual symbols of the Nazis, the shout of
'Heil!' and the extended right arm, were not ori-
ginally Nazi at all. 'Heil!' was a greeting carried over from the Middle Ages, and used well over
thirty years ago by the Roamers, and in 1923 there
were several Youth Movement sects in which the
ramrod arm was a standard gesture."

The continuity between the Youth Movement and
National Socialism is just as apparent in Becker's
statement that "anyone observing a squad of Hitler
Youth on an expedition (at least before 1939)
would see lutes, fluttering ribbons, knapsacks,
and cooking pots, and would hear roaming songs
which, although not drawn from The Pluck (which

364

the Nazis have prohibited), would sound much like
the old repertory. Even the uniforms would not
strike an utterly false note, for the alliance
youth of the 'twenties had abandoned the individualistic raggle-taggle of Karl Fischer's boisterous
crew. The same observer could overhear talk about
the extraordinary qualities of the squad leader,
the sense of fusion, folk community, and Germany's
mission which would sound strikingly like the
stock-in-trade of the Free German Youth."

National Socialism and Hitler. It's significant that Laqueur says that National Socialism became ascendant as a party composed of young people.
Even though Italian Fascism glorified youth more
than in Germany, and even named its hymn "Giovi-
nezza" relating to youth, Hitler repeatedly said
that his Nazi movement was, among other things,
"a revolt of the coming generation against all that
was senile and rotten with decay." Beyond the
youth aspect, Laqueur says that National Socialism
had its roots in the long sweep of German history.
It did not represent a "sudden break" in trends
that were established much earlier in Germany.
Even the Nazi's racial anti-semitism was not
"thinkable without the different kind of anti-
semitism that preceded it."

David Schoenbaum has written a thoughtful
book about the National Socialist internal policies,
Hitler's Social Revolution. In it, he observes
that "the most general theory -- that National Socialism was a revolution of the lower middle class
is defensible but inadequate . . . National Socialism was no less a revolt of the young against the
old." He recounts that "the average age was thirty
to thirty-two, corresponding to the age of Hitler
himself who was thirty when he arrived in Munich.
A war of the young against the old was as great a
possibility as the mobilization of the dé classé
against the established. This opportunity Hitler
was quick to exploit with his organization of an
'active' Party auxiliary, a 'sport' group organized
from the remnants of the anti-communist militia of

the first postwar months . . ., to ride around in trucks, pick fights with the Communists, and be seen. Of the twenty-five members of the first SA group, formed in 1921, only one was over thirty, and fifteen were under twenty, too young even to have been in the war."[9]

The Nazis came to have considerable strength in the universities, and this flowed out of the fact, which Laqueur reports, that during the Weimar Republic in the 1920's the universities were "bulwarks of anti-democratic thought." The national climate was so favorable that at a time when the National Socialists had still enjoyed only minor electoral success they had already achieved a plurality in many academic communities, and "in some they had an absolute majority."

Militant German nationalism was already present among German young people and "needed only systematic expression and propagandizing," Becker says, "to bring it hand in glove with Nazi doctrines." He notes "the hatred of internationalism; the reiteration of the 'stab in the back' legend; the demand for other territories reassigned by the Treaty of Versailles; and the identification of efforts to develop a peaceful Germany with spineless pacifism."

Schoenbaum gives considerable detail about the flavor of Hitler's administration. I have been especially interested in the nature of Hitler's socialism. Schoenbaum quotes Hitler as having said that "we are not a charitable institution but a Party of revolutionary socialists." Combining a number of ingredients, "the new regime was, by its own definition, revolutionary, socialist, egalitarian, and elitist at once." The result was "a verbal radicalism in the old socialist tradition . . . As the worker was declared the pillar of the community, the bourgeois and the capitalist were excoriated as the enemies of the people." Schoenbaum says that "what characterized its socialism was not the ownership of capital but its relation-

ship to the State. Capital remained in private
hands because this seemed expedient. But the
threat of intervention was always present and
generally adequate to produce the desired cooperation." He tells us that "a Party editorial in
1939 declared free enterprise to be the very basis
for Germany's socialism." In characteristic socialist fashion reminiscent of Britain's R. H.
Tawney, the Nazi E. R. Huber "defined the right of
property as a function of duty."

　　Even though Schoenbaum points to a gap between Nazi rhetoric and Nazi practice (and here he
fails, I think, to give sufficient weight to the
brevity of the Nazi civil administration before
the onset of war), he believes that socialist
ideology and rhetoric were important to Nazism.
"As an affective concept," he says, "socialism had
a very real meaning in Nazi attitutdes. It was
hortatory and defined a state of mind." He tells
us that it "referred principally to a basic social
egalitarianism with a streak of social welfare,
and a considerable element of militancy." In the
ideology, a "socialist" world was set off against
a "bourgeois" world. The farmers, workers and
soldiers were identified with socialism, while
"the enemies of National Socialism included not
only the 'Jewish Marxists,' and the Catholics, but
'certain elements of an incorrigible, stupid,
reactionary bourgeoisie.'" During the brief period
before the war Nazism hadn't gained complete control of the economy, but in its ideology it "claimed total control of the economy; total command over
resources; total direction of wages, prices, production; total organization of credit, manpower,
transportation, and planning." Nazi law authorized
the Fuhrer "to limit or expropriate property at will
where this limitation or expropriation was consonant
with the 'tasks of the community.'" Schoenbaum says
"the Third Reich was notable for the far-reaching
transfer of managerial decisions from the managers.
Wages, prices, working conditions, allocation of
materials: none of these was left to managerial
decision, let alone to the market. It was expedience, not ideological bias, that left property

367

in the hands of its owners, something made evident
by the regime's own free-wheeling entrepreneurial
activity, its theoretical treatment of the right
of property."

The social egalitarianism that existed within
Nazism is illustrated by Schoenbaum when he quotes
the petty human concerns of a prison camp gaurd:
"Formerly when I went to the theatre with my wife,
there was always trouble. We got a seat in the
twentieth row. But Huber, our chief accountant,
and his wife were in the tenth row. And afterward
all hell broke loose. Why can the Hubers afford
the tenth row and not ourselves? Nowadays, six
nights a week, all the seats in the theatre cost
the same. First come, first served. Sometimes
the Hubers sit in the tenth row, and we sit in the
twentieth. But my wife knows that's because the
Hubers live nearer the theatre."

As has been true with a great deal of socialism both in and out of Germany, the egalitarianism
was also elitist. Schoenbaum quotes the Nazi Ley
as having said that "there are no longer classes
in Germany. In the years to come, the worker will
lose the last traces of inferiority feelings he
may have inherited from the past." He points out,
though, that a Dutch correspondent heard Ley say
that "people are children. They have childlike
wishes. The state has to care for these and see
to it that they get their presents if they are to
be happy."

The Nazi program worked toward a number of
ends. One objective was to cause employers to improve conditions at work, and to raise living standards. Schoenbaum says this resulted in better
housing and even in such quality-of-life extras as
symphonies, plays, excursions and swimming pools.
Hitler wanted to make the cities smaller, the concentration of capital less; to increase the rural
population; to return women to the home; to reduce
inequalities of income. And it was all done to a
litany of ideology and propaganda. An inexpensive

but durable small car, the Volkswagon, was put on
the market for the purpose of making the auto-
mobile available to everyone, not just to the bourgeoisie. In industrial relations, considerable
attention was focused on an organization known as
"Strength through Joy."

The circumstances of Hitler's rise. I have
stressed the continuity of National Socialism with
the anti-bourgeois alienation and with several traditional socialist values because it is in those
things that the main lessons are to be learned
from it. But it is probably true, as people are
quick to see, that Hitler wouldn't have acquired
power if it had not been for the straitened circumstances of Germany in the 1920's and early 'thirties. The experience of World War I and of the
defeat in that war, especially when combined with
the humiliations of Versailles and the severe re-
parations, not to mention the traumas that were
involved in run-away inflation and in brief Communist take-overs, were all factors which worsened
the crisis that existed independently in the German
mind and spirit. The social turmoil and economic
difficulties placed a strain on democratic institutions in other nations as well as in Germany.
And we must not lose sight of the fact that the
Weimar Republic was a new democratic experience
for Germany, so new that it seemed alien to a milieu which detested precisely its democratic aspect. Laqueur points out that "in Germany large
sections of the middle classes believed that political democracy was a foreign importation unsuited to German conditions, and there had been signs
of anti-liberal and anti-parliamentarian unrest
since the very first year of the Weimar Republic."
A number of circumstances in Germany militated
against liberal institutions.

It isn't hard to see, then, why it is almost
totally irrelevant whether Hitler was or was not
psychotic. An understanding of the rise of Hitler

and of the advent of World War II calls into play
all of the factors that I have discussed in this
book. In the broadest sense, the horrors of
National Socialism reflected the problematical
condition of contemporary Western man as the in-
heritor of a deeply rooted division and immaturity.

NOTES

1. Walter Z. Laqueur, Young Germany (New York:
Basic Books Publishing Co., Inc., 1962), pp. 152,
87, 179-180, xviii, xxi, 6, 8, 11, 116, 139, 165,
9, 31, 44, 53, 52, 60, 74, 75, 105-106, 117-118,
168, 191, 197, 140, 141, 179.

2. Adolf Hitler, Mein Kampf (Boston: Houghton
Mifflin, 1943), p. 491.

3. José Ortega y Gasset, The Revolt of the Masses
(New York: W. W. Norton & Company, Inc., 1960),
p. 75.

4. Howard Becker, German Youth: Bond or Free
(New York: Oxford University Press, 1946), pp.
145, 51, 73, 100, viii, ix, 189, 158.

5. George L. Mosse, The Crisis of German Ideology
(New York: Grosset & Dunlap, 1964), pp. 4, 14, 25,
27, 29-30.

6. George L. Mosse, Nazi Culture (New York:
Grosset & Dunlap, 1966), p. 97.

7. Ludwig von Mises, Bureaucracy (New Haven: Yale
University Press, 1944), pp. 94-95.

8. Laqueur, Young Germany, pp. xviii, xxi.

9. David Schoenbaum, Hitler's Social Revolution
(Garden City: Doubleday and Company, Inc., 1966),
pp. 44, 18-19, 27, 53, 55, 56, 57, 69, 119, 154,
157, 299, 112, 117, 298, 110, 111.

17

LATIN AMERICA AND THE COLD WAR

So far, I have discussed the "modern predicament" only in the context of Europe and the United
States. In the present chapter I will want to
emphasize that historic circumstances have made
the predicament within the West also the most important fact so far as the future of the so-called
"Third World" of Asia, Africa and Latin America is
concerned.

I don't want to seem ungracious toward civilizations which have, and have had, their own heritage and greatness, but I think it is important to
realize that these other continents contain a
serious void with regard to the prerequisites of
liberal society. I say this even though I wish
them well in every sense of the word. This void
combines with their dependency on European and
American intellectual sources, so that in an important sense all three continents are in a situation that is analogous to Russia's in the nineteenth
century. Rapidly expanding masses of people are
appearing in Asia, Africa, and Latin America at a
time when their own dependency causes them to import the neuroses which have plagued the West for
so long.

This unwitting reliance on the worst aspects
of Western civilization in an age of existential
lostness has led and will continue to lead to some
of the major tragedies of the modern age. The impact of the reliance is reflected, for example, in
the pages of Solzhenitsyn's The Gulag Archipelago,
where he vividly describes the enormous suffering
of the Soviet people under the regime of imported
nineteenth-century Marxist ideology.

It is entirely inappropriate for the non-
European peoples -- in Russia, in China and else-

where -- to have absorbed the thinking of the many fevered descendants of Rousseau, Hegel and Marx. But they have done so because of the great pulse of alienated literature that has come from Europe during the past two centuries. We can imagine how different the world would be today, and how different its future would be, if these peoples had drunk deeply instead, say, from the teaching of such men as Benjamin Franklin and James Madison.

Since World War II, the pressing question has been whether these peoples would succumb to Communist totalitarianism. But actually it is a broader question that hangs over their heads, because in a more general way we know that they remain susceptible to the neuroses of Europe and America. Even if Communism were to disappear from the world overnight, there would still be reason for profound doubt about these peoples' ability to develop advanced liberal societies.

In all of this, I see the key factor as being the nature of the West's intellectual leadership. If that leadership continues to inject the West's own void into the weakness that is already present in those other continents, their future -- and ours -- will remain dangerously problematical.

It's hard to imagine how Asia, Africa and Latin America will find the way to embrace the principles of a free society if alienation continues to stream from European and American thought. Little in their own past or current condition will lead them to these principles. But if, on the other hand, some profound change were to occur in the ontology of the West to reconcile its own divisions, the affirmative leadership that would result would be immensely constructive for the emerging peoples everywhere. In turn, this would remove, or at least substantially alleviate, one of the main threats to the future well-being of the new world civilization.

As it stands, the world is poorly prepared for

the precipitate rise of these peoples. Nevertheless, they are coming rapidly into their own; they
are taking their places as participating members
of a vastly expanded human community. A gradual
process of globalization has been underway for
thousands of years. It is perhaps two-thirds of
the way along toward completion. Vast changes are
still to come, but even now these other peoples are
no longer cast in the role of "superfluous people"
who exist in the shadow of a primarily European
world order.

They are here -- and they're growing, both in
numbers and in assertiveness. This raises towering questions: What is to be their future -- and
ours, as affected inevitably by theirs? How will
they affect liberal civilization? What will their
contribution be?

Ortega felt the "palpitating danger" of what
he called "the revolt of the masses" in Europe.
If this has rendered Europe problematical, how much
more so must it make doubtful the future of the
peoples of the Third World! As has been true with
Europe, there is an element of great hope: the
rise of "average humanity" to a higher plateau is
actually the fulfillment, at least in part, of a
basic human aspiration. It is a major step along
the way toward an abundantly rounded, fulfilled
humanity. There is enormous dynamic potential
that goes along with the dangers. It may even be
-- and we certainly hope so -- that the positive
aspects, based on the energies and intelligence
of countless people, will predominate. Certainly
I wouldn't want to underestimate that possibility.
But it is easier by far to identify the reasons
for doubt.

I have chosen Latin America for specific discussion in this chapter, with the idea that it
will be helpful to get somewhat closer to at least
some of the concrete aspects of the subject. In
what follows, I will want to survey some of the
factual highlights about Latin America.

373

1. As the peoples absorb the techniques of applied science, there is a rapid expansion occurring in the population. Estimates are that the population will more than double to between 500 and 700 million people by the end of the twentieth century (and if this occurs, the population will far outstrip the projected food supply).[1]

2. Because of a number of factors, there is little chance for truly liberal development.

The burgeoning population will, as in Ortega's Europe, come to fill all of the places and will fully establish the cultural tone. It will know and demand the amenities of advanced civilization, but its peoples will have only the most superficial understanding of what it takes to create and maintain those benefits. In their present "have not" status, these peoples are often prey to envy, resentment, impatience and direct-action techniques. Unfortunately, these characteristics continue into advanced civilization in the form of spoiledness and shallowness.

In many of the countries a majority of the people can't read or write. Preston James cited the following literacy percentages for 1959 (which was almost twenty years ago, but the percentages nevertheless give us a picture of the situation): Argentina, 87 per cent; Bolivia, 31; Brazil, 50, Chile, 81; Columbia, 56; Costa Rica, 80; Cuba, 76; Dominican Republic, 43; Ecuador, 56; El Salvador, 42; Guatemala, 30; Haiti, 11; Honduras, 44; Mexico, 55; Nicaragua, 40; Panama, 72; Paraguay, 69; Peru, 42; Uruguay, 85; Venezuela, 69. These statistics show the presence of a void that makes rapid progress extremely difficult. It's a monumental task just to motivate so many people to learn to read. But of course we know that even 100 per cent literacy won't assure that these peoples are more than minimally educated. In fact, it might even increase their vulnerability to neurotic social movements, since there has been a certain protective conservatism in the ignorance and apathy of largely rural

374

masses of people in the past, just as there was with the peasants of nineteenth century Russia.

The population of Latin America comes from three main sources: Indian, Negro and European. It is the mixed-blooded mestizo who predominates, but it's significant that we are told that "the Iberic-Negro-Indian mixture is not notable for mechanical skills and lives at odds with the technocratic world of the twentieth century."[2] The Europeans have made up the cultural elite; the negroes and mulattos live mainly in the hot coastal regions and are almost all the descendants of slaves. They have produced some leaders, but in Latin America, An Interpretive History Donald Dozer tells us that generally they are indolent. "They perform the minimum physical labor required for a hand-to-mouth existence." Of the Indians, he says that they "are agricultural traditionalists, living close to the land as have their ancestors for thousands of years."

Most of the peasants live in extreme poverty and hardly participate in the societies in which they live. According to Dozer, "their only trade is the trade in merchandise carried on men's backs. They do not enter into the life of the countries in which they reside and in which their ancestors have resided for generations. They still live in a precapitalist economy and supply their needs largely through barter." He reports that if the real per capita income continues to rise at the slow rate it has been rising, "Latin Americans will require almost two and one-half centuries to reach one-third of the per capita income now enjoyed by citizens of the United States."

These economic conditions are made even worse by inflation and land monopoly. There has been chronic inflation since World War II. Dozer gives us the following figures about the price index, using 1953 as a base of 100 and giving the comparative figures for 1960: Argentina, 622; Chile, 944; Bolivia, 2,398; (but the Dominican Republic

375

only 98). Land monopoly has been the target
of various land-reform programs, but these
haven't been very successful. Dozer says that
"where land redistribution has been undertaken it
has often failed to create greatly improved living
standards, important increases in production per
hectare, or democratic institutions in rural society." Land reform has been more successful in
Mexico, but there the socialistic techniques that
have been used have kept the farmers from becoming
capitalists. "Members of the collective ejidos
show little desire to care for land that next year
may be worked by others. On parcelized ejidos the
plot of ground may pass out of the hands of one
family to another. On private lands, even those
which conform to the legal size limits prescribed
by law, there is always the lingering threat of
expropriation resulting from a change in the Agrarian Code . . ."

3. Even though there is an immense void in
Latin America, stopgaps have come in to fill it,
and it is almost certainly due to this that communism has not been more successful. In 1830, Simon
Bolivar, in despair over the failure of his Gran
Columbia, exclaimed that "our America will fall
into the hands of vulgar tyrants; only an able
despotism can rule America."[3] His prediction seems
to have accurately described the political future
of the continent. Almost a century and a half
later, a more or less innocuous form of Latin
American neo-fascism serves as the bulwark against
Communist seizure. A combination of intense nationalism and welfare statism led by a mercurial
leader known as a caudillo, or by the military, has
been the pattern. Even though Dozer says that
"democracy is everywhere latent in Latin America"
and that "even the most ruthless dictator cannot
indefinitely and with impunity ignore public opinion," he also observes that "constitutional government is only a facade and the observance of the
forms of representative democracy only a ruse designed to placate local visionaries or foreign public opinion." He makes it clear that "personal

376

leadership or caudillismo continues to be the salient feature of Latin American politics." He even goes so far as to say that "to ask whether or not Latin America is becoming more democratic is to pose a question which is immaterial in the Latin American milieu."

Nystrom and Haverstock point out that "military governments, since the formulation of the Alliance (for Progress), have seized power in more than half of the Latin American republics."[4] Fortunately, this military rule hasn't involved intense armament or expansionist military policies. Nevertheless, Dozer says that "the aspirations of these people for a better life . . . have come to be bound up with an ardent, even a fanatical nationalism."

In this context, the state has become a major instrument for accomplishing social objectives. Dozer gives a good description of what this involves: "Many of the so-called 'dictators' of Latin American countries, particularly those of the nineteenth century, remained in office in order primarily to serve the interests of wealthy oligarchic classes, such as large landowners, the church hierarchy, an entrenched military organization, or foreign business interests. This type of dictator still continues, but more typical in the twentieth century is the dictator who comes to power and maintains himself in power in order to satisfy the material aspirations of the mass of the population in his country. He responds to their importunate demands for economic relief and social justice, and he resorts to the methods of dictatorship and uses the enlarged powers of his office in order to crush out the traditional oligarchies who are held responsible for the plight of the masses. As the glamorous caudillo of the people he becomes the instrument for achieving a social revolution."

All of these factors justify the conclusion that, as judged by classical liberal values, there is a significant civilizational void within Latin America.

377

This is made considerably worse by the void coming
in from Europe and America in the form of alienated
intellectuality. Since nothing really points in
the direction of truly liberal institutions, the
caudillo's stopgap nationalism is probably as
satisfactory a solution as we could hope for, at
least as long as it remains separate from any world-
wide expansionist totalitarian system. The question in the long run is whether the growing peoples
of Latin America can move gradually into the new
age without catastrophe for themselves and without
endangering liberal values elsewhere. This is
equally true for Africa and Asia (although I
wouldn't have us ignore the fact that in all three
continents there has in fact been Communist
encroachment, often very extensive).

The West's effort to inhibit the spread of
Communism in these continents is bound to be a
frustrating effort. Wherever there is no viable
liberal middle (and that is rare), we are forced
to stand more or less behind the status quo. And
this status quo is usually inconsistent with our
own ideals. Our will to resist Communism in such
a situation is sapped by the fact that our own intellectual subculture, which is left in its orientation, does not understand the problem in this
light. Instead, it tends to minimize the threat
of Communism and to overplay both the possibility
of finding a viable middle and the unworthiness of
the status quo. Here again, we get back to our
own divisions as a root cause of difficulty.

If I were a military strategist on a global
scale, I would emphasize that the most important
aspect of the struggle against Communism lies in
overcoming the alienation of Western intellectuals
against Western culture -- although I would recognize, too, that this problem, which is crucial to
the military picture, is not subject to military
solution. Were the alienation overcome, the world
would be a vastly different place, and the future
would be a great deal less clouded. Until the
fundamental existential division is healed within

378

the West, alienation, hatred and class-division will continue to seep out to the Third World. This is something to which military and economic assistance to the countries of Asia, Africa and Latin America is almost totally irrelevant. The assistance can at best provide additional stopgaps. The struggle against totalitarianism must be resolved primarily within ourselves.

NOTES

1. In his Latin America, An Interpretive History (New York: McGraw-Hill Book Company, Inc., 1962), Donald Marquand Dozer (at p. 15) projects the increase to 550 million people on the basis of a 2.5 per cent rate of annual increase. In Preston E. James' Latin America (New York: The Odyssey Press, 3d ed., 1959), at p. 4, the projection is to 500 million. J. Warren Nystrom and Nathan A. Haverstock, in their The Alliance for Progress (Princeton: D. Van Nostrand Company, Inc., 1966), at p. 17, speak of 600 million, based on a 2.6 per cent rate.

2. Dozer, Latin America, pp. 11, 13, 555, 556, 20, 562, 554, 559.

3. James, Latin America, p. 63.

4. Nystrom and Haverstock, Alliance, p. 112.

EPILOGUE: LOOKING TO OTHER DIMENSIONS

The review I have just made of some of the
specific historical consequences of the immaturity
and division within modern Western civilization
certainly doesn't exhaust the subject. We have
just scratched the surface. Even so far as actual
events are concerned, we could go on discussing
the consequences indefinitely.

It seems to me, though, that the most pervasive and life-molding consequences of the alienation and of our immaturity have been intellectual.
In Chapter 1, I pointed ahead to the fact that
much of what I have called "the modern predicament"
consists of the strange social reality we have
created out of a mixture of fact and interpretation.
We need to understand that no one perceives social
reality directly. Human beings can only mediate
it through a process of mental organization and
selectivity. This means that we always create
our own social ontology. And when this process is
affected by gigantic warpings arising out of
immaturity and division, the result must be understood as being something that is quite far from a
straight look at the world. The interplay of the
mediation with the many forces I have sought to
describe (and, to be sure, with many others I have
neither described nor thought of) has brought about
the large contrasting systems of interpretation
which we refer to as the modern ideologies. These,
in turn, are not only interpretations of reality,
but themselves become vastly important parts of
our social reality, affecting everything they touch.
The main schools of thought -- such as positivism,
pragmatism, social Darwinism, legal realism and
many others -- can also be best understood in the
context of this dynamic mediation and warping; and,
in fact, they bear a close relationship to the main
ideologies.

These patterns of perception react on policy
and on the entire range of topical issues that we

381

face in the "agenda" of a society at a given time.
The ideas often even define what it is that we
consider to be an issue. If our ideas were different from what they are, many things that we consider to be important issues would be dropped unceremoniously from the agenda, and many other
things that we don't even notice today would become
important to us. This molding of the political
and social agenda of a given society arises directly out of the fact that the issues are, in at least
one of their dimensions, the product of our interpretation of social reality. Ideas form the fundamental parameters within which the practical
world acts. Richard Weaver was right on the mark
when he said that "ideas do have consequences."

What I have done in the present book has been
to spell out what I consider to be some of the
main ingredients in a sociology of modern thought.
It isn't a complete or exact sociology because the
factors I have discussed can't be quantified and
because there are no doubt many elements I haven't
considered. (It is this admission that separates
my thinking from the many dogmatic "philosophies
of history" that allege to have captured all processes leading into the future in a nutshell.)
But it lays a foundation which I have found quite
useful in trying to understand why people hold the
ideas they do -- and especially in understanding
why various ideas which are outwardly disassociated
are so often found linked together. The sociology
of the forces I have described gives us a way to
see the common threads, and to see them not so
much in terms of a static "model building" analysis
(even though that is important in its place) as in
terms of an on-going human process in which much
can, in fact, be explained.

It will be in light of all of this that my
ensuing books will consider each of the major
modern ideologies. The important thing to remember
as I discuss them will be that I see them in the
context of this sociology. I won't be discussing
them just for their own sakes. They exist as vital-

382

ly important extensions of the factors I have been discussing in this book.

INDEX

385

387

388